Footsteps of a Life Jour...

DESTINED BY GRACE

James R. Willis

By

James Beverly Willis

ISBN-13
9781500257316

Cover design
by
Bonnie Powell and Dan Elkin

Printed in the United States of America

First Edition

James B. Willis
Born April 23, 1924

DEDICATION

This book is dedicated in loving memory of my parents and my wife's parents:

Floyd H. and Inez G. Willis

and

James O. and Melissa M. Barefoot

They taught us Christian principals of living and gave us good moral training in our youth by their word and deed. They had faith in God to direct us toward a successful life and a future in Heaven.

TABLE OF CONTENTS

AUTHOR'S PREFACE

My name is James Willis. I am not the first to carry this name, but I may be the first one with this name to carry a Purple Heart.

For several years I have been writing down the memories I have about events I've lived through. Most of those were ordinary events, and yet, some of them quite extraordinary indeed. Who else could tell these stories? There is truth in the saying that when a person dies, a library of information is lost forever. Through God's mercy I have lived a rich and full life with many meaningful experiences.

As I have reached the latter years of my life, it is due time I put my writings into a book to leave as a dedication to those who have passed before me and to those who follow. The result my writings is a compilation of part history and part remembered experiences.

My early memories take me back to my childhood. The formative years of my life took place on my parents' farm during the 1920s and through the Great Depression of the 1930s. It was from those early beginnings that my life has been shaped. Stories of my youth and my life, which led up to college, give the reader a brief insight as to what country life on the farm in southern Indiana was like during those years.

I have clear memories of my years of school, military career, marriage to my beautiful wife and raising our children. There are many events that seem as if they happened yesterday. My life story would not be complete without the telling of a variety of my adult living experiences and family adventures.

One chapter of this book is a brief account of my military experience. In my previous book, *The Odyssey of a Purple Heart Vet,* I have written a more complete account about my experience in the Battle of Okinawa during WWII. It is only by the grace of God that I survived to write about it and I encourage the reader to refer to that book for the full details.

Everyone who reads this book has some ancestor(s) who

traveled to this country from somewhere else in the world. Like many others who have studied their genealogy, in my research I found some fascinating details about my ancestors who struggled to come to America before it was a nation. A section at the beginning of my life story is devoted to them. I have also included a little of the Willis family history that is known and experienced during my lifetime. There is a complete Willis genealogy, which is traced back to our ancestors that came to America from Wales, in a book written by my brother, Imel H. Willis, called "Plow a Straight Row (Willisville Beginnings and Beyond)".

The beginning chapter of my book is of special interest to me. I trust others, especially descendants of the Willis ancestors, will find it meaningful to learn about some of the Willis origins. Perhaps it will make Willisville (formerly Clark's Station), which is in southern Indiana, a special place on the map for you.

All of us have had certain life experiences that are more memorable and important than others. I have lived through a fascinating period of history and could not tell of all the marvelous discoveries humanity has made nor all the social and cultural changes I have seen. Even if I could remember all the turns of my life, it would take a very large book to tell it all.

Throughout all of these pages no intent is for my own glorification or to be boastful of any deeds or accomplishments. Though my accounts of my and my family's adventures may not be complete, I have composed my story as best as I am able to remember.

Perhaps my greatest joy in life has been the gift of God's blessings of a loving wife and beautiful children. If I have anything to boast about, it is this fortune. I am very thankful to God for giving me loving parents, patient teachers, and the wisdom and instruction of others who have guided my footsteps through my life. I hope you will be blessed as I share with you my journey and how God's grace shaped my destiny. My prayer is that you will find Him to guide you as well.

ANCESTRY REFERENCE

Following is a list of my Willis ancestors for the last 5 generations discussed in this book. It is not intended to be a complete ancestry listing but just for a quick reference. The underlined names are my direct ancestor lineage.

Thomas Willis and Anne
begat:
Thomas, Rachel, George, James, Hanna, and Adam

George Willis and Margery
begat:
Nancy, George (Duck), James, Jane, Thomas, Maxwell

Maxwell Willis and Nancy Jane Miller
begat:
Jasper, Henry Jackson, Beverly, Louisa, George, Elizabeth, Martha E., Mary J., Nancy Amanda

Jasper Willis and Sarah Ellen Dean
begat:
Cordella, Maria, Beverly B., Louisa, William Emery, Charles L., Catherine, George M., Nancy Elizabeth

Beverly B. Willis and Isabelle Hilborn
begat:
Rozina (Rosie), Louisa Mae, James Edmund, Clarence, Ola, Floyd H.

Floyd H. Willis and Goldie Inez Parker
begat:
Imel, Marybelle, Wesley, James Beverly, Lelah, Morris, Orace Wayne

Chapter 1

ORIGIN AND A FAMILY LEGACY
RIDING THE WAVES TO A NEW WORLD

...the Lord thy God shall bless thee in the land whither thou goest to possess it. (Deuteronomy 30:16)

Introduction

The Willis family has its roots in Wales of Great Britain, and it was from there Thomas Willis, my great, great, great, great grandfather was born in 1734.

The work of several Willis researchers share a consensus of Thomas Willis as our immigrant ancestor. They agree that Thomas and Anne came to America as part of a group of Willis kinfolk in the mid-1700s and were first documented in this country on the tax listing for Rowan County, North Carolina, in 1768. Thomas' will, probated in Rowan County in 1794, clearly reveals he had settled in the locality and acquired considerable acreage. Over 400 acres, as well as, a stock of horses, cattle and hogs are designated to beneficiaries.

According to the records, at about age 20, Thomas married Anne who was two years younger than himself and whose maiden name is unknown. Their marriage is estimated to be around 1754.

Brief Willis History

Many of us look to history for an understanding of our personal identity as well as for knowledge about our past. That history matters to us is why so many devote time and energy to learn of their family tree and study their roots. In doing this, each generation asks different questions about their past and finds different answers.

My wife's maiden name is Barefoot. We know that our

families, both Willis and Barefoot ancestors emigrated from Great Britain. What impelled them to do so and how would their decision affect the course of history? There is no evidence either family knew of the other, neither before nor after their migration to America, even though they both chose to settle in the same colony of North Carolina. It was destined by God that these two families, each with their own fascinating stories, are now joined in the tree of life. How did this come to be?

The region of Wales consists mainly of moorlands and mountains with scattered villages and small farms. Coming from Wales, Thomas Willis would have learned to speak Welsh, the native language as well as English. All his life, even after he immigrated to America, he spoke with a thick brogue.

It was a time of great social conflict in England. The Industrial age had begun causing the uprooting of many people from farms to work in factories. However, economic growth was slow resulting in wrenching poverty in the cities and stirring the fires of discontent in many British subjects. Added to that was an awakening desire for religious worship free from the dictates of the government.

The Monarchy was slow in adapting to these social changes. The common man was not represented; only five percent of the population had a right to vote. Laws were passed making it a crime to be jobless. Many people struggled to survive and riots erupted in cities over rising food costs. Poverty was rampant and the gin-soaked city slums were degrading tremendously. In the face of those troubles, a few brave and determined folk were finding relief by making the journey to the New World where they were promised land.

When Thomas Willis married Anne, they were full of hope and enthusiasm about their future. They discussed the wonderful opportunities that were available in the American colonies, having seen advertisements in the form of handbills posted in the town commons. The postings promised rich fertile land in the colonies to all who came. However, what would it cost and could they afford it?

There were two ways one could get to the colonies–as a free person or as an indentured servant. If you didn't have the money to buy your way on a sailing ship, you could earn passage by agreeing to work a certain number of years for a proprietor or wealthy colonist, thus becoming an indentured servant until your debt was worked off. For many poor British, indenture servitude worked. Many poor families were lifted out of poverty and made a prosperous life for themselves in that manner. However, the Willis families were landowning farmers. They were wealthy enough to be able to afford their own passage. Due to their heritage of being self-sufficient farmers, they would not have found indentured servitude a palatable proposition in any case. By wise management of their finances, they could raise the money needed to make the move to the New World. Other members of the Willis clan along with my great great great great grandfather worked together, saved their money, and planned to go together to the New World. Eventually, five Willis brothers decided to find passage on a sailing ship to the colony of North Carolina.

As they made their inquiries into available shipping companies for passage, they found differences in rules about what they could take; varying rates for groups such as theirs; different levels of trustworthiness of companies and more importantly...the ships' crews.

The fare for traveling in questionable conditions on a sailing ship during that era was advertised at 31 pounds for first class passage. That would be about the equivalent of $15,500 in today's currency. Steerage was more affordable at five to eight pounds (about $2,500 to $4,000 in today's currency). For their money they were given meager quarters.

Ship owners relied on sufficient cargo to fill the ship's holds, which provided for a return on the money they had invested in their ships. Freight filled the ships' cargo holds first. Passengers were carried as an accommodation and they did not travel in comfort.

The Perilous Ocean Voyage

It is believed that in 1760 the Willis clan set off for their long journey to America. Thomas and Anne would have been traveling with four small children. Winter provided the best sailing times when an average crossing would take about 30 days. Yet, it was not unheard of for the journey to take up to 50 days. As the Willis brothers and their families made the crossing, one wonders how many times the parents answered the eternal travel question of all children: "Are we there yet?"

Sailing the wild Atlantic was dangerous even for seasoned sailors. For land dwellers and curious young children...the perils would have been numerous. The craft of sailing involves as much knowledge of the mysterious devices used as it does an art of understanding nature. There were many strange devices with odd names like: fife rails, hawsers, belaying pins, braces, bails, bitts, and more. Sails and lines are repeatedly changed and adjusted in a carefully choreographed dance with the wind. It was common for the sailors to chant and sing songs as they performed their work in unison.

Following is a story, written by an anonymous sailor ca 1800, of what the Willis families faced on their journey on a cargo ship of that era:

> Most of the passengers were young and in their composition was the best blood of Europe. The dwarfs and crippled were kept at home.
>
> These young people, with their hopes burning high, braved the dangers of the Atlantic on the loaded ship and were stowed away in the "tween decks" with little air or light, and all seasick. The wet, dirty, and dismal "tween decks" with its seasick occupants mingled their moans with the creaking of the ships joints as the ship rolled with the waves.
>
> The provisions, too, were severely plain, the principle item being Indian (or yellow) corn meal, which was

served out in the raw state to the emigrants themselves twice a week. The daily allowance of this food they carried to the galley to be cooked.

Often the passengers were saluted by a large green wave as they tried to reach the galley and were swept off their feet. They would be piled in a heap, on top of each other, in the lee scuppers in a most helpless condition and the food they were taking to be cooked was washed into the sea.

When the ship was pitching, some would lose hold of the man-rope while trying to reach the steerage with cooked food. They would tumble down and lay prostrate at the foot of the ladder, with their yellow meal scattered around the decks and on their cloths.

It took six weeks to make the passage. When the ship anchored, the passengers (some dancing, more singing) soon forgot the hardships of the long journey—as if it were a dream.

A Dream Come True

Lining the rails of the ship, when land was sighted, they caught their first glimpse of the shores of the New World. They anchored off the coast of North Carolina, anxious to offload and begin their search for a new home.

The nickname Tar Heel was used to refer to residents of North Carolina and gained prominence during the American Civil War.

Some of the Willis clan remained on the coast to settle. Thomas and a couple of brothers turned inland, looking for a place where they could spread out, build homes, and farm the land as was their custom. They may have been lured to the area of Rowan County perhaps because of its resemblance to the countryside of their homeland.

Thomas and Anne found the land they were looking for in Rowan County. There the soil was good, the neighbors friendly, in addition there was plenty of room for the family to grow and prosper. It seemed God had truly blessed the land.

Both Thomas and Anne Willis listed England as their birthplace and were in their 30s when they appeared on the North Carolina tax list about 14 years following their marriage. The children born to Thomas and Anne, as listed in the ancestry records are: Thomas, Rachel, George, James, Hanna, and Adam. The spirit of Thomas and Anne was later reflected in their grandchildren, who surely must have heard the adventures and stories recounted many times.

Thomas, through hard work as an independent farmer and with keen financial sensibility, eventually came to live quite comfortably; the family was part of a thriving middle class. Colonial Americans fretted over the cost of living and worried about how the increasing burden of taxes imposed by the Crown were eating into their finances.

Sadly, the quest for religious freedom that drew many to America was not always fulfilled. The various denominations in the colonies did not freely mingle without friction. Many were hostile to one another. Catholics were tolerated only in Maryland and Pennsylvania. Quakers were not welcome in New England.

Half the population in that area were loyalists, but Revolution was brewing in the Northern Colonies and the peaceful back-country of Rowan County would soon hear the sounds of war. Life in the colonies was not as spartan and uncivilized as we may imagine. The colonists enjoyed one of the highest living standards in the world. The people worked hard but they also found time to enjoy themselves, to relax with neighbors and form bonds of friendship.

In that era, social gatherings such as rural corn husking bees (contests) were popular. There were also songfests and in nearly any gathering, a fiddler would be there to entertain and lead dances. Those country dances were the forerunners of the square dance we have today. It is likely that at those events Thomas and Anne's growing children began to discover the rituals of courtship. It may have even been at one of those events my Great, Great, Great Grandfather George Willis met a young country girl named Margery.

George and his elder brother, Thomas, joined their father in expanding the farming operations, but their brother James had other ideas. Although most of the Willis families were farmers and did not pursue an education beyond the basics, James decided to become a doctor. Medical men were few and far between in the 1770s. There were less than 200 in all of the 13 colonies with actual medical degrees. James persisted to become a doctor, with the help of his father, and returned to Rowan County where he established his practice.

The Willis family, like typical colonists, took pride in their abilities to tame the wild frontiers of America. There is a family legend that Daniel Boone was once a neighbor. In 1775, Daniel Boon blazed the Wilderness Trail through the Cumberland Gap, a natural passage through the Cumberland Plateau of the Appalachian Mountains near the junction of Kentucky, Virginia, and Tennessee. In time, a group of Willis families would follow that trail in their search of new land to settle.

Effects of the Revolutionary War

Most of the early settlers eventually began to think of themselves as Americans, not as British subjects. Those independent thinking colonists began to pass their own laws and resisted the heavy taxes the Crown imposed. They were American Patriots and they soon resolved to declare their independence from Britain.

By 1776, the colonists formally documented their intentions with the Declaration of Independence. The people declared themselves a sovereign nation of the United States. The British promptly declared war on America!

In the year of 1778, during the middle of the American Revolution, British born George Willis married an American born young woman named Margery. As Margery's last name is unknown, some have speculated that she may have been of American Indian descent. If so, she would not have had a last name. George and Margery built their home near the Willis family farm in Rowan County.

The war seemed far away and for a while it remained so. Two years after George and Margery were married the British Army, led by Lord Cornwallis, seized control of the North Carolina coast. The Willis families who lived there found their lands occupied by the British army.

The American General, Nathaniel Green, was commissioned by the fledgling new American government to gather a force of militiamen to fight the British in both North and South Carolina. General Green used the sharp shooting skills of the militia's frontiersmen to great advantage. The two armies left a trail of devastation in their wake as Green lured Cornwallis away from the coast. General Green used hit and run skirmishes to lead Lord Cornwallis on a chase through the interior of the Carolinas.

The two forces converged on Charlotte, North Carolina, less than a day's march from Rowan County. The Willis farms were squarely in the path of the marching armies! There is no record of how the Willis families prepared for the impending ravages of war that threatened everything they had worked for. What is certain, though, is they knew the fighting was near and they took steps to protect their properties. They did what they could to save their homes, livestock, crops, and other items from the pilferage that follows in the wake of marching armies.

By the miraculous hand of God, the northward march of Green and Cornwallis turned at Charlotte missing the Willis farms by about 20 miles. Nevertheless, scouts and hungry troops looking to take what they needed to survive could have confronted the Willis families.

An intriguing question is whether any of the young Willis men joined in the fighting. There were several Willis men of the right age whom would have felt the call to protect their way of life.

General Green's tactics gradually weakened and demoralized the British who were unused to fighting on long marches under constant harassment of hidden sniper fire. In the end, Lord Cornwallis retreated to Virginia where he was surrounded. He surrendered at Yorktown giving the new nation, the United States, victory in the war for independence. Although Great Britain signed the Treaty of Paris in 1783, recognizing the United States as a sovereign country, it was not the end of hostilities.

Becoming Tar Heels

The end of the War of Independence brought new prosperity to Thomas Willis and his family. Rowan County records show that in 1783 Thomas was granted 565 acres of land from the state. It is unclear why he was granted such a large tract of land although two possible answers are available by reading accounts of historical documents.

One scenario is that he was being rewarded for his support to General Green when the war was being fought on the doorstep of the Willis farms. Undoubtedly, Thomas lost crops and livestock to both marching armies. Another possibility is that some British loyalists fled back to England at the end of the war giving up ownership of their land. There are accounts of British loyalists who were lynched or otherwise mistreated by embittered ex-neighbors. Perhaps the land grant was the result of abandoned loyalists' property being awarded to a patriot.

For the next 11 years, life was peaceful in Rowan County. In 1794 Thomas Willis died at the age of 60. An actual record of his Last Will and Testament has been found in the Rowan County Library. It tells much about how God had blessed this hard working farmer from Wales in the 34 years since he and his family arrived on the shores of North Carolina.

The will reveals he set aside for his wife 100 acres where their home was built and the buildings for their horses, cattle, hogs and farming equipment. Thomas bequeathed 100 acres to three of his sons. To Hannah, one daughter, went a cow and a calf. Another daughter, Rachel, received a colt. The youngest child, Adam, may have been in poor health and it is believed that he was sickly. Adam died the same year as his father.

At first glance, it may appear that his daughters' inheritance was not so generous. However, considering the primary mode of transportation was by horse and buggy; a good horse would sell for about $100 (about $10,000 in today's currency). Likewise, Hannah's inheritance was very valuable because her gift could provide a livelihood.

Three years after Thomas died, George and Margery had a son. He would be my Great Great Grandfather Maxwell Mackenzie Willis. Maxwell was the first of my grandfathers to be born in America. The year was 1797 and John Adams was President of the United States; the second man to hold that position. The spelling of Maxwell's middle name has been written as Mackenzie and Mackenzey. Even on his Marriage Bond his name is spelled two different ways on the same page! For the sake of consistency in this writing, the spelling Mackenzie is used.

The War Years

When Maxwell was 15, America was again at war with Great Britain and it is possible he joined the fight. Maxwell would have heard stories from his dad (George), his uncles (Thomas, James, and Adam) as well as from others who lived through the *American War of Independence* when the armies of Green and Cornwallis skirted the edge of the Willis farmlands.

Since the time of the Revolutionary War, the British had repeatedly attacked American trade ships. By 1812, the United States congress, fed up with the British aggression, declared war on Great Britain. At the time of the War of 1812, the tiny American Navy was no match against the might of the powerful English fleet. However, America had two things Great Britain lacked: vast resources with which to build ships and the interminable American spirit. Yet, the blows from the British were painful.

After two years of war, in 1814 the British invaded the U.S. Capitol and burned the White House. In early 1815, the final battle of the war was the *Battle of New Orleans*.

There was news in 1816 that Indiana had become the 19th state of the union. With such news and discussions of U.S. expansion, the seeds of migration and exploration were sown. It was Indiana that Maxwell Mackenzie would one day call home.

The ensuing years were prosperous and filled with technological advances as great as any today. The steam engine became America's new workhorse. Railroads crisscrossed the land with telegraph poles springing up alongside. The horse drawn reaper was invented. John Deere developed the steel plow. Steamboats began plying trade up and down the rivers.

According to a local Rowan County Newspaper article, Captain Maxwell Willis was wed to Nancy Jane Miller in 1825. A copy of their Marriage Bond has been found. In the wording of the bond we read that Maxwell was required to post a bond before a Marriage License was granted. It is unclear today what the purpose of a Marriage Bond was, but such a regulation would seem to have the effect of reducing the number of insincere intentions. Maxwell and Nancy Jane's first son was born in 1826. He was called Jasper and was my great grandfather.

Among the Willis families in Rowan County, there were discussions about the expanding American Frontier and the pioneering of Western plains. For the younger generation there was a lure of open spaces, abundant land, and the hope of a good future for their children. By the standards of the time, Rowan County was starting to feel a little crowded and the Willis families in Rowan County were intrigued by the possibilities of adventure.

In 1834 George Willis (Maxwell's father) died. It may

have been the event that gave Maxwell the courage to decide to move to Indiana. Eventually a few Willis families decided they would like to be a part of the pioneering movement. In fact, it was pretty much a family decision since George's sons and his wife, Margery (then 75), banded together to resettle in Indiana. One of his daughters stayed behind in Rowan County.

Westward Bound

It was Maxwell's turn for adventure and he paid mind to the wisdom of his elders as he and other Willis families planned to move to Indiana. George died two years before those plans materialized and one year before a great storyteller named Samuel Clemons (Mark Twain) was born. Among those leaving for Indiana were all of George Willis' sons, their families, and my Great, Great, Great Grandma Margery.

To guide the party across the mountainous terrain of the Cumberland Gap, Indians were hired. The Cherokee tribe, originally living in southern Appalachian Mountains, provided the logical choice of guides. Their knowledge of those mountains had been learned over many lifetimes of explorations and travels; it was their homeland. The Cherokees were one of the remaining tribes who were, at least marginally, friendly with white men. They had even tried to adapt and live in the white man's culture. Sadly, it was the white men who rejected the Cherokee's efforts to become a cultured people.

It is believed the Willis party began their journey to Indiana early in 1836. It would take them a little ways north, then west across the Cumberland Gap. Soon after Maxwell's move to Indiana, the Cherokee Nation was driven from their ancestral land, in an overland journey that became known as *The Trail of Tears* because of the death and suffering along the way.

Lineage from Thomas and Anne Willis (who first came to America), through Maxwell Willis (my great grandfather):

Thomas Willis 1734 - 1794
Anne Willis 1736 - 1794

Children of Thomas and Anne Willis:
Thomas (1755-1808), Rachel (1756-1823)
George (1757-1834), James (1759-1828)
Hanna (1761-1861), Adam (1763-1794)

George Willis 1757 - 1834
Margery Willis 1760 - 1841

Children of George and Margery Willis:
Nancy (1780-1837), George [Duck] (1784-1896)
James (1786-1846), Jane (1790-?), Philip (1790-?)
Thomas (1794-1847), Maxwell (1797-1856)

Maxwell Willis 1797 - 1856
Nancy Jane Miller Willis 1736 - 1794

Children of Maxwell and Nancy Jane Miller:
Jasper (1826-1901), Henry Jackson (1827-1875)
Beverly B. (1829-?), Louisa (1830-?)
George (1831-1864), William (1836-1864)
John (1838-1858), Elizabeth (1840-1895)
Martha E. (1842-1920), Mary J. (1842-1895)
Maxwell (1845-?), Nancy Amanda (1847-1924)

Maxwell Willis
Migrated from North Carolina to Indiana in 1836
My Great Great Grandfather

Chapter 2

MY ANCESTOR'S JOURNEY WESTWARD

*But I will for their sakes remember the covenant
of their ancestors, whom I brought forth out of the land...
that I might be their God: I am the Lord. (Leviticus 26:45)*

My Family Tree

Louisa Mae Willis Evans (she was called Mae), born in 1882, was my father's older sister. She remembered stories about our family, from her childhood and even into her adult life, which had been passed from past generations of ancestors. She recounted them in remarkable vividness, which might have never otherwise been known to future generations. I have included a few of those stories as a reminder of some of the unique happenings among people in those early days.

Treacherous Mountain Journey

Great Grandfather Jasper Willis would have been ten years old when their covered wagons, pulled by oxen, lumbered down the road heading north toward Indiana through the Cumberland Gap. Of course, Jasper was thrilled about the adventure, as only a young boy would be. However, the roads soon became trails, and the narrow treacherous terrain across the Appalachian Mountains was extremely hard and dangerous.

Later in life, Jasper would tell his children and grandchildren about the long rough journey. He told how white oxen pulled their covered wagons exclaiming, "It was an awfully rough trip!" It was especially hard on his mother, because she was with child. That child would be her sixth, which they named William, and the first Willis to be born a Hoosier.

The trail through the Cumberland Gap was
tiresome for the animals and the families.
[A.E. Willis illustration]

Jasper also described how they got lost along the way. They were fortunate to find some friendly Indians who, along with the hired guides, helped them find the right direction. Jasper recounted that they spent a lot of time observing the many things the Indians did, for their ways were quite different. He told how they made corn cakes by grinding corn into meal, adding water and other ingredients, then patting out cakes by hand to bake over an open fire. He noted that was all done without them ever washing their hands, which were filthy.

Settling in Indiana

The Willis families reached southern Indiana late in the year of 1836. Maxwell had been granted 640 acres to homestead in Pike County, about five miles south of Petersburg in Washington Township. The area would become known as Clark's Station. Great Great Granddad Maxwell built a log cabin and cleared the land to begin farming.

Young Jasper did not have a soft life growing up. In

addition to helping with the family farm, he worked with other Willis men building roads. That required clearing under-brush, cutting down large trees, and digging out rocks. Then the grading and scraping of a roadbed using mule teams could begin.

They worked hard but they found time to socialize too. There was always a need to exchange news, conduct business, and make new friends. Perhaps it was at a church meeting or other community gathering that Great Grandfather Jasper met a young woman named Sarah Ellen Dean. She was a rather small woman with fair skin, pronounced cheekbones and very soft blue eyes. On March 22, 1846, they were married.

Jasper and Sarah Ellen rented farmland and when it was possible they bought a 40-acre farm in the same area. It promised to be productive in measures equal to the labor they put into it. In 1846, he acquired another 120 acres giving him a total of 160 acres of good fertile farmland. Jasper aspired to own a large, successful farming operation. Of course, to farmers in that era, large families provided the needed labor to operate the farms.

In 1848, Jasper and Sarah Ellen's first son, Beverly B., was born. Bev, as he was called, was my grandfather and was the third of 12 children. Besides being a good father, Jasper was described as a *jolly* man, weighing over 200 pounds. His love for jokes and pranks has been handed down over the generations. He was also a shrewd businessman. He managed to buy and sell several tracts of land at a handsome profit. He had been able to enlarge the farm to 160 acres, making it one of the larger spreads in the county. In 1856, he sold their farm. The sale gave him a nice return on his investment. Jasper then moved his family from Washington Township to Logan Township. They were highly respected by the community in which they lived.

In 1856, Maxwell Mackenzie, the man who led the Willis families to Indiana, died. His wife Jane, my great great grandmother, lived until 1891. They both were buried in

Johnson Cemetery south of Petersburg, Indiana, on Line Road.

It was a time of great turmoil in the United States. The war between the North and the South had left no one untouched. Many families were torn apart, sometimes politically and sometimes through bloodshed. It was frightening to realize the enemy was not some foreigner from another country.

In 1868 Jasper moved his family back to Washington Township where they bought another farm. Jasper made improvements to their new farm and bought more land in the surrounding area. The evidence of his successful land deals is revealed by records that show he eventually amassed a large estate with 440 acres of good fertile land, much of what was cleared and farmed.

Aunt Mae was Beverly's second oldest living child. Mae was rather large, stout, and strong as an ox! She would get out and work on the farm, driving the wagons, and any other farm duties there was to do. She was quite capable of doing her share of work, just as any man on the farm. Jasper always called her "the old Irish" because she was always ready for a good joke. She loved joking with him and pulling jokes on him.

Aunt Mae told some interesting stories about her Grandpa Jasper. Following is one of them:

> "He was a jolly old man weighing over 200 pounds! One time Grandpa and I were on this wagon headed over to the riverbed. He let me drive the team of horses into the water. We weren't expecting it to be so deep, but all of a sudden, the river water came clear up to the wagon bed! We had to get out of the wagon. Well, Grandpa had on a brand new pair of doeskin trousers. They fit him rather tight, but he was quite proud of those new, expensive pants. When he jumped out of the wagon he slipped on a corn cob, fell, and ran a brick up his pant leg! As we worked our way back toward the house...here came Grandma

running out! Not knowing whether to laugh or to cry, she exclaimed, 'Now, Jasper, you're in a terrible shape!' He retorted, 'Well, don't tell me something I already know?' The brick was securely lodged and could not even be coaxed out! 'Guess I'll have to get the scissors and either cut your leg or cut the trousers,' she jokingly declared. So, she began to cut the pant's leg, until the brick finally came out. Grandpa was so upset to have his brand new doeskins ruined!"

Mae went on to exclaim, "But I would be [upset] too, because they were a specialty item and cost more than regular trousers."

Very little is known about the children of Jasper and Sarah Ellen Willis. Of the 12 children born to them, only nine lived to adulthood. The most information recorded about any of them–that our family has–is about their oldest son, Beverly, my grandfather.

In 1883, the Pike County Democrat (the local newspaper) published an article about the 58th birthday celebration of Jasper Willis. It was an event celebrated by his children, neighbors, and friends at his home in Pike County. There were 85 people present to enjoy the baskets of good things to eat. The article did not name the children in attendance, but it is very likely that my grandparents, Beverly and Isabelle, were at that celebration.

Jasper died December 5, 1901 from Bright's Disease (a kidney disease). The probate records show that Jasper had been cared for by two doctors. One was Dr. W. M. Hunter, whom Floyd Hunter Willis (my father) was named after. The other doctor was Dr. Imel, whom Imel H. Willis (my brother) was named after.

Sarah Ellen, my great grandmother, outlived Jasper by two years. She was born September 9, 1825 and died October 19, 1903 from gangrene. Jasper and Sarah were highly respected members of the Missionary Baptist Church. At the time of their deaths, they were among the oldest residents of

Pike County. They were laid to rest side by side in Walnut Hills Cemetery at Petersburg, Indiana.

My Great Grandfather
Jasper Willis
1826 - 1901

Sarah Ellen Dean Willis
1825 - 1903

Jasper and Sarah Ellen Willis with their children taken ca 1908
L to R: Emery, Delia, Charles, Kate, Lou, Mariah, Bev, George, Liz

The children of Jasper and Sarah Ellen:
Cordella/Delia (1846-1908), Maria/Mariah (1847-1927),
Beverly B./Bev (1848-1911), Melissa Jane (1850-1865),
Sarah Ellen (1852-1854), Louisa/Lou (1854-1920)
William Emery (1857-1916), Charles L. (1858-1931)
Catherine/Kate (1861-1912), George M. (1864-1936)
Mary Ellen (1866-1886), Nancy Elizabeth/Liz (1868-1932)

Beverly and Isabelle Willis

My grandfather Beverly was born, lived, and died in Pike County, Indiana. Not much is known about his childhood, but he would have had the usual farming responsibilities that were required of boys in the 1800s. His education, typical of the time, included enough that he could read and write.

Beverly was around 19 when he met a young woman at church named Isabelle Hilborn (she was known as Belle). Isabelle's birth is recorded in the Hilborn family Bible as Isabel, born April 10, 1856. For the sake of consistency, in this writing the spelling *Isabelle* is used. Beverly fell "head over heels in love with her" which resulted in marriage October 17, 1872. At

21

the time, Beverly was 23 and Belle was 16 years old.

Nine children were born to them, three died in their youth. Their living children who established their own homes were: Rozina–called "Rose" or "Rosie" (married James Nance), Louise Mae (married Lawrence Evans), James Edmund–we called him Edmund (married first to Alice Able, who died during childbirth. Edmund later remarried to Mary Coleman), Clarence (married Esta Mable Willis), Ola Gertrude (married Roy Kincaid), and Floyd Hunter (married Goldie Inez Parker).

My Grandparent's Homestead

When Beverly married Belle, he owned 60 acres of land in the area of Clark's Station. Of that 60 acres, a 40-acre square was on the west side of the main road that ran north to Petersburg. The reconstruction of that road began in 1939 to become State Highway 57. The new highway bypassed what had been the Wabash-Erie Canal and my old homeplace.

Beverly and Belle built their house, barn, and other farm buildings near the center of the 40 acres. The other 20 acres was a strip to the south on the east side of the road, where the Wabash and Erie Canal had been dug diagonally across those 20 acres. When the canal operations stopped, the railroad was built parallel and adjacent to that section of the abandoned canal. The canal and the railroad consumed approximately six acres leaving only 14 acres of tillable land. The remaining acreage of the estate included cropland, woodland, and some pasture. My father would eventually own a portion of that property and build the home where I was born.

Soon after my grandparents moved into their small two-room home, Beverly built a large modern four-room frame house east of the original two-room home and just west of the main road. The new structure did not have plumbing and electricity because there was no electricity in the rural areas at that time. There was a wide porch across the front of the house. That was an important feature as it was the common gathering place on summer days. It was where family and friends came to relax, share news, and enjoy time together. After the new house was completed, they moved their two-room house down the hill to join the new house. A space of 10 feet was left between the two structures and enclosed to serve as a breezeway between the two sections. The old section became a kitchen and the newly built section was the living quarters.

That is the house I remember as Grandma's home. I have fond memories of family gatherings as well as countless hours working, playing, and spending many nights with Grandma. It was in their "modern home" that the Lord blessed them with a large family and comfortable living. The old canal actually became part of the farm and served as a source of water for livestock.

Bev and Belle were called Pa and Ma by their children. Aunt Mae recounts two stories about her dad:

> "Pa and me had a pet chicken snake we called Ezra. Ezra's hang out was the corncrib but he also had yard privileges. He was fed milk in a pan. Now, Ma wouldn't set foot in that corncrib for anything! One day Ma went out to the pump to fetch a pail of water and stepped right on Ezra, barefooted! Pa came home and saw poor Ezra dead and said, 'Oh, Belle you've killed our pet snake!' 'Oh, Bev,' Ma said,'I'm sorry! I was so scared that I did not think what I was doin' until it was too late!' "
>
> "Pa was a great hand for jokes and tricks, which seemed to be a traditional family character trait. Bev and his younger brother, William Emery, were always good at playing tricks on people. One day Bev saw some boys going to drown some cats. He told them that Doc Tisdale was buying cats for 5 cents a piece. The boys took the cats to him. Doc got so mad that the next day he filled the Willis yard with cats. I guess the doctor thought that would show him a thing or two."

Farming was Bev's main occupation and he had ambitions to be successful at it. He purchased some extra land and put aside part of his farm for a fairly large apple orchard. He also planted a variety of other fruit trees, as well as a raspberry patch. Their livestock consisted of two teams of horses, four milk cows, two sows, several chickens, some ducks, and ironically–plenty of cats.

Aunt Mae recalled an accident that happened one day while Beverly was plowing with a team of horses. He had been plowing most of the day and he was using the harrow. He was hot and tired as he maneuvered the team around the field. As he was pulling on the reigns with his sweaty hands, the reigns slipped out of his hands and fell between the horses. They spooked and took off running, upsetting the harrow and dragging the rig with Beverly under the harrow some 20 yards.

Aunt Mae had to ride the mule to town to fetch the doctor while Belle was putting any kind of rag on him she could find, to stop the bleeding. The doctor said he was blessed to be alive but his extensive injuries would be slow to heal. It was a long time before Beverly was able to work again. The neighbors came to our aid and helped with the farming.

That accident happened in 1897, the year William McKinley became the 25th president. It was in March of that year Floyd, my dad, was born. Belle had her hands full that summer as she had both Bev and Floyd who needed round the clock care. She was grateful for the help of all the neighbors. They pitched in and helped as they could with the farming and anything else that was needed.

Beverly slowly recovered from his accident but his health was never the same afterward. The winters were especially hard on him and by 1908, he became very sick with tuberculosis. His health gradually worsened. His lungs started filling with fluid and it got harder for him to breath.

During that time, the tragedy of Edmund losing his first wife struck the Willis family. When Alice died while giving birth to their only child, Arba, his head was damaged as a result from the use of forceps in the efforts to save his life. Edmund did not have the experience or the inclination to raise a handicapped baby, so Bev and Belle took in Arba. Always the tenderhearted one, Belle cared for Arba and loved him as one of her own.

Grandpa Beverly died on May 7, 1911 at the age of 62. The doctor announced his death was from "that killer pneumonia." He was buried in Martin Cemetery near Hosmer (the town was renamed Glezen in 1939), Indiana, south of Petersburg. Grandma Belle outlived Beverly by 23 years, which is why her offspring remember more about her than they do about Grandfather Beverly.

Unfortunately, I never met my grandfather Beverly because he died when my father was only 13 years of age. However, he left a legacy of good Christian morals and taught his children the value of honest living. At the time of his passing all of his sons and daughters, with the exception of young Floyd, were married with homes of their own. Floyd was still a boy but was given a man's responsibility, as it fell on his shoulders to take care of his mother and run the farm.

Grandfather Beverly B. Willis
1848 - 1911

25

The Matriarch Belle Willis

The history of Isabelle (Belle) Hilborn Willis is an interesting one. We always knew her as just Grandma or Grandma Belle. Her father was James Rose Hilborn. His family had immigrated to Newark, New Jersey from Holland. In New Jersey, the Hilborns became well respected and influential in society. James Rose Hilborn's mother's name was Martha Rose.

Family lore has it that Martha Rose and President William McKinley's mother were sisters. James Rose Hilborn sought his fortune in Indiana and it is there that Isabelle was born in 1856.

Grandma Belle was among the first women to be able to vote in presidential elections after women won the right to vote in 1920, which was an outcome of the woman's suffrage movement. Aunt Mae provided some of the history about Grandma Belle.

Her parents, James Rose Hilborn and Rozina (also spelled Rosanna) Ellen (last name unknown), were married on July 3, 1846, in Pike County, Indiana. Both had other children by previous marriages. Isabelle was born on April 10, 1856. She was the second daughter born to James and Rozina Hilborn. Isabelle's older sister was Louisa and the younger siblings were Tempie, Jane, and Charles.

The matriarch of the Willis clan was truly Grandma Belle. Everyone loved and respected her, even if they didn't always agree with her. She was the person that many went to with their troubles and concerns, looking for advise, or just comfort. She truly had a big heart for everybody's problems, whether it was family or not. But she especially loved her grandchildren. So naturally, advice was given out to us all (especially when we needed it).

Isabelle Hilborn Willis ca1927
Grandma Belle
1856 - 1934

Grandpa Bev and Grandma Belle family ca1908
(L-R) The Nance family: Norman, Arthur, Elizabeth, Dellie,
Rose Willis Nance (holding Myrtle), Lura (back), and Jewel.
Uncle Edmund (standing), Grandpa Bev Willis,
Floyd (my father), Grandma Belle Willis, Aunt Ola (standing),
Aunt Mae Willis Evans with her daughters Ruby (back) and Opal.

Floyd Hunter Willis

My father, Floyd, was born on March 20, 1897, in the modest country home of his parents in the community of Clark's Station, now known as Willisville, and it is where he lived throughout his lifetime. He was the youngest of nine children. Aunt Mae, his older sister, was 15 years old at the time. She loved her little brother very much and it became her responsibility to take care of him. Mae has told that she watched over him like a mother hen. Floyd was a homebody and never liked to go anywhere. There wasn't much of anything he could hide from her because she knew him better than anyone. She said one of the things he liked best was for her to take him horseback riding. Their ma was afraid he might fall off, but Mae would explain to her "I sit him right up behind me and he clings to me like a tick."

On Election Day one year, while the men went to vote, Grandma Sarah Ellen invited all her daughters and daughter-in-laws over to stitch, chatter, and cook up a big dinner at a quilting party. At that time, women were not yet allowed to vote. Aunt Mae claimed their house was busier than an "ant heap" once all those large families got there. When Grandma Belle and all her brood were ready to go, they found Floyd all wrapped up over in a corner with tears in his eyes. He didn't want to go! Mae stayed with him while the others returned home. She played games with Floyd and finally tricked him into riding the horse to Grandma Belle's house.

One time Floyd was riding with his pa in the wagon, when the horses got spooked and bolted down a steep bank throwing Beverly out of the wagon. Then the horses barreled it up a hill and around the barn three times before coming to a stop. Floyd was still in the wagon and yelled to his ma. She came running thinking he was hurt. He said, "I wasn't scared. I just wanted you to see what a nice ride I's taking!" Beverly never used bad words and he didn't let Floyd say them either.

When Floyd was about three or four, he wanted a door open for some reason. So he said to his pa, "D*#$& open this door!" Bev said, "that is a naughty boy to say such things. Don't say words like that again." Floyd piped back, "D### I will. Open the D### door!" So, guess who got a thrashing!!

Following are a few short stories Mae told about Floyd:

> He was very unhappy about his sister, Mae, getting married. Floyd told her husband, Lawrence, that she could not leave because, "She is my part."
>
> Mae bought Floyd a dog and where he went, the dog went–even to school. The teacher put the dog out, so Floyd would leave, too. He said, "If my dog can't go to school, then I won't either!" Floyd was about as excited about going to school as an apathetic camel! He would hide under the bed, in the corncrib, or under the house. Sometimes he could not be found. He was known at times to hide under a bridge all day until time to go home from school.
>
> Some time after Beverly died, Floyd would write notes to his ma and sign some unknown man's name to the letter. She would get angry about it until finally she learned that it was one of Floyd's tricks. Floyd was often up to some kind of trick or mischief.
>
> Floyd was the only child living at home when his pa died. All the other children were married and living in their own homes with their own families and responsibilities. Not only did he assume all the general upkeep to the property, he and his ma earned a living from the approximately 40 tillable acres of the remaining 80-acre farm. They had enough food coming from the land, but managing to purchase other necessities and having extra cash to pay property taxes was very difficult. It was a lot of strain put on a 14-year-old boy and his mother. They put their faith in God to help them and they made it. To complicate the situation further was the "watching

after" or taking care of his younger nephew, Arba, who lived with them. Since Bev and Belle had cared for Arba, Floyd then felt he needed to take on the additional responsibility of being the father image to him.

Aunt Mae described Floyd as growing up to be a fine young man. He was tall (close to six feet), slim, and handsome, with beautiful blue eyes that were full of kindness. Sometimes there would be that spunky twinkle in his eyes letting you know he was up to something or getting ready to tell one of his funny stories. Even though he was tall and skinny, he was as strong as an ox! He was very active. He was also an avid, expert hunter and fisherman. Floyd's parents had taught him the meaning of honesty and integrity toward his fellow man such that his word was as good as gold. His word on any kind of agreement or business deal was as good as written and sealed on paper. His jovial and humorous disposition not only won many friends, but also helped to brighten the lives of those he daily came in contact with.

My father ca1912

Goldie Inez Parker Willis

From inside the house we heard the sound of familiar footsteps approaching. As I looked up from where I was playing in the yard with my brothers, there stood my mom–an apron on over her blue dress, which matched her warm blue eyes. She would look to where my dad might be working. I watched as she put her hand to her forehead to shade the evening sun from her eyes and put the other hand to her mouth to summon us to dinner. That was her routine to call the family in for the evening meal. Then she would raise her voice up a notch louder so my dad could hear from wherever he was working. She waited for a response, but if there was none, she would send one of us to find him. We would all usually be hungry enough that we did not have to be called twice.

Even though time has moved forward, I can close my eyes and still see those moments replay. Those times have always been etched in my mind. It is just like yesterday that I can see my mom's tired face and love in her eyes, smiling as she watched us kids enjoy our meal. Even though we must have been a burden at times, her love for us was a reflection of the unconditional love of Christ. These are just a sampling of the memories that I will always cherish in my heart about Mom. My mom was a woman of high character, strong, and yet tender. She was only about 5 feet tall but packed a lot of influence with those around her. Her family background was a strong ingredient in molding her childhood, as she came from a family comprised of businessmen, farmers, and merchants.

Her grandfather, William Harrison Parker (also called Bill or Will), made a big move from Kentucky to Spencer County, Indiana. He purchased a farm between Richland City and Rockport where he raised hogs and cattle as the main source of the family income, which is how he gained his nickname "Hog Bill". Grandpa Bill was tall and thin in stature in contrast to his wife, Mary Stillwell Parker, who was short and stocky. They had three children. Their first child, a girl, died at a very young age. The second was a girl and they named her Ida. She was very bossy to her brother, Harry, who was the last child. Harry was my mom's dad. When he was old enough he helped his father on the farm, which had extensive acreage. After his father's death (July 21, 1921), Harry inherited a share of the farm, which he traded for a store.

Upon Harry's marriage to Grace Gilliland, they moved into their new home on land his dad had given him, which was west of his parent's home. Grace stood a little taller than her husband, but then most people did. Harry was a good looking man with dark hair and stood only 4½ feet tall. Their first child was Goldie Inez Parker, born on October 7,1897. Goldie Inez was a beautiful baby and very healthy, but very tiny.

Following are some stories my mom told about her childhood (in her own words):

"Sometime during my highchair years, I had an accident that could have had far more serious consequences than it turned out to be. My mom had tied me in a little rocker so that I would not fall out, but the tie came loose and I fell head first toward the fireplace. My crying and the dog barking brought the adults to my rescue. The fire had burned a spot on my head causing terrible pain and later caused a bald spot. Hair would never grow in that spot again."

"There was another time, which I can barely remember hearing my mom crying in severe pain as she pulled a rusty nail from her foot that she had stepped on out in the hen house. Not long after this, she got very sick. I remember trailing after her as she went to the mailbox where there was some medicine waiting for her. I was only three years old when that happened–when she took lockjaw and died. I cried and cried because I missed her so much...because I knew she loved me very much. I couldn't understand why she was gone and wouldn't come back."

"When my mom died her dad (John Gilliland, my grandfather whom I called Pa) and Ma (Melissa Bassinger Gilliland) moved in with Poppy and me. I assume this arrangement was made because I was only three years of age and needed to be cared for. They were very good to me! They were loving grandparents and they seemed to know how to comfort me, especially at night, as I would cry a lot because I missed my mom so much."

"Sometime afterward, my dad [Harry] married again and returned to the homeplace with his new wife. His new wife Minnie gave birth to a daughter (Willie Beatrice). I now had a baby stepsister and I was very happy about that."

"At the age of five, still living at "poppy's place" (my dad's home), I really wanted to go to the school that was just across the field from the house. I must have begged hard enough that the decision was made that I could attend. I worked hard and did well enough to please my dad. After finishing first grade, he gave me a little trunk, which was filed with candy. I opened it up and discovered my first grade reader and a scratch book laying neatly in the bottom. This trunk was a very special treasure to me. I stored my stuff in it; such as pictures and letters and cherished it as one of my fondest memories of my Poppy."

"I was about six years old when my grandparents Gilliland and me moved to a farm between Gentryville and Lincoln City, Indiana. This is where we lived for the next four years. I really loved that house! It was a big two-story house with a nice large upstairs with lots of rooms. Behind that house, was a two-story brick building located on the same property. I had fun turning that whole upstairs into my very own playhouse. This entire estate was known as the Kerchavel Farm."

"I met a neighbor girl, Ruth, who turned out to be a very special friend to me as we had so much in common with each other. We were nearly the same age and enjoyed doing many things together. Ruth and I always took the long walk to school together which was two miles. On extremely cold days, the hired hand would come to pick us up on horseback, bringing with him an extra horse for us to ride. I do not remember the hired hand's name, but I do remember that he was very kind and resourceful. He nicknamed me "Golden Heart" because I would always give him my desert from my sack lunch. It was easy to give it away because I didn't like it anyway. One day he told me not to tell Grandma that I disliked the butter and sugar on bread. If I didn't tell her, she would continue to put it in the sack lunch and he could continue to feast on it on the way home from school."

"While we lived on the Kerchavel farm, Grandpa (I called him Pa) raised tobacco on a large scale. He bargained with me, one day, that if I would raise a little patch of tobacco, he would buy what I raised and pay me some money for it. I agreed and worked that small tobacco patch til it produced very well. This is when I realized I might have a "green thumb" after all. That turned out to be very good business training. The experience helped me develop business skills that I have since put to good use. I have my Pa to thank for these opportunities as they have been beneficial throughout my years."

"Pa also raised sorghum as a secondary crop. Ruth and I worked at the sorghum mill riding the horse round and round as the stalks of cane were fed through the wheel. We did this all day long, but sometimes we would get so tired of riding and decided to take turns leading the horse around on foot. After so much of that, we decided that riding was better because our feet were getting very sore from walking so much. When the horse would get thirsty, it was our responsibility to make sure he had enough water and feed to keep going."

"It seems like I had lots of aunts and uncles in the

Gilliland family. Some of these uncles were Ted, Don, Jock, and Arthur...along with Aunt Florence (Dougan) and Aunt Pearl (Ranger). Shortly after we moved to Lincoln City, my cousin Roy Dougan (Aunt Florence's son), stayed with us to go to the local school where Ruth and I attended. We didn't get along very well because he was a bully and would push us around. I was determined he wasn't going to get the best of me and I soon learned to outsmart him."

"My grandpa, John Gilliland, was short, stocky, and stout with dark hair. Pa (Grandpa) was an intelligent and a very innovative man. He decided to set up a blacksmith shop near a pond in Lincoln City. The school had purchased a boat with oars for the neighborhood kids to play with on the pond. It wasn't long until the bigger boys, including my cousin Roy, monopolized the boat and would seldom let us girls use it. They proceeded to break the oars and put this nice plaything out of commission. Grandpa made a special set of oars just for me and asked me to take good care of them. I would then take my girlfriends out in the boat without the boys around and we would have so much fun. I knew I had to guard those oars from the boys and was very successful in doing so. One day Roy asked for those oars and I told him flat out, 'No way!' I said, 'if you had not destroyed the original oars, you would still have them and I am not having you do that with mine.' Roy searched high and low without success, because I had them hid in the cellar where he did not think to look."

"Behind my schoolhouse, at Lincoln City, stood the *Nancy Hanks Lincoln* home [Nancy Hanks-Lincoln was President Lincoln's mother]. On each anniversary of her birthday, regardless of weather conditions, all of us kids had to march out to her gravesite. The Lincoln Memorial Park was just being started at that time. The Lincoln log cabin was built near Little Pigeon Creek in December of 1816. Nancy Lincoln was buried on a wooded hill south of the cabin."

"In 1907, when I was 10 years old, our big two storied house in Lincoln City burned to the ground. Nobody seemed to know how the fire got started, but one thing that got saved from the fire was my little trunk. After the fire, we moved to Petersburg, Indiana, where we lived two houses away from Mrs. Grable and my girlfriend, Ruth. They also had recently moved to Petersburg. Ruth and I went to the same school again. It was a long walk! We walked all the way to the top of what was called *Bell's Hill* to get to the Smith School. I attended there for three years and then dropped out to help care for Grandpa who had become ill that summer."

"Grandpa (Gilliland) died November 7, 1911. Now it was just Grandma and me, so we packed up our belongings and moved over near the sawmill on the west side of town. To help Grandma I went to work in the tomato-canning factory. I was 13 at that time and there were many assorted chores to do while still working at the factory. I always enjoyed staying busy doing gardening, sewing, cooking, etc., but I preferred being outdoors, which is why my skin was tanned most of the time."

"Grandma and I were very close and really enjoyed working and doing things together. We attended the First Baptist Church in Petersburg. That is where I got baptized. I was 15 years old then. Another thing I remember about Grandma is that she had a large loom. Boy, we made a lot of quilts."

Smith School at Bell's Hill was just south of Petersburg, on the main road that went south to Clark's Station. The school no longer exists but I remember passing it when I was a youth. There were classes still being held at there at the time I attended high school. I didn't realize until later in life, that my mom had at one time been a student there.

Inez Parker (age 4) - 1901

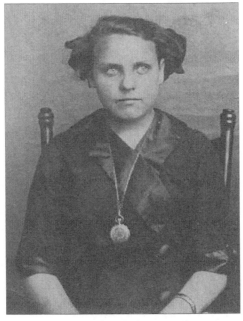

My mother in her youth

My Maternal Grandparents
Harry Parker 1878 - 1938
Grace Gilliland Parker 1881 - 1901
(photo taken ca1899)

Home of Harry and Grace Parker
Birthplace of Inez (my mom)
east of Richland City, Indiana

My mom's paternal grandparents
William Harrison Parker 1846 - 1921
Mary E. Stillwell Parker 1845 - ?

My mom's maternal grandparents
John Gilliland 1845 - 1911
Melissa Bassinger Gilliland 1850 - 1920

John and Melissa Gilliland home between Gentryville and Lincoln City, Indiana. This large two-storied house is where Inez had the entire second floor as her personal playhouse.

The Perfect Set-Up

Five years after my mother moved to Petersburg with her Gilliland grandparents, she met my father. It was a real set-up! This story, told by my mom, is how she and my dad met:

"I was 15 years old at the time and a girlfriend and I were invited to the home of Norman Nance, a nephew to Floyd, on a Sunday. Floyd Willis had seen me before (I didn't know about this plan) and asked Norman to invite us both over so he could meet me. Norman and him cooked it up that he would "just happen" to be walking towards town on the railroad tracks about the same time."
"Norman's girlfriend asked me if I wanted to take a walk down the track with them. 'How far are you going?' I asked. She said, 'Maybe to Clark's Station. A

certain feller out that way reckoned he'd meet us part way.' Well, that decided the day! I grinned and caught my friend's eye. O' yes, it must have been planned all along. I decided to go nonchalantly pretending there was nothing extraordinary about this Sunday afternoon walk. In a way it wasn't out of the ordinary because folks walked down the tracks all the time. Just so you were in pleasant company enjoying the idle chatter. It was a little awkward because the guys hadn't decided exactly how to arrange it. Looked pretty flimsy to me!"

Norman said, 'That must be him settin' way down yonder.' So Norman hollered at him, 'Howdy, Mutt.' He looked up and hollered back, 'Howdy.' I watched as his long thin form pulled himself together, stood to full height, and turned to come toward us. I had seen just a glimpse of him a couple of times before."

" 'You'll probably have to do some extra talking cause Mutt's awful shy around girls,' my friend said. I replied, 'I'd like to know why they all call him Mutt. Maybe I'll ask him that.' 'Well,' she said, 'I don't recall hearing him called anything but that. But I guess it's just a nickname.' While we walked along in silence, I took time to study him. He was well tanned and had a long lock of hair that came down across his forehead, which caused him every now and then to give his head a sideways sling to throw it back. A big grin filled his face and he grinned the rest of the way there, with his head ducked slightly a bit because of shyness or maybe it was because of awkwardness."

"As Norman stumbled through some simple introductions, I was startled to see what striking blue eyes Mutt had. They were kind eyes...shy eyes and an honest open face. The brief introduction was the most difficult moment of the day. Mutt's sudden *little boy look* and awkwardness caused a funny little twinge in my heart. At the moment, I knew he had just stolen a small piece from it."

My mom, Inez, learned to manage her own affairs very early in life. She was blessed and greatly loved by her grandparents who brought her up. The Gillilands had high spiritual and moral values and exhibited those in the manner in which they lived. While my mom was a teenage girl, those values were taught to her as a part of her everyday life. She was quite active in church. She had made a full commitment to the Lord, which proved to be a guiding factor in her life. Some of the fondest memories and earliest recollections of her childhood were woven into the very fiber of her character as a young woman, then as a mother. All of us children were blessed by the living influence of the moral, spiritual, and ambitious standards set before us by our parents throughout our growing years.

My mom taking Aunt Mae for a ride in her buggy

Inez and Floyd ca1916

Chapter 3

EARLY FAMILY AND HOME LIFE

The Spirit of God hath made me, and
the breath of the Almighty hath given me life. (Job 33:4)

Our Family

Floyd Willis and Inez Parker (called Pop and Mom by their children) were married November 5, 1914. They started their married life living with Grandma Belle. Even though they were starting their own family, it was necessary for them to continue the maintenance and operation of Grandma's farm and home. While living with Grandma, their first three children were born.

Mom holding Imel not long after he was born in 1917

Inez and Harry Parker (Mom's dad) standing
William and Mary Parker seated with Imel 1917

Mom and Pop with first two children
Floyd holding Marybelle and Inez with Imel ca1919

Mom and Pop moved into a house across the road from Grandma's, in the latter part of 1921. In the summer of 1922 they moved into a cabin that was close to where they would begin building their own home. Grandpa Beverly had deeded an acre of land to each of his sons and daughters who were interested in establishing a home there to raise their own families. Pop chose an acre that was near a remaining section of the old Wabash and Erie Canal. In the late fall of 1923, my parents moved their family into their new four-room house.

This photo is of our homeplace taken ca1967. Our house was one of the better homes in the community at the time it was built. The large hickory tree in the foreground is gone now, but it supplied almost a bushel of hickory nuts each year. The house is still standing yet today and looks about the same as it did when I was a child.

Pop was criticized by many relatives and friends and strongly advised that he would surely have children drown in that body of water by building his house in that location. In response, he assured the pessimistic people that he would not permit any of his children to drown. Pop had a secret plan, which he promptly practiced with each of his seven children.

47

As soon as we could crawl we were taken to the canal and taught how to swim. None of us even remember learning to swim, but we all learned to do a good job of it. I have never known or heard of anyone drowning in the canal. Today I have fond memories of living on the banks of the old Wabash and Erie Canal.

This is a portion of the Wabash-Erie Canal that still exists near the home where I was born in Clark's Station (now called Willisville), Indiana.

The Wabash and Erie Canal

The idea behind building Indiana's historical Wabash-Erie Canal was to improve the transportation of commerce through the state. In 1843, early sections of the canal in northern Indiana started operation. By the time the canal was finished, the railroad boom was in full swing and provided faster transportation for shipping. The canal was in full operation for only about 10 years and was considered a colossal failure because of huge financial losses.

The canal was originally intended to connect Lake Erie in northern Ohio with the Ohio River in Evansville, Indiana. Many crews were working on various sections of the canal continually for five or six years. The objective was to carry commerce to the Fort Wayne and Indianapolis industrial centers; then across the state to Terre Haute for access to the Wabash River; then back through the middle southern part of the state to Evansville, connecting with the Ohio River. A large turning pool, for the boats to turn around, was built where the Evansville Courthouse now stands.

The southern section of the Wabash-Erie Canal went through Petersburg and on to Evansville. During the early 1850s the canal cut was made through the area where the Willises had settled south of Petersburg. Grandma said that some of her ancestors and distant relatives worked on digging the canal.

The last canal boat in Indiana made its final docking in 1874, but many areas of the canal had already shut down years earlier. In many places, the tow-paths of the canal were used for the train system rail-beds.

In 1861 the canal boat operations ceased in the area south of Petersburg, where my relatives lived. According to historical research, it is likely the community was given the name of *Clark's Station* around the time the tracks were laid for the railroad and the train was put into use. The canal was abandoned after all sections of it became useless and no one was denied the use of it as if it were public property.

The Willis Children

The signs of spring appeared with trees sending forth their new leaves, flowers blossoming, and birds singing their cheerful songs. All of nature seemed to be celebrating a special event. God's handiwork, shown in the wonders of spring, was a grand reception for my appearance. Born on Wednesday, April 23, 1924, I was the first child born in the new home (my old homeplace). Perhaps that is why, yet today, I appreciate the beauty of spring that celebrates my birthday each year.

At birth, I was given the name Beverly James. However, in the recording process, my name was changed to James Beverly. I still consider it an honor to be named after

Grandfather Beverly Willis. I was the only one of Grandfather Bev's seven grandsons to be named after him. (*A good name is rather to be chosen than great riches... Proverbs 22:1*) That is a wonderful truth in God's word. I consider it a good name, but I never gained any great riches!

My oldest brother, Imel Harry, had just turned seven just before I was born. He was born March 14, 1917. Later in life, I learned that Imel had been assigned the responsibility as my caretaker. He was to be my guardian, my teacher, my boss, supervisor, and my mentor. Because of his Christian life, high morals, and great ambition in life, Imel set a good example for not only me, but for all the other siblings, too. We all respected his word as truth and the justice of his correction as right.

I do not remember there was any time that Imel had to use physical punishment to get me to do as I was told. I just knew his instructions were the law–so to speak. I doubt if he ever gave orders in a way that would cause any of us to rebel. Since he was my caretaker, it is quite likely that I got a spanking on the behind a few times to teach me to be an obedient child. If so, I was too small to remember it.

Others of the family reported that I was very slow at learning to talk. They may have thought I was going to be a retarded child. Evidently, there was little need for me to talk. Five other people were probably busy talking most of the time, so I hardly had a chance to get in a word anyway. Besides, they had a way of knowing my needs and desires without me telling them. I was not interested in exercising my vocal chords for anything other than grunting and crying in time of disaster!

Even at the table, it only took a grunt and a point to let them know what I wanted. I remember there was some discussion about my way of expressing my needs but I don't remember being reprimanded for it. When Lelah began to talk, she taught me a more civilized way to communicate. That was the end of the grunting, but there were still special occasions for crying. It must have been frustrating or maybe laughable to others of the family.

That was about the time I learned to swim. Pop was living up to his promise to teach each of us to swim almost by the time we could walk since we lived close to the old canal. He was determined to eliminate the possibility of any drowning accidents in the canal. In addition to those early swimming lessons, we all learned respect for home and family, the rules of good behavior, and even to work at simple things within our ability.

In our youth, Morris, Orace Wayne, and I were good boys but sometimes we carried on with a lot of foolishness. We watched for certain comic strips in the daily paper...to name a few: *Alley Oop*, *Li'l Abner*, *The Mountain Boys*, and *Chief Wahoo*. That was our main reading for the day, and we would take some of the things those characters said and repeat them over and over until others of the family were really tired of hearing us. For example: "There's nary a dry drizzle cloud in the sky", "Mommy, here I is", or "Uug, chili heap hot". There were many more!

Mary Isabelle was born September 18, 1918. Her middle name was a namesake of her paternal grandmother. We called her Marybelle–I don't know why or how that got started, but it stuck. Marybelle is what everyone came to know her as...most people never knew her true given name.

At Christmastime when I was in the sixth grade, Marybelle and her boyfriend, Gerald Gray, told us that they had an announcement to make on Christmas Day. They had been going steady for about two years, and we thought they were going to announce their engagement. To everyone's surprise, the news was that they were already married and had been for a few months. At that time, married students could not attend school and she was in her senior year. Everyone wanted her to keep the secret until school was out so she could finish high school. However, no amount of coaxing would get her go back to school. Sadly, she stopped short of graduating by only four months.

The third child was Wesley Bassinger and he was four

years older than me, as he was born June 17, 1920. The unusual name was the name of the doctor who delivered him, Dr. Bassinger, and it was maiden name of my mom's grandmother (Melissa Bassinger Gilliland). When I worked with Wesley, I respected his opinion on what we had to do and how to do it because he was more experienced in how to get the job done. Wesley had to start serious and difficult farm work at an early age because of our family's dependence on the farm for a living. It was interesting to work with Wesley. I always knew of him as a fast hard worker, who knew how to get a job done right with quick efficiency. Quite often, the motive for his fast work was to get some free time after a job was finished.

After me came Lelah Grace who was the fifth child and the second girl in the family. She was only 16 months younger than me. Lelah Grace was born on August 26, 1925. Her middle name was a namesake of her maternal grandmother's name. Probably, it was much to Mom's delight that she had a second girl in the family instead of another boy. It is reported that Lelah taught me to talk by mimicking her as she began to talk.

After having taught me to talk, Lelah and I were chums in many ways throughout our growing years. Since she had no sister her age to play with, she joined in many of the games and played with us younger boys. She entered in the outdoor games of pushing bottles in the dirt, pulling the wagon, climbing trees, tending to the chickens, and many other activities with me and the other boys. Lelah never cared much about playing checkers until Grandpa Parker came to live with us.

For the lack of someone her age with which to play and seldom any girl for a playmate, Lelah sometimes coaxed me into playing house, cutting out paper dolls, or some other girl type of game. I was careful not to let any neighbor boys see me or to know that I was playing "sissy" games. Lelah even joined us boys when there was work to be done. We all pitched in to do our chores with the same enthusiasm and effort as we did with our games, but not with the same pleasure.

Our family continued to grow and on July 14, 1927, the

sixth child, Morris Eugene was born. I was only three at the time, so I do not remember that blessed event. Morris and I played together peacefully most of the time, but sometimes he would balk at my trying to be the boss and we would argue about it. We never settled any dispute by physically fighting. I could usually subdue him or let him think he won the argument, so Pop or Mom would not know about our scrap. We knew their disapproval might result in the switch. Morris was the only one of us that had natural curly hair all over his head. Sometimes he would get sleepy at the supper table and drop his head down into his plate of food–into whatever was on it. Morris and I were near enough the same age that we worked together on some assigned chores as we grew old enough to take on responsibilities. Morris was never a slacker and could very well do his share of the work.

On a day in the late summer of 1929, the doctor came to our house and we children were made to stay outside and play, but did not know the purpose of the doctor's visit. Later, when we were called to the house, we were told that the stork had brought a baby boy to Mom. Since we did not see any stork, we thought the Doctor must have brought him. It was the 27th day of August that Orace Wayne joined our family as the seventh child. As soon as Orace Wayne could walk, he joined in our playtime. Orace Wayne, Morris, and I (and sometimes Lelah) were playmates during our early childhood and enjoyed many happy days in our various and sundry activities.

Orace Wayne soon outgrew the baby stage and became as lively and spunky as the rest of us. At a very early age, he could pick up a hoe and work in the gardens with the others or work at almost any other childhood chore to be done. There was never a lazy streak in him. Morris, Orace Wayne, and I were serious playmates at pushing bottles in the dirt for roads, digging a tunnel in the canal bank, *scooper and wheel*, hauling stuff or riding in the wagon, pushing the *wheel*, swimming or skating on the canal, and just anything we could think up to do.

Scooper and wheel was a common outdoor game that

many children played, using a small metal wheel pushed by a stick. The wheel was a small metal rim from a child's wagon or buggy. The stick had attached at the bottom, usually a loop of heavy wire or a small strip of wood placed crosswise, something that would allow for pushing the wheel...thus making it a scooper. Pushing the *wheel* was a simple activity but we really enjoyed it. It was using an iron wheel, which was about two feet in diameter and had a short pipe sticking through it (like an axle). The pipe did not move as it was rusted in and we pushed the wheel by rolling the pipe with our hands. We rolled the wheel so often that we made the pipe slick...it even made our hands slick.

There was never a dull or boring time at our house! I can assure you that we never lacked for activity nor ever said "I don't have anything to do." We all learned a good work ethic and a spirit of cooperation that has been an important factor in our adult lives.

The Willis Home

This drawing is typical of our homeplace and the surroundings
[A.E. Willis illustration]

Our simple four-room home was one of the better houses in the community at the time. Of course, in those days, country homes had no electricity and there was no indoor plumbing. The only running water was from the outdoor pump, which we ran to fetch. During the winter, after getting water the handle of the pump had to be lifted (to unprime it) to keep it from freezing. Then it had to be primed again with hot water when we needed another bucket of water.

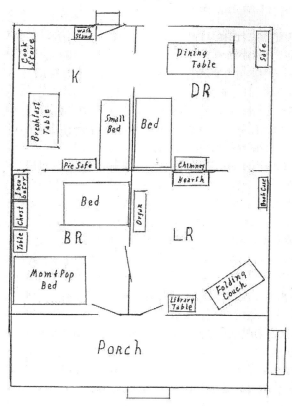

Interior diagram of our home at Clark's Station

In cold weather our baths were taken in a washtub, which was in the kitchen. We took a bath that way once a week (usually on Saturday), whether we needed it or not. In warm weather, the canal served as our bathtub.

For other personal needs, we had a path that led to an

"air conditioned" outhouse. The inside temperature changed automatically with the outside temperature. Pop had our outhouse anchored to two stout garden posts with some heavy wire so it would eliminate the possibility of being overturned by Halloween pranksters. There were no such things as indoor bathrooms in our community. Our relatives who lived in the city had indoor bathrooms and so did some public places, like the courthouse. When we visited our relatives or went to the courthouse on business we were reluctant to use the restroom facilities because of the noise the toilet made when it was flushed. We didn't like for people to know what we were doing.

One of my earliest memories about our home was watching it being painted a beautiful yellow color. A tall ladder was standing against the house and my dad was on it painting the side of our house. I wanted to climb up to where he was at, but Pop called down to me, "No, James! You stay down. Do not climb this ladder!" Everett Hilborn, a cousin, was standing on the ground helping with the painting. I must have been about three years old.

A long multipurpose building was just beyond the back yard. It served as a corncrib, chicken house, and cow shed. Pop had built a cellar with a building on top called the cellar house or sometimes referred to as the smokehouse. Those much–needed buildings were in use all year.

The cellar house also served as a place where one of us might have to *spend time* for some kind of misbehavior. The few occasions I had to "serve time" in the cellar house for a mischievous deed or behavior problem, I did not consider it punishment. I rather enjoyed plundering through the abundance of interesting tools and things stored in boxes and on shelves. I even enjoyed being in the cellar house in the evening, because when it started to get dark and I couldn't see to plunder–I could listen to the outside night noises and maybe even hear a rat or mouse scurrying around. All those noises were fascinating to me! I never told anyone that I really liked the cellar house.

The term smokehouse got its name from earlier days

when people smoked their meat to keep it from spoiling and stored it in such an outdoor building during winter months. I never did know anything about the smoking process because Pop cured his own meat with a special curing salt, sometimes called smoke salt, then stored the meat in the cellar house/smokehouse during the cold winter months.

The smoke house/cellar house served as a place to keep cured or smoked meat. Sometimes it was used as a detention center.
[A.E. Willis illustration]

During the school year, I always looked forward to the time of day when my older siblings arrived home from school. One winter Imel, Marybelle, and Wesley were staying home from school for a few days, not because of the weather, but because of being quarantined due to some contagious disease whereby they were required to stay home from school. Our parents were conscientious about them keeping up with their schoolwork and that was the standard they always had for all of us children when we were in school.

The older three children worked their school lessons around the kitchen table because it was the only place they had for their studies. Of course, we younger children thought it was great that we could have school with them and we did our "play study" of coloring and drawing, such as it was, and pretended we were also doing schoolwork. We younger children sat on a homemade bench that was on the side of the table–next to the wall.

One time, as I started to get off the bench, I fell off the end onto the floor and struck my head on a small piece of coal that was lying loose on the floor–instead of in its proper place in the coal bucket near the stove. One of the kids yelled for Mom, "James has cut his head and it's bleeding." The blood made it look serious, although it was just a small cut on my right temple. I can still remember it bleeding quite a lot and Mom patching up the wound with some of her home remedies. The school lessons continued after the interruption. Being very young at the time, my preschool had not taught me how to express my thoughts. *My* story of explanation, to any who asked, was that I got the bad place on my head by falling on a "piece-of-a-lump-of-a-coal." Yet today, after 80 plus years, I still have a scar high on my right temple.

Marybelle was a big help to Mom and she learned at an early age to take over many household responsibilities. We younger children also learned to obey her and respect her authority over us. Marybelle was not overly demanding, but she did expect each of us to do our assigned chores and to stay out of fights and other trouble. In later years, I learned just how much Marybelle helped Mom in so many ways.

Mom often helped with the fieldwork and depended on Marybelle to take care of the housework. Many times we all came in tired after all day hoeing corn, working in a potato patch, or other arduous work and Marybelle would have supper ready.

Monday was washday and Marybelle was always doing her part to help Mom scrub clothes on the washboard. During the busiest time of the farm season, Marybelle may have done it all by herself. The four of us younger children did not realize just how much work Marybelle had with all of the household chores or we might have tried to be of more help instead of an aggravation that I'm sure we were at times. She often scolded us for our misdeeds, but only one time do I remember her using the switch on any of us.

Marybelle had taken the four of us younger children and a couple of neighbor kids down the gravel road beside the canal, it could have been to Joe Hurst's Store. It was evening and as we returned home we reached a place on the railroad tracks where some men and boys gathered at their regular loafing place.

Elden Kincaid, Aunt Ola's oldest child, is on the far right.
He had a peg leg until he was 14 years old (ca 1937).

We were all acting silly and yelling at one another, maybe just showing off! We were not walking along like sensible kids. It was very embarrassing to Marybelle for us to act so uncivilized in the presence of all those loafers sitting on rails. She never said a word to us until we got home, which was just a little ways further up the road. She stopped on the south side of the house with all of us and said to wait there until she called us one at a time to the north side. She said she had a surprise for us. As each of us, including the neighbor children, were called to the north side, we learned what the surprise was. It was several keen licks with a cherry tree switch and a warning to never act like that again. We all knew we deserved that switching and held no resentment. We loved her just the same!

When I was older, at about the age of 9 or 10, Imel gave me some very serious and lasting advice that I took to heart. Imel knew we were neglecting the reading of more wholesome material and he said to me, "James, you need to be reading the Bible. There are many good stories in the Bible." He probably had some other words of advice along that line. But, the main words that stuck with me was his statement that I ought to be reading the Bible. Very soon, I started doing just that. The red letter words were the most interesting to me at first, but I soon learned that reading the other lines also made the words of Jesus more meaningful.

Imel was more than just the big brother of the household. He gave us many lessons in living just by his own character. Many instructions on successfully completing chores and necessary jobs were taught by him as well as by Pop and Mom. He was a reliable source of advice and council in many decisions that confronted us in our growing days and throughout life as well.

Hog Butchering Time

The main source of meat for our family was one or two hogs that were fed well and fattened for that purpose. Pop would decide on a hog butchering day during the colder days of November. Sometimes Pop would team up with Uncle Edmund for that project because it was a big job and the two could work at it better than each doing his own butchering. Much preparation had to be made, such as: heating water, making a platform, and arranging a large barrel for hot water.

Even though it was rather cold weather in the fall, we kids donned our coats and caps to watch the process. It seemed to be an exciting event for us but maybe not for the pig.

Much fat was carved away from the edible meat and put

into a big iron kettle to be rendered for lard. The job for us children was to keep the fire going under the kettle. As the fat was heated, the grease would be cooked out and it would be very hot. All the fried pieces of fat were scooped out onto a cloth and squeezed to remove all possible grease from them. Those little bits of cooked fatty pieces left in the cloth were crunchy and called *cracklins*, which we enjoyed for snacks.

Next, one of the adults would dip the hot grease into buckets to be stored and used for cooking purposes. It made a very good supply of lard. That was the shortening Mom used for all her cooking. It made delicious biscuits, fried potatoes, and other scrumptious food. Never mind the unhealthy use of lard! Somehow, we all survived and were healthy normal children.

A small amount grease would be left in the bottom of the kettle. Next was our fun job! We would throw in some popcorn, sprinkle it with salt, and watch it start popping. Our popcorn party was as good as eating pork chops. It was the best popcorn we had all year.

After the meat cooled sufficiently, the final process was to carve the different sections for storage. Those sections were salted down to keep from spoiling and then were placed in the cellar house. The cooler weather was an important factor for the salt to begin the curing process before the meat could spoil. The tenderloin was the best part of the meat and we would feast on it for a few days without having to salt it for storage.

That was a very common practice in all the surrounding community as most people depended on pork as their source of meat. Not many people could afford to buy meat at the store, so they raised their own. I do not know of anyone who raised a calf or a steer for their source of meat. In today's world, health officials claim pork is not healthy. However, it was our main source of meat and we all thrived on it; I do not remember that any of us were taken to see a doctor as a result of eating pork.

The Family Garden

It was an exciting time when Pop took the horses and plow into the garden to make it ready for our spring planting. Our garden was near the bank of the old canal bed, which gave it good drainage. Therefore, it could be plowed and tended earlier than most fields and gardens. Pop had built a fence around our garden to keep the chickens and varmints out. The fence was sufficient most of the time.

Mom and Pop would decide where to plant various vegetables and show us kids where and how to plant the seeds or set plants and cover them properly with soil. All available family members got involved in making the garden. The large garden supplied much of our food in the summer and for canning purposes to be used during the winter.

Early in life I learned to enjoy making garden and watching things grow. I found a small corner by the raspberry patch that was not tended and usually left to grow up in weeds. For a few years, I claimed that space for my own personal garden. I dug it up with a shovel and produced some additional vegetables for the family. I have continued the joy of gardening and working in the soil all my life.

We also had a variety of fruit trees that supplied delicious fresh fruit for the table and some was stored for the winter. Mom made jam, many fresh fruit pies, and she canned the fruit. A hickory tree stood beside the entrance of the drive leading to our house. It was a very large tree that was there when Pop built the house. I was glad he did not cut it down because it supplied an abundance of hickory nuts each year. It was always a thrilling time when the nuts were mature and began to fall from the tree. We would hurry to the yard each morning to see who could gather the most nuts to fill our pockets or containers.

These are some of the things I remember most about my small world in which to play and enjoy life during my early preschool years. Eventually my world began to expand to include the neighborhood of several families, who were mostly of some relation to us.

Inez with the first six children 1927
(L to R) Wesley, Inez holding Morris, Lelah, James
In the back - Imel on the left and Marybelle on the right

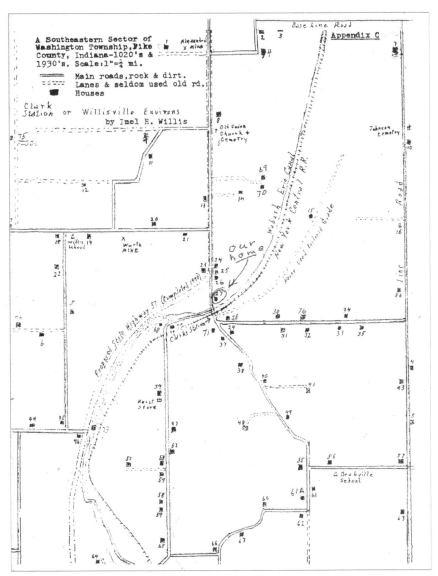

Map of the Clark's Station community
[Illustration provided by Imel Willis]

Chapter 4

THE TIME OF MY YOUTH

Children, obey your parents in the Lord:
for this is right. (Ephesians 6:1)

Barnyard Business

Farm animals were a basic necessity for our livelihood as I was growing up. The horses were for work and for that purpose only. We seldom rode them except when necessary for some type of work or to run an errand. Tom and Bill were our workhorses that I remember well. They toiled many long hours pulling the equipment for plowing the fields, planting, cultivating, harvesting, and many other farm needs. I remember us four younger children going along to play in the dirt while Pop and Imel were both using teams to plow and plant a field at Uncle Casper's place. (Evidently there was another team of horses we used at times, but I don't know who owned the other team.) At noontime, the horses were given feed and water then were allowed to rest while we all had lunch.

When working at Uncle Casper's farm, Mom would walk up the railroad and bring a basket lunch to us. Sometimes one of us children would help her carry it. Our lunch was served under a large oak tree in the yard in front of Uncle Casper's cabin. While we were eating, the horses had their lunch of corn and hay from the bed of the wagon. When working close to home, the horses were taken to the barn for feed and rest in their stalls. After lunch, the horses were hitched back to the plow for a long afternoon of work.

At the end of the day, the team would be hitched to the wagon for the trip down the trail and back to Grandma Belle's. At the barn when their harness was removed, the horses would usually roll on the ground a time or two. We never knew why they wanted to do that; maybe it just felt good to their backs after wearing the harness all day.

Cultivation of crops was an important part of our farming and generally we used a riding cultivator pulled by a team of horses. However, there were times when Imel and Wesley would each use one horse to pull a single cultivator such as a double shovel, a five shovel, or a mower wheel used as a drag. That helped preserve the ground moisture. When they were cultivating like that, Wesley used Tom and Imel worked with Bill.

Sometimes Lelah and I would ride the horses to keep them in the middle of the rows so they would not step on the plants. At the end of the rows, we would help turn them to avoid trampling the growing seedlings. I let Lelah ride Tom, because he was the good-natured horse. I rode Bill because he was a little ill-natured and would occasionally turn his head back trying to nip the rider. I had to always be on the alert for that. We never had a saddle–we just used a grass sack or some other padding. Even with a little padding, sitting on the backbone of the horse was like sitting straddle of a fence rail and would get mighty tiresome by the end of the day.

While Grandma was living, the cows and horses were kept at her place. Pop, Mom, and Imel did the milking of the cows. Some milk was given to Grandma but most of it was carried in the milk buckets to our house, which was a five-minute walk from Grandma's. I do not think Arba ever helped with the milking. He was not good at making friends with the cows and I think the cows did not like him. It is necessary to be friendly with the cows for them to let you do the milking.

The horses were essential to our farming and we had to take good care of them. There was a pasture near Grandma's barn that had a cool natural spring of water, which formed a small pond at the edge of the woods. The field gradually sloped into the water. Sometimes the horses would wade out into the water to drink and they would sink down into the mud. When they tried to get out...the more they struggled to get free, the further they sunk into the mud. Often they would "get down" in

66

so far their bellies would be touching the water. On more than one occasion, Old Bill lost his footing and "got down" in the spring. After being there in the cold water and getting chilled, it made it more difficult for him to have the strength to get out. One Sunday morning Old Bill did not show up at feeding time. We found him stuck in the spring again. Pop asked Mr. Wertz, a neighbor, to bring his team of mules to pull the horse out.

When they got Old Bill out and on his feet, he was shaking all over. He was taken to the barn where Wesley and I brushed and curried him to remove the mud. It was critical to stimulate his blood circulation, to get him dry and keep him warm. We could not afford to lose a horse...Tom and Bill were very important to us. The next day Bill was ready to be hitched to the wagon with Tom, his teammate, and start working again.

One day when cultivating in a field at Aunt Ola and Uncle Roy's place, we had not quite finished the field by the normal quitting time. Wesley and Lelah took their horse to the barn, but Imel and I worked about another hour to finish the field so we would not have to come back the next day. Such was the work ethic of Imel. He taught me to finish a job rather than to put it off until tomorrow.

When times got a little better, Pop got to work on the WPA (Works Progress Administration) projects. The horses eventually died, first one and then the other. However, I had fond and vivid memories of some hard working days with the horses. I had experienced the satisfaction of learning how to work with them and care for them.

When we no longer had any horses, we would borrow a team for plowing our small garden and other little jobs. Wesley and I once borrowed a team from Uncle Jim Amos, who lived two miles from us on the Line Road. It was common to call older people uncle, that is why we called him Uncle Jim. We didn't know he really was a great uncle. Later in life I learned Jim Amos was married to Nancy Elizabeth Willis (a sister to Grandpa Beverly).

While returning the horses back to the Amos farm in the

evening, we noticed a dark cloud that looked like a storm approaching. After Wesley and I delivered them and headed back home, the storm reached us. We got under the lean-to of a haystack to shield us from the driving rain. After the rain had ceased, we started ahead although much lightning and thunder continued. When we were halfway down the Beckville Hill, a bolt of lightening struck nearby and knocked us to the ground. There was a great ball of fire in front of us. We got up, took hold of each other and said, "Let's run!!" Within a short distance, we realized how foolish it was and Wesley yelled, "It's all over now. We don't have to run!"

Upon returning to the area the next day, we looked up and saw a tree on the high bank that had the bark split from top to bottom. It was a narrow escape for the two of us!

Farm Chores Galore

At a very early age, I watched the adults and older siblings working at many chores and I was required to help when possible. We planted and harvested most of what we ate, especially during the depression of the late 1920s and early 30s. I can remember the long days of hard work by the older ones of the family and each of us younger ones helping as we could. There were long rows of corn that had to be hoed to keep out the weeds and grass. As soon as we were big enough to handle a hoe, each of us had to do our share. By the end of the day, those rows got longer and longer. It was music to our ears to hear that it was supper time.

Pop usually sowed the oats in the spring to make feed for the animals. One of my first memories of that part of our farming was when I was watching Pop in the old orchard area just south of Grandma's house. I asked him what he was sowing and he replied, "I am sowing oats." To me that meant something we would harvest and eat for breakfast. Since my favorite cereal was Post Toasties instead of oats, I thought he should plant some of that. I asked, "But, Pop, why don't you plant some Post Toasties?" The only response I remember was his big jolly "ha, ha, ha." Later someone tried to explain it all to me, but I still couldn't understand. It was a subject of my thoughts for several nights before I would go to sleep.

As small children, even before we could be of much help on certain jobs, we were usually out where the work was going on. On one occasion Wesley was cleaning out the barn at Grandma's and hauling the manure to the field for fertilizer. I was along giving moral support by riding to the field with him to scatter the manure. I liked to tag along with Wesley and help him when possible because I thought he was a very good worker. When we were back at the barn, I got in the feed-way to watch and ask questions while Wesley worked. I may have been more of an aggravation to him than help, but at least he had some company and I felt like he liked to have me around.

He finished filling the load and was ready to head back to the field. As usual, I jumped from the feed-way to go with him, but my feet did not reach the ground. I was caught... hanging by the seat of my pants on the sharp point of a nail that was sticking out the top of the railing. The nail made quite a gash in my buttock.

Wesley hurriedly took me to the house where Grandma applied an old reliable home remedy. She bathed the wound in salt water and applied *Cloverine Salve* to keep out the germs. Although I could not comfortably sit for a while, the wound healed without getting infection and left a lasting scar on my bottom. I well remember that old-fashioned treatment taking place in the same pantry room where the big dinners were usually set for the threshing crews.

Learning to tend to the chickens was an easy and fun chore for the small ones of the family–except in cold weather. That chore involved pitching out the feed and using a small basket to gather eggs from the row of nests in the hen house. We always had quite a flock of chickens, which was a source of eggs and meat. Anytime company came, a hen or rooster was prepared to complement the meal.

Our chickens had the freedom to go anywhere except in the garden which was off limits. The garden was fenced all around but some hens would find a way to get under, over, or through a hole in the fence to feast on the tomatoes or other garden goodies. Any chicken caught in the garden was subject to a shower of clods of dirt. Some of them might wander across the road in search of better scratching for food. Sometimes while crossing the road, one of them would have a fatal accident with a passing automobile.

The poultry flock was replenished each summer by letting some hens that became broody, or took on a mothering instinct, to hatch and raise a family of baby chicks. It was quite common for Mom to have 10 or 12 hens, each setting on 12 or 15 eggs. We always referred to the hens *setting* rather than *sitting* and the number of eggs was called a "setting of eggs". A hen will lay one egg each day for several weeks until she decides it is time to raise some little ones. Then she will take on a clucking mood, stop laying eggs, and stay on the nest day and night. When that happened, Mom would put the hen with her *setting of eggs* on a separate nest made in a crate or box, away from the others. The hen would sit on her eggs continually for 21 days; the amount of time it takes for the eggs to hatch. She may leave her nest one or two times each day for a short period of time for food and water.

It was exciting to watch each nest for the baby chicks at hatching time. It was always amazing to me how the hen had no instructions about when it was time to begin the setting mood, how many eggs to lay in her nest, the importance on turning each egg everyday to keep those eggs constantly warm, and to go scratching for food for the babies when they hatch. It just is part of God's design to give her those natural instincts as He does for all animals.

We always thought it so interesting that sometimes a hen would decide to steal a place somewhere to make a nest out in the weeds or bushes and lay herself a setting of eggs. There were times we found a hen during the incubation period, but just as often it would remain a mystery until she came to the house with her brood of baby chicks.

We also had a small flock of ducks that lived mostly on the canal. Each evening they knew to come to the house at feeding time. During their short laying season, we would drive them into the hen house for the night because that is when they lay their eggs, whereas chickens lay their eggs during the day. Duck eggs were favored as a special breakfast treat and Mom liked them for cooking. To replenish the ducks each year we would collect 10 or 12 duck eggs and put them under a setting hen. The hen would have to sit for 28 days for the duck eggs to hatch.

Sometimes a duck would steal a place out in the weeds to make a nest somewhere along the canal bank. After she set for 28 days on her nest, she would come swimming down the canal with a string of little yellow ducklings. We would catch the little ducks and keep them in a pen until they got about half grown. Otherwise, they would not survive in the water with their mama because they would become food for the turtles.

In addition to the salted pork in the cellar house, our supply of meat was supplemented with wild game; fish, rabbit, quail, and turtle. Wild rabbits were quite plentiful and they ended up on our menu regularly in season, which lasted through most of November through February.

We always had two or three hogs that would have a litter of pigs. The pigs were a source of income when they got big enough to sell. Two or three of the pigs would be kept to be fattened then butchered for our own use.

One of the sows took deathly sick in the fall before her babies were to be born. She just lay lifeless in the shelter that was built for them. Pop said to us boys, "We cannot afford to lose that hog. We must get some food down her or she'll lay there and die. I'll make a thick soup of milk with fine hog feed. James, I want you and Morris to crawl in there and feed it to her. You'll have to raise her head to make her swallow the soup."

Morris and I crawled into the shelter where she lay. One of us would hold up her head and pry her mouth open so she would have to swallow the nourishing soup as the other one would put spoonfuls of it in her mouth. We did that three times a day and in about three days she began to raise her own head for the food. Within two weeks, she was able to get up, join the other pigs, and eat her food. Pop was ever so thankful we saved the hog, but he did not have any money to reward us. Neither did we expect any pay for a job well done! Our reward was the satisfaction of pleasing Pop, successfully saving the hog, and in due time...seeing her litter of pigs.

In addition to the regular feed for the hogs, Pop thought they needed some green plants as long as the growing season lasted. We boys were expected to pull a pile of weeds and grass for the hogs each day. That was an undesirable chore, but seeing how eager the hogs were to eat the green plants was a reward for the difficult task. We usually used the cart or the little red wagon to haul the green plants to the hogs.

Daisy and June

Milking the cows was an every day project. Most of the time we had two cows named Daisy and June. They were waiting for us at milking time each morning and evening. The adults, including Imel, took care of the milking for a long time. When Imel was working away from home or at college and pop was unavailable, the milking was left up to Mom. When I was 10 years old, Mom said to me, "James, I need help in milking these two cows. I want to show you how to milk a cow so you can help me. Just remember that you always milk on the right side of the cow. Most cows will not let you milk on the left side." On my first try, I only got a pint of milk by the time Mom had two gallons milked from the other cow. At first my hands tired quickly, but in a few days, as my hands gained more strength, I could obtain almost as much milk from a cow as Mom could.

When our pasture would get picked too close, we took the cows to a field at Jimmy Shepard's house (about a half mile from home) where he had a good unused pasture. For the twice-a-day milking, Mom and I would walk up the railroad and over a stile (stairs built over a fence). The lush green grass in his field helped the cows produce plenty of good creamy milk. They would stand perfectly still for us to do the milking and we would have three or four gallons of milk to carry home. We brought the cows back home when our pasture had suitably regrown.

During the winter months, we kept the cows in the shed at night where we gave them feed and hay or fodder. Eventually, Wesley and I were given the responsibility of tending and milking the cows. If there was only one cow to milk, we would take turns or at least we were supposed to share the job. However, there was a problem. There was often a personality clash between Wesley and the cows! Cows can be temperamental when they are not treated properly. The cow might kick the milk bucket, not stand still, or just refuse to let all her milk down. Because of his difficulties in making friends with the cows, I assumed the job of milking. For a few years I would be up early to milk both cows before going to school and then again in evening.

Wheat Harvesting Time

We were very fortunate to have parents who were thrifty, worked hard, and planned ahead so we would have something to eat. Pop always planted a field of wheat that was supposed to supply our flour for the year. Harvesting the wheat was such a big ordeal that a few farmers would join together to help one another with the harvesting. There might be only one binder, which took three horses to pull it instead of the regular team of two horses. With three or four farmers sharing their horses, they could occasionally switch teams to the binder because it was such hard work for them. The binder would cut the wheat and tie it in bundles and the men came behind to stack the bundles into shocks.

After the wheat stood in shocks for a few weeks to become thoroughly dry, farmers would come together again for a threshing time at each of their fields. Someone who owned a threshing machine would come through the country to thresh wheat. When I was a young boy, those threshing machines were pulled to the fields by big steam driven tractors. A large leather belt connected the tractor's flywheel to a pulley on the thresher to power it.

Because most farmers had little or no money, it was common for them to pay for the job by giving the threshing machine owner a percentage of the wheat. For a few years, when they were threshing in Pop's field, my job was to carry drinking water to the workers. I carried two jugs that were one gallon each. The weight of those jugs would get almost unbearable before I could get to the men. Sometimes it seemed like I just could not make it, but I knew the water needed to get to those thirsty men! I would have to stop and rest a couple times along the way. When I stopped for each man to drink from the jugs (no cups furnished), I would get another little rest. By the time I got around to the dozen or so men, the jugs would be empty. Then I would trek back across the field to the pump for more water. By the end of the day I thought I had done more work than all those men in the field.

Wheat Shocks

Threshing Machine

Hay Wagon

On one occasion a threshing crew was moving to another field by way of the dirt road going up Beckville Hill. The hill was rather steep and the steel wheels of the steam engine started spinning on some soft dirt. As the steel wheels would spin, the steel cleats dug deeper into the ground. The men dug, pried, and blocked for several hours. Finally, some teams of horses were hitched to chains, which were attached to the front of the engine. They were finally able to get the steam engine and threshing machine up the hill. The place where the engine got stuck was close to where, a few years later, Wesley and I were nearly struck by lightening.

On wheat-threshing days, the women gathered at the home of the farmer, whose wheat was being threshed, and prepared a *threshing feast*. It was a custom in those days that the men would eat first at any such gathering. After the men had eaten, smoked, gossiped, rested, and got around to leaving the table, then the women and children would eat whatever was left. It seemed to take forever and ever for us to get the chance to eat. I was not old enough to eat with the men during my earliest years of being the water boy. I would be very hungry from my hard work and I thought it seemed very unfair that I had to wait to eat later. However, that was the custom and we lived by it.

After the wheat threshing, it was time to change the filling in our straw ticks for our beds. We had no mattresses, but each bed had a big cloth bag made purposely for holding straw. Those bags were called *straw ticks*. We liked to get to the fresh straw from the large pile left by the thresher before any rain. If we could not get to it before the rain, it was necessary to dig away the top layer and get straw that had not been blemished by water. Those ticks would be about 12 to 16 inches thick when filled with new fresh straw. They would stay fluffy for several weeks. What a delight it was to sleep on a newly filled straw "mattress". Gradually the straw would mash down until, by the time to refill them the next year, they were almost flat mats.

Wagon Excursions

It was a great delight, when I was a small child, to go with Pop wherever he went in the wagon. A few of those occasions remain a vivid memory. One of the first times I remember was when he went down the trail by the canal, across a couple of meadows, crossing a creek, and up a hill to a large white house. That house looked almost like a castle compared to our little four-room home. It might have been the home of Sid (Sidney) Wyatt, who was a distant cousin by marriage to Permelia Willis. The woman brought out a delicious looking piece of pie on a plate for me, but I was too bashful to take it. However, Pop told me to go ahead and eat it. That made it OK, because whatever Pop approved–I knew was all right for me to do.

There was a special trip, which I went with Pop, to take a wagon load of corn and some wheat to be ground at the mill in Petersburg. It was about four miles from home. He did not have money to pay for the grinding, but the miller was willing to take a portion of the grain as payment. That was the customary way many farmers paid for services and goods. On the way to town, Pop let me take the reins to guide the team. He taught me to keep the slack out of the lines without holding them too tight, which would cause the horses to stop. If the horses slacked up on their gait, I was to slap the lines on their rump and yell "giddy-up". That would make them step more lively. When going up a hill, about half way up we might let them stop for a rest—especially if they were pulling a heavy load.

Main street in Petersburg, Indiana, as I knew it in the 1930s when I rode to town with Pop in the wagon. We parked the team and wagon in the middle of the street like other wagons and a few cars. I held the lines of the horses while Pop went into the store to take care of business.

One spring day Pop was going up Beckville Hill, past where Aunt Ola and Uncle Roy lived, with the wagon. For some reason, none of us children were permitted to go along. I did not know the reason nor did I know where he was going. However, as he was leaving the driveway I sneaked and got on the coupling pole. It was a four-inch timber, which connects together the front and back part of the wagon chassis, which stuck out about a foot behind the wagon bed.

About halfway up the hill, past Ted Fowler's house, Pop

said, "whoa!" and stopped the wagon. I wondered why he was stopping! Then he said, "Alright James, you can get up here on the seat with me." How did he know I was back there on that coupling pole? Years later we were told our parents and teachers have eyes in the back of their heads! Anyway, the trick worked and I was never punished for it. Rather, I got the joy of riding with Pop on the wagon seat! Maybe he was glad to have my company while traveling, but he would not go against Mom when she said we could not go.

When I was about eight or nine years old, Pop gave me a driving test with the team hitched to the wagon, as he probably did with all the other children. As we crossed the railroad, there was a sharp turn into the lane that went to Uncle Casper's farm. A concrete railroad post was on the left side at the entrance and a big ditch on the right side. The test was to make the turn without hitting the post with either front or back wheel of the wagon and not allow either wheel go into the ditch. That had happened several times before, when people carelessly made the turn. I knew how to handle the team and felt confident I could make the turn successfully. I do not know if Pop was ready to grab the reins in case I missed the turn or if he was just going to let me experience whatever happened. By holding the reins just tight enough so the horses would feel the pull on their bridle bits, I made a big swing and went straight into the lane exactly as intended. I passed the test!

A Thankful Thanksgiving

In 1929, the electric flashbulb was invented. Although this invention had no effect on the stock market, its brightness followed by a rapid burnout is a metaphor of the Wall Street crash of 1929. In an instant of time, company after company came to financial ruin as their stocks collapsed. The domino effect shattered the economy of the entire country over a period of hours. Millions of factory workers were thrown out of their jobs. Rich people became poor overnight. I remember hearing about breadlines springing up to feed the hungry, especially in the cities.

That was the beginning of the Great Depression of the 1930s. The effects were felt around the world. China imploded into civil war, which led to the overthrow of her fledgling republic...pushing the country into communism. I was too young to understand all those events at the time. I just knew we lived meagerly but we had always lived that way.

It was in the midst of those events, on a cold November day in the early 1930s, I had my first and special memory of Thanksgiving Day. I would have been seven or eight years of age at the time. I recall many of our relatives gathering for festivities at Grandma Belle's house.

Those days of the Great Depression were tough for everyone. I think the worst hardships did not touch the lives of country folk like us who were accustomed to living simply and close to the land. We were more fortunate than many because the women could always bake some goodies with homegrown or even wild fruit. There were chickens to dress, pork from the smokehouse, fresh vegetables, and home canned goods. It was Thanksgiving and we had much to be thankful for.

Many relatives came for the big dinner and it was a grand occasion! A long table was set in the breezeway area, which separated the main house from the kitchen. After the long wait of the meal preparations, the men ate first as was the custom. That meant we kids and the women had an even longer wait while the men had their fill. Then after they ate, their conversation lingered while still sitting at the table–while we continued to wait!

During the endless period of long waiting, I remember two special things. One of the men had arrived in a truck, which was an exception for ordinary country folk. He let us children take turns sitting in the driver's seat; examining the steering wheel, the knobs, levers, and pedals that did mysterious things. That may have been my first experience behind the wheel of a vehicle. That afternoon we had our first snow of the season, which was exciting for the children.

Finally, the children were given permission to enjoy a scrumptious meal and barter over who would get the chicken drumsticks or the pulley bone! That was the only Thanksgiving dinner I ever remember celebrating at Grandma's home. It seems like thereafter, all families went their separate ways for the Thanksgiving celebration.

Laborious Coal Mining

Pop's brother, Clarence, was also a farmer and usually had a good team of horses. He shared work with Pop occasionally when either of them needed extra help. Uncle Clarence managed his farm well and lived about the same as us. He had two sons, Melvin and Millard, who were very good helpers on his farm.

Pop and Uncle Clarence in the 1940's

Pop had a closer relationship with Uncle Clarence than with any of his other siblings or at least it seemed that way because they worked together on so many projects. They were both farmers, had similar interests in life, and even resembled each other in appearance.

Around 1930, during the depression years, there was little or no money for families to buy things–even basic necessities. Pop and Uncle Clarence dug their own coal on the property that had belonged to Turner Willis. Turner's daughter, Esta, was Uncle Clarence's wife. Turner was deceased at the time but he was a distant cousin to Pop and Uncle Clarence. He was a descendant through another son of Thomas and Anne Willis. Turner's great grandfather was Thomas, the oldest brother to George (my great great great grandfather).

The widow of Turner, Sienda (known as Si–pronounced *sigh*) Beck Willis, still lived on their property where there was a good vein of coal fairly close to the surface of the ground. Sometimes the coal would be cropping out at the base of a hillside. Uncle Clarence made the arrangements with Si Willis, to strip the ground off to get the coal. It was a hard laborious task to uncover and dig out enough coal to supply six families for their winter's needs. Not only would the coal be dug for Uncle Clarence and our family, but it was agreed they would also dig enough coal for Si and other members of the family: Melvin, Grandma Belle, and Uncle Edmund.

Pop and Uncle Clarence would go into the wooded areas or the Turner field searching next to the hillsides to find what seemed a likely spot that would have a good vein of coal not too deep under the surface of the ground. When they found a good place, they would spend about two weeks uncovering the coal with two slip scrapers pulled by teams of horses. That meant plowing the ground, which got harder and harder as the pit got deeper. That would loosen the dirt enough so the horses could pull the scraper with a person in the pit loading it. The team would drag their scraper load of dirt outside the pit where another person would be there to dump it. Round and round they would go until all the top layer of loose dirt was removed. Then it was time for the struggle of pulling the plow all over the area again to loosen more dirt. After about two weeks, they would finally get down to the slate that covered the coal. The slate was a little easier to remove.

Many days we children would go along and watch the process of stripping off the dirt, uncovering the coal, and digging out the coal. Imel and Millard managed the teams except when it was time to plow the hard dirt. Pop, Uncle Clarence, and Melvin did most of the work in the pit. It was two miles from home, so Mom would fix a lunch and bring it to us. By lunchtime, I would be as hungry as the men who had worked hard all morning. The lunch Mom fixed for us consisted of things like: boiled eggs, beans with cornbread, fried potatoes, home canned fruit or some pie. It was an enjoyable treat for ravenous appetites and seemed like a picnic regardless of how simple it was. No one objected or complained about whatever Mom prepared.

After the dirt and slate was removed from the area of coal, it was time to start blasting the layer of coal to loosen it up. Pop and Uncle Clarence would drill a hole deep into the bed of coal and insert a stick of dynamite with a long fuse cord. Everyone cleared away and Pop would light the fuse, then we watched for the explosion. That would loosen up a large area of the coal bed, which was then dug out with picks and shovels. Pop, Melvin, and Uncle Clarence did most of the digging. Wesley also helped some with both the digging and loading the wagons, although he was not old enough to do real heavy work.

After the wagons were full, Imel and Millard would deliver the coal to the various families. Each of the wagons would hold 25 bushels of coal, which was equal to a ton. They would dig out enough coal for each of the homes to have 8 to 10 loads of coal. The wagons were a heavy load for the teams to pull over the hills.

Imel made the longest haul (two miles) taking loads to our house, to Grandma Belle, and to Uncle Edmund's place.

Millard had a shorter route to deliver the coal (one mile) to his dad's house, to Melvin's house, and then a short distance to Si Willis' house. When he was done with those deliveries, Millard would haul a few loads for Imel. It usually took four weeks or most of August to get the winter's supply of coal.

A horse drawn wagon (such as this one) was used for hauling the coal, transportation, and many other purposes until pop ceased farming.

On one occasion, Melvin invited me go home with him for lunch. I remember I was very shy. It was a new experience for me to be invited to eat at someone else's home. Mildred, his wife, was very nice to me, and she had a good lunch for us to enjoy. After lunch, Melvin asked me, "James, do you have a pocket knife?" I explained to him that the older boys had a knife but I did not have one. Melvin went to a drawer, got out a neat small knife, and gave it to me.

That was the very first pocketknife I ever had. I was very proud of it, because every boy thought it was important to have a pocketknife in those days. That was the summer before I started to school and I carried that prized possession throughout my elementary school years. Among other uses, it was very handy for playing mumble peg with the other boys at school. On several occasions after that, when I would see Melvin, I would thank him for the knife he gave me. Melvin and Mildred did not have any children at that time. I suppose my gratitude may have amused him a little. Yet, he always acknowledged my appreciation with solemn dignity and a smile.

I rode with Imel on many of his trips hauling the loads of coal to our house and to Grandma's place. When we had to climb steep grades like the Wertz Hill, Imel would let the team rest once at the mid point of the hill and again at the top of the hill. By the time we reached the top, those horses would be lathered up with sweat and breathing hard from pulling the heavy load.

Going down the hill required a different strategy. While the team was resting at the top, Imel would tie a chain to one wheel in such a manner to act as a brake. By locking the wheel, it would slide to prevent the heavy load from running away or running over the horses as we went down the hill. Once we were down the hill Imel would stop and remove the chain.

After the men dug all the coal out that had been uncovered in the pit, they would start using their picks to dig into the vein of coal that ran under the hillside. That would create a cave with an overhang of dirt. They would go back as far as possible to take advantage of all the coal they could get before abandoning or closing up the pit. One year, a crack in the earth began to appear above the area where they were digging. I was scared the over hanging *cliff* of dirt would break off and bury the men working down under it. I kept calling to Pop every few minutes telling him they better get out, because the crack was getting bigger. They were aware of the crack and the eventual cave-in, but they kept on digging and shoveling until the crack became about 12 inches wide. It was big enough a person could fall into it. I was getting desperate! I yelled to Pop, "You better quit digging and get out from under the bank, because it's goin' to fall."

Finally, they knew time was running out. They collected their tools, got out of the pit and waited for the *fall*. What a relief it was to me when they were finally out from under there! We all waited and watched the crack get bigger and bigger until after a short time the bank crashed down into the pit with such force that the earth shook beneath our feet.

That was the end of the coal digging for the season. All the families had enough coal to heat their houses and keep their cook-stoves going throughout the winter months. For four years during the depression, Pop and Uncle Clarence took the month of August to get their winter's supply of coal.

Mystery at the Log Crossing

One mile south of the place where they mined for coal was where Uncle Clarence lived. However, to walk to his house from our home, we would take a different route. We would go down to the railroad, follow the rails to a path that led through a wooded area, across what had been the old canal bed to a creek. We walked across a tree that had fallen over the creek, up a steep bank and out of the wooded area to the road that was close to his and Aunt Esta's home.

A few times we went there for a Sunday dinner. It was always interesting to go to their house because they kept things so neat and they did not have a family of young children to disrupt the orderliness of things. Their place had many things we did not have; a big barn, a large corn crib, a coal-house, an orderly smoke house, and a hammock in the front yard. Most of our visits with Uncle Clarence and Aunt Esta were in the evening whereby we might just sit in front of the fireplace and hear the adults tell stories of their past experiences or talk about current events. Aunt Esta would serve apples or popcorn as a treat to pass the time.

When we left their house at night, it was usually not difficult to find our way back down the steep bank to cross the log and through the canal bed to the path that led to the railroad. But, one night it was so dark we could barely even see the road; there were not even any stars to give a little light. When we reached the canopy of trees over our path, we knew it was going to be quite difficult to find our way down the embankment and the log across the creek. But something happened! As we found the path to go down the bank toward the log, for some mysterious reason a light from somewhere lit up the area, which made it easy to cross the log. Just after we all got across, the light disappeared.

This photo was taken in the vicinity of where
we crossed the log over the creek

As we walked, we began to think about what had just occurred and wondered where the light came from. The most logical explanation was a few moments of the parting of clouds to let some light shine for us. On the other hand, perhaps it was a will-o'-the-wisp as some suggested! Regardless of any explanation, it was definitely a light from heaven, which showed us the way. This is a good example of how, at seeming dark times or troubles in our lives, we can look to the light from above. God will lead us and help us to see clearly how to overcome the obstacles in our path.

Christmas Cheer

During the depression years, our Christmas was very slim but we thought nothing of it. That's just the way it was and we knew no better. On one of those Christmas mornings, we younger four children might each receive two tiny toy animals and/or some trinket along with an orange or apple in our stocking. It was Christmas time and we enjoyed what "Santa" had brought us. During those years of hard times, Mom made our candy with sorghum molasses. There were a few years the *High Y Club* from the Petersburg High School delivered a Christmas basket with food and other goodies to our family. It was quite a delight to all of us.

When Pop got a job working in the coal mine, things got a little better. There was a very special time one "night before Christmas", as the family was enjoying the usual time of cracking nuts and perhaps eating apples around the fireplace. The evening was filled with chitchat and story telling, when suddenly Pop announced, "I think I heard a noise out on the porch. I wonder if Santa has made his trip early this year and left our Christmas presents on the porch."

We jumped up and ran out barefooted onto the cold porch to see what the noise was about. Sure enough!! There was a big red toy wagon with some other presents and goodies piled on it! There was even a doll buggy, for Lelah, with a doll in it. Of course, we three younger boys assumed the wagon was just for us to share and it was our main delight. Most other things were of little interest to us. Even with limited space, we made roads through the house pushing one another in the wagon. It was as if we had to wear off the newness of it that very night. That wagon was the highlight of our outdoor play for the next few years.

By the time I was old enough to start school it became obvious to me that it would be impossible for a *Santa* to deliver things to children everywhere. I then knew it was a fairytale that parents and older people got us to believe, so I just went along with the game for a while. It was still a few years before I learned about the real meaning of Christmas.

When I was in the fourth grade, I asked Morris to go with me to find a Christmas tree. We found a small cedar tree about three feet tall. We set it on the library table and fixed it so it would not fall over. We younger children decorated it with some tinsel and a few ornaments.

The next year I could not find another cedar, so I cut a small sassafras tree. I wrapped each limb and twig with white crepe paper, then the other kids helped me to decorate it. All the family liked my new kind of Christmas tree. The only other Christmas decoration at our house was red and green decorating rope stretched diagonally across the living room two ways with a paper bell hanging in the center of the room. That was the same decoration year after year at our house. After Christmas it was all taken down, put in a box, and saved for the next year.

The Myth of the Easter Rabbit

In our home, in the 1920s and 1930s, the egg was the symbol of Easter to us children. On Easter morning, it was a custom at our house for each person to see how many eggs they could eat for breakfast. I could eat only three or four, but one time I do remember eating six. There were several years that Pop ate 12 eggs and I do not know how he did it!

We believed the Easter rabbit brought us Easter eggs during the night before Easter morning until we were old enough to know that was also a fairytale. The three older children had gone through the same experience of being led to believe in the Easter rabbit when they were small. Each of us four younger ones would make our own nest, which might be just a cap or a small basket and put it close to a window leaving the window open just enough so the rabbit could get through.

I think Mom got a special thrill from seeing us get excited about making our nests and finding the eggs the next morning. She liked to buy the candy eggs for our nests when possible. There may have been times when regular eggs were colored for the nests when money was very scarce.

When Imel, Marybelle, and Wesley were small, Mom

made up an Easter game, which Imel remembered with fondness all his life. One night the three children made their nests for the rabbit and put them in a dark room. They kept going into the room frequently and felt around in the nest to check if the rabbit had been there. Mom slipped in the room without their knowledge and put a fur cap in Imel's nest. When they went back again to check the nests, Imel felt that fur and thought it was the rabbit. They all three went running back from the dark room telling about it. Mom told them, "Now you must stay out of the room quite a while to give the rabbit enough time to lay eggs in each nest." When they finally went to check again, with Mom's permission, guess what! There were some candy eggs in each nest! The retelling of that story, to the rest of us young children, strengthened our belief in the possibility of an Easter rabbit.

The rabbit would lay the Easter eggs outside if the weather were nice. One year the rabbit failed to leave the eggs in our nests before we got out of bed. Needless to say, we were about to lose faith in the rabbit. Evidently, the rabbit overslept or forgot to get things set for us. Moms usually have a solution to difficult problems! She told us that since it was such nice weather, the rabbit might have made the nests somewhere in the orchard. While we were searching there, the rabbit sneaked out to the garden to plant the eggs. When the eggs were not found in the orchard, she suggested that rabbits like gardens. In our excitement, we quickly ran to the garden barefooted, even though it was not barefoot season yet, to search for his tracks. Sure enough, we found some eggs planted in the garden–four nests neatly lined with straw each containing a few candy eggs. We just thought that was real funny for the rabbit to play that trick on us.

Even with our early childlike faith in the rabbit, each of us children came to know the truth about Easter through the teaching of the church and reading of the Bible. The four gospels tell the story, each giving a little different detail but all of them share the same truth. After His crucifixion, Jesus was wrapped and laid in a tomb furnished by Joseph of Arimathea. On the third day, the huge stone was miraculously rolled away from the tomb and an angel appeared telling those who came to look for the body "He is not here, He is risen." After Jesus appeared to different ones, at different times, He ascended to heaven. Some people do not believe the story as is told so vividly in the Bible, but I am thankful that I have learned the truth about Easter.

I have never held it against Mom and Pop for not teaching us the real meaning of Easter and Christmas. Even though we were not taught the real meaning of these celebrations when we were small, the Lord had a way of leading all seven of their children in the right direction to a Christian life and the true meaning of salvation.

Mom and Pop never took us to church. Imel said that he could remember going to church with Mom as a very young boy and hearing her testify about her salvation and her love for the Lord in the church service. Pop regularly read the Bible and would often comment on things that were right and wrong according to God's word. He could quote many of the scriptures that he had learned.

Mom and Pop left us a legacy of cooperation, hard work, and good morals to live by. I am thankful I had such wonderful parents who loved their children and did all they could for us to have a good home.

My mom and dad 1940s

Chapter 5

TREASURED STORIES

For thou, Lord, wilt bless the righteous; with favor wilt thou compass him as with a shield. (Psalms 5:12)

Our family was fortunate to live close to a remaining section of the old Wabash and Erie Canal, which had water still standing in it. The canal section was only about ¼ of a mile long, but it was a source of much activity for us children and sometimes the neighbors too. We used it for swimming in the summer, boating and fishing in spring and fall, and ice skating in the winter.

My first ice-skating experience on the canal was with a pair of hand-me-down skates already used by the older children. They were just the right size for my shoes. I was down more than I was up, but it did not hurt to fall because I was so bundled up to keep warm.

After a few days, I was almost skating right along with the others. When we would get a snow on top of the ice it was great sport to make a fox and geese game. That was a large circled pattern shoveled in the snow with some cross paths. One person, called the *fox*, would chase and try to catch the *geese* (the other skaters) as they ran or skated around and through the circle.

We did not have very good skates so it was hard to get them strapped on real good. It was so difficult that we did not want to take them off until we had to quit skating for the day. We used straps, twine, wire, or anything we could find to tie them onto our shoes. Mom, in her sympathy for our problem, would occasionally let us wear the skates into the house for lunch. I think we would have slept with them on all night if she would have let us.

Sometimes we skated on another section of the canal, down the road from our house, when the ice became real thick.

On one occasion when were skating there, the neighboring boys, Ralph, Donald, and Alvin Church, showed up with their skates. They were near the same ages as the younger of us four Willis boys. Wesley and Ralph, the oldest of the bunch, decided it would be a fun adventure to skate down an overflow ditch at the far end of the canal to see where it went. Naturally, all the rest of us followed in single file down through the frozen ditch. After some distance, the ditch opened into one of the coal mine pits. We all skated right on through the open pit which was plenty safe because the severe cold had frozen the ice very thick.

We stopped to rest at a place where the water pit ended and the workers had been digging for coal. We noticed that Orace Wayne, our youngest brother, was so cold he was crying. Providence had led us to a barrel of burning hot coals left by the workers. Wesley and Ralph punched up the fire and added more coal, which fired the barrel up very hot. Everyone enjoyed the heat, but we especially wanted to get Orace Wayne up close so he could get warm before we started back. If we had not found that fire, Orace Wayne would have been in real jeopardy trying to make it back home and might have had serious frostbite.

It was suppertime when we got home. We were glad for the rest, to remove our skates, and call it quits for the day. Our bold adventure was one of our secrets that we did not tell anyone at the time. We did not always talk about our misadventures unless we were questioned. Our parents would not have liked us to venture down through the coal mine pits because of the potential danger.

We were reluctant to give up the skating privilege when the ice began to melt and sometimes we would challenge the ice at the shallow end of the canal, where the water was only one or two feet deep. When the ice became unsafe, it would sag as one person at a time went across. Finally, when the first kid broke through and got wet, we would put away our skates!

In the springtime, Pop would let us be our own judge as

to when the water was warm enough to swim. We would sometimes push the season and take a swim when the water was quite chilly. However, we at least let all the ice melt a few weeks before attempting to swim. At our noon break from working in the fields in the summer, a dip in the canal was a real treat. Although we were only allowed to stay in the water for 20 minutes before we ate lunch. Time could not be "wasted" by swimming in the canal. There was work to be done!

The Willis Brothers
just back from the swimmin' hole
Wesley, baby Orace Wayne, and Imel
Morris (curly hair) and James

95

Growing up during the hard days of the Great Depression had its knocks and bumps. It was not easy for the adults attempting to raise a family with meager resources. But there were so many pleasurable times that we children did not recognize those were hard times. We were very poor like other families at that time, but no one told us we were poor. Therefore, we did not know it and we enjoyed life anyway. Some of our relatives would come to visit us from St. Louis who seemed to be rich because they drove automobiles, dressed fancy, and talked different. Very few people in our community could afford an automobile. We children sometimes felt sorry for them because they lived in the big city and missed the opportunities we had in the country. They did not know how to have our kind of fun and enjoy the wide-open spaces. Ours was a rich and wholesome country life.

Weathering the Storm

The front porch of our house faced the west whereby on pleasant evenings we could sit and watch the sun setting. The gathering of storm clouds was also an interesting sight to observe, especially when we were in the need of rain that might be in the making. One such dark cloud brought with it much more than just rain! It resulted in a terrific hailstorm that punctured holes in the roofing of our house. When Pop built the house, he had to use the least expensive materials possible. He had used a plain roll roofing, a material that could not endure the large hail. The roof began to leak when rain followed the hail. We quickly got in the attic and, by lamplight, placed buckets and containers of all kinds to catch the water to prevent the leaks from damaging the ceiling. We were thankful when the rain finally stopped.

Pop went to the lumber store in Petersburg the next morning and told the owner, who was a good friend, about the problem. He needed to get enough metal roofing to cover the house on credit because he had no money. That very same day, the man delivered a pile of metal roofing and stacked it in our driveway without even a down payment. He knew Floyd Willis would pay the bill, as he could, without fail. Pop and some other men began installing the new roof immediately. It took Pop two years to pay for the roofing. That roof has been there standing the test of weather for over 60 years.

Blessed Assurance

As children, we attended various church services and our parents never objected. Sometimes during summer months, we walked about two miles south to the little settlement of Hosmer to attend Sunday school. Frequently there would be a revival, in a schoolhouse, tent, or brush arbor, which provided an opportunity to go and hear some preaching. When there was a revival or church meeting at the Willis School on Sunday afternoons, we would always attend. Our serious and regular attendance to church did not begin until later years when we were in our teens. However, we were getting an introduction to the meaning of God and Christianity by attending those various church services every time there was an opportunity.

There was never a dull moment nor a time when we said, "there is nothing to do!" During the summer months we played with the cart, pushed bottles in the dirt–pretending they were toy cars, played marbles, climbed trees, played hop scotch, *shinny* (a rough type of hockey), and many other improvised activities and games. Those games were played anytime when work was finished. Sometimes neighbor kids would come to our house to play, but we seldom went to play at some other person's house. There was always plenty of work to do or things to play with at our own home. Saturday was just another day of work or play as usual. No work was required on Sunday–other than just the necessary chores.

We always had chores to do before we could play. Sometimes there was schoolwork to do and we sat around the dining room table for that. We would also use the dining room table to play board games.

When the weather was too bad to play outside and during the long winter evenings we played table games, similar to those that we played at school, like: checkers, dominoes, monopoly, and book cards (we were not allowed to play with gambling cards). Some of those games created considerable excitement. On many cold winter nights we sat around the grated fireplace cracking nuts, peeling and eating apples, eating popcorn or other snacks while telling stories, riddles or jokes.

The Music Man

For several years our house was also a gathering place for adults. Pop and the three older siblings, Imel, MaryBelle, and Wesley, were all string instrument players. Pop had learned to play from Harley and Harrison Willis, Uncle Casper's sons. Pop had become somewhat accomplished on the banjo, fiddle, guitar, mandolin, and the piano. Imel usually played the mandolin, banjo, or guitar. Marybelle played only the guitar. Wesley played the mandolin and guitar, he also liked to play a French harp and became very good at it.

Other musicians in the neighborhood would come to join them on Sunday afternoons and occasionally during the week. Often other neighbors would come just to socialize or listen to the music. The younger siblings, including me, never learned to play music, but we enjoyed hearing the performance of old time country music played by the musicians.

One special guest we younger children really liked to have come was Ed Cottrell. Ed lived two miles from us and he would bring his accordion when he came. We truly enjoyed the beautiful music he played on the accordion. Sometimes Pop or some of the others would play their string instruments along with him. Ed usually came expecting to spend the night because of the distance for him to walk home.

The Lost Coin

My earliest time of attending a county fair that I can remember was when I was about the age of seven or eight years old. Some of our family went to the fair with a neighbor, who had a car. At that time, the Petersburg fair grounds was out on the south end of 6th street. It was so exciting to see all the hustle-bustle and swarms of people. The fair consisted of two main rides, the Ferris wheel and the merry-go-round. There were several places to buy refreshments such as very hard ice cream (they called hokey pokey), hot dogs, cotton candy, snow cones, and a many other of delightful treats. Several tents lined the walkway where men were yelling for people to try their luck at winning some sort of prize. I was not interested in trying that because I had only one dime to spend. I did not even want to buy those things, much less take a chance of loosing my dime on a game. It was a form of gambling that we were taught against. The Ferris wheel cost 10 cents and that would have taken all my money. In order to stretch that dime I decided to buy an ice cream cone for a nickel and ride the merry-go-round with the other nickel.

I remember a few years later when Gerald and Marybelle had a 1930 Model A Ford Coup with a rumble seat. The rumble seat on those old cars was a trunk that opened backwards with an open-air seat back of the cab. Two or three of us younger children rode in the rumble seat to go with them to the county fair, which was still held at the old fair grounds in Petersburg. Even at that time, which was about 1935 or 1936, we all were still feeling the effects of the Great Depression and no one had much money. Evidently, our parents were able to scrape up enough that each of us could have 10 cents to spend at the fair. I bought myself a 5-cent ice cream cone but was not interested in paying for a ride and I could not see anything worth spending my other nickel on.

Close to the entrance of the fair was a machine (a slot machine as I learned later) that contained pocketknives, silver dollars, and other interesting things. I watched when people played it; an arm would go out to pick up one of those valuable items. It just seemed so simple. I thought I could easily make the arm go out there and pick up a pocketknife. As we were getting ready to leave, I picked up nerve enough to try it. In went my last nickel and just like the instructions showed–the jaws reached down but picked up nothing! There went my nickel with not a thing to show for it. That was a big loss to me! It confirmed to me that my parents were right in teaching us not to gamble. Since that time I have never wanted to visit any places where you take a chance on a seemingly great possibility of winning something but equally the chance of losing your money. I call them "gyp joints"!

Some years later, about 1940, the County Fair was held out southwest of Petersburg by Hornaday Park. I attended the fair out there a couple times but only spent a little money on some snacks but not at the *gyp joints*. For me, the main attraction at any of those fairs was the 4-H exhibits. I especially enjoyed the animals and plants. In addition, whenever there was a horse pulling contest or a tractor pull, I liked to plan my visit on that date.

The Night Hunt

Wesley like to hunt at night for "coons", groundhogs, 'possums or whatever he could find. One time he wanted me to go with him. I did not much want to go but he made it sound exciting. I did like to work and do things with Wesley, so I decided to go along.

There had been a story or rumor about a wildcat that had been sighted roaming the woods in that area, but it did not bother me. I just thought if we ran onto that varmint, Wesley would shoot him.

We started on our *night hunt* just before it was dark and walked for what felt like miles through the woods until late into the night. It looked as if we might go home empty handed, so I told Wesley we just as well go home. He finally consented, but soon thereafter our dogs began barking as if they had spotted something. They had "treed" a skunk!

I do not know why Wesley wanted to bother with a skunk, but as I recall the hide possibly could have been sold for some cash. We got the skunk, but we arrived back home with an aroma that prohibited our entrance into the house without removing our clothes. The dogs smelled like skunk perfume for many days!

Radio Fascination

In the summer of 1936, we took a trip by wagon to Uncle Jim's. He and his grandson, Grester Amos, lived alone. They invited us to come for a visit to hear their new radio. Even Aunt Ola climbed in the wagon and went with us. That was to be a grand occasion because no one in our neighborhood had a radio. No one out our way even had electricity, so the radio had to be operated on a special battery. Mom and Pop sat on the spring seat to drive the team while the rest of us all sat in the wagon bed.

Imel gave us a lesson in astronomy to pass the time on our 30 to 45 minute ride. The moon was shining bright so he explained about the different phases of the moon, what caused eclipse, the distance of the stars, the formation of the galaxy, and other things about the solar system. We thought he must have learned about those things in college.

Upon arriving at the Amos house, we hurried inside with great anticipation to see what a radio looked like and to hear the extraordinary marvel of science. Uncle Jim thought he had the new radio all connected up properly with the battery and a good long outside antenna...ready for us to hear it. He tinkered with it for a long while and we finally heard some voices. However, we did not hear any music and he finally gave it up as a bad time for the radio. Pop had brought along the musical instruments, so they made a music party instead. We enjoyed the music and the ride in the wagon regardless of the disappointment of not hearing the radio.

A year later, in 1938, radios were becoming more prevalent. Mom bought a battery operated radio for $35 on credit–to be paid at $5 per month. We cherished the times when the radio could be tuned to our special programs. Some of our favorite programs were *Lum and Abner, Renfro Valley, Grand Old Opera, Fibber McGee And Molly*, and the news. We also started receiving the Evansville Press daily newspaper by mail. The comic strips in the daily paper and the radio were a new form of entertainment for us.

Switching Seats

From the earliest time I can remember our mode of transportation was always by wagon or by foot. When we needed to travel to Rockport, Indiana (where Mom's relatives lived) or some other distant place, Pop would ask Dello Robinson to take us in his car. Before I was born, the family had a fast horse and a buggy they used to travel to distant places.

We had no automobile until 1938 when Pop became Township Dirt Road Supervisor. At that time, he bought a 1930 Chevrolet for $50 so he could have transportation for his job. Wesley was to be his chauffeur because Pop could not drive. Pop tried to drive one time, by following Wesley's instructions, but he had trouble combining the operations of the clutch, accelerator, and the gearshift all at one time. He especially had trouble finding the right gear with the floor shifter. Most alarming though, was the car would not stop when he said "Whoa!"

The old car gave considerable trouble and finally completely quit running. Wesley attempted to repair the carburetor and the distributor. Those things needed someone with experience and he was not successful with the repair. The Chevy was traded for a 1929 Model A Ford for $75. Pop again attempted to learn how to drive. He got so nervous about trying that he just gave it up. Repairs were easy to make on that Ford. Wesley and I both learned to fix about anything that went wrong with it.

1929 Model A Ford

The 1929 Model A Ford was a very popular and good serviceable car. Wesley and I were the main drivers of our Model A. We drove it many miles around Pike county taking Pop over the roads he was to look after and for many personal family needs.

Imel taught me how to drive his 1934 Chevrolet pickup truck. Then, when Wesley was not available, I drove Pop around to investigate and repair roads–even though I did not have a driver's license yet. When I became 16 I was able to get my Indiana driver's license, then I was legally Pop's driver!

During the summer, I was usually the one who drove him to work and over the roads as needed. When we went out on the roads, to repair a bridge or other repair jobs we would be gone all day. I usually helped him with any of the bridge repair or other work to be done.

The Runaway Boy

We had to report to the county garage each morning before going out to any repair or inspection job. One morning, on the way to town, a boy of about eight or nine years old was riding his bicycle in the same direction. I slowed and watched him carefully to see that he was beside the road and not in my path. As we got almost to him, he suddenly turned right in front of us. Even though we were not going over 20 miles an hour on the dirt grade, there was no way I could avoid hitting him. Of course, we stopped as quickly as possible and got out to check on the damage. We saw the bike was in bad shape but the boy was nowhere to be seen. He had taken off running as hard as he could go for home, which was just a short distance. We set the damaged bike on the front bumper and took it to his house. His dad was Darwin Bell who ran a filling station and country store on Bell's Hill. Pop offered to pay for the bike, but Darwin would not let him pay. He knew it was the boy's fault and was just glad that he was not hurt.

The New Mechanics

In 1941, Imel bought a new Chevrolet pickup truck and decide to sell his 1934 Plymouth to Pop to replace our Model A Ford, which was in need of much repair. Pop paid him $150, on payments, for the Plymouth and disposed of the Ford. Our mode of transportation was much improved. The '34 Plymouth was a luxury car in its day.

The next year the transmission went bad in the Plymouth. It was going to cost $50 to $80 to get it fixed. Pop did not have that kind of money and thought it was probably not worth fixing. I asked him if he would let me try to fix it. He said, "James, if you think you might repair it, go ahead and try. Even if you take it apart and cannot get it back together, we are not any worse off!"

I got Eldon, my cousin that lived across the railroad, to

help me with our crude tools. We spent a whole day in getting the transmission out and taking it apart. Before we even got it apart, I found the problem. With the top plate removed, I saw a small gear that was stripped. None of the other gears were damaged.

I finally got it taken apart enough to remove the damaged gear. I took it to a dealer in town and he found one just like it. I paid only $2.50 for the new gear. It took Eldon and me another day to get the transmission back together. We were surprised that it worked as if it were new. Pop thought I was a real mechanic, although I did not think that was true. It was just an experiment for me! However, I was elated to be successful with what seemed to be a major repair job. The Plymouth was a great car and gave us several years of reliable service.

1934 Plymouth

Chapter 6

COMMUNITY OF FAMILY AND FRIENDS

*Iron sharpeneth iron; so a man sharpeneth
the countenance of his friend. (Proverbs 27:17)*

Uncle Edmund

Floyd (L) with elder brother James Edmund Willis
by Edmund's house ca1918

Edmund was Pop's oldest brother. He was a very likable man and always had a playful disposition toward us. He had eight children in his own, seven of which were at home during those early years of my life. Their ages corresponded very close to the ages of the children of our family and that set many of us in the same grades at the Willis School. Much of the time we walked to and from school together.

Uncle Edmund and his family lived in a house that was on the north edge of Grandma's 40 acres near the wooded area.

I never did know if he built the house or if the piece of ground was deeded to him as was the case with the other siblings. Edmund worked at the coal mines and various other jobs. One job in particular that I remember was him and his son, Randall, shearing sheep for some farmers.

Edmund never owned a team of horses during my lifetime, so he was not engaged in any farming except the raising of some pigs and chickens which would help supply their need for food. His family also raised a large garden during the summer months. Each fall he usually shared the work with Pop in the butchering of the hogs. His son acquired an old automobile, which furnished them transportation to their jobs and an occasional family trip. Unfortunately, Uncle Edmund met an early death by a gunshot wound in 1935. He was buried in the Martin Cemetery (south of Clark's Station) where his parents, Bev and Bell, were buried.

We often played with Uncle Edmund's children at our house, at their house, or at Grandma's house. The children of our age were all girls, so we boys did not like to play at their house very long.

The straw hat was a personal and valuable item to every child. Agatha thought her hat was gone forever when it fell in that deep well.
[A.E. Willis illustration]

When at Grandma's place one day, some of us were leaning over the well curb looking down the well to see what things Grandma had hanging down there. In those days everyone wore straw hats, girls and boys. Well, along came Agatha wearing her straw hat and when she looked over the edge there it went tumbling down into the well.

It so happened that Pop was there at the time. She began to yell for him to get her hat out of the well. Pop heard the commotion and instinctively knew the problem, so he came for the grab hooks that were always kept handy for such purposes. While Pop was getting the grab hook ready to fish it out, Agatha was getting impatient...thinking the hat was sinking. She kept yelling, "Hurry Unc' Floyd, it's a goin' under!" Pop was able to get the hook on her hat and pull it out of the well. Agatha was very happy! We were all promptly instructed to remove our hats in the future when we wanted to look into the well.

Another Close Uncle

Floyd with Clarence enjoying one of their similar interests

I knew Uncle Clarence, Pop's next older brother, quite well because he came to our house often and visited. Also, he was involved with my dad in the farming and coal mining.

Uncle Clarence always made a "hot bed" where he sowed seeds early in the spring. The seedlings he grew could be put in the garden quite early. Often some of us children would buy plants from him. For a nickel or dime we could buy about all the tomato and cabbage plants we needed for our garden.

Many times, especially on a Sunday afternoon, Uncle Clarence would walk to our house to visit for a while. I do not remember Aunt Esta ever visiting our house; she was kind of a homebody and did not go anyplace except to town when she could get one of her boys to take her.

Saturday night was a big time when many people went to town. Some would go for shopping but many would just go to window shop or walk the streets to see people they knew.

One Saturday night, close to Christmas, three of us kids rode to town with Gerald and Marybelle in order to buy presents for our gift exchange at school. At that time, I was in the seventh or eighth grade so I was about 13 years of age. While I was shopping, I saw Aunt Esta walking down the street. She looked so lonely that I thought it would be good to buy a present for her, thinking it might cheer her up. Immediately, I went in the 5 & 10 store and bought a woman's handkerchief. When I caught up with her, I handed her the bag containing the handkerchief and said, "Merry Christmas, Aunt Esta." I neither wanted nor expected anything in return. I just wanted to do something to brighten her day with some joy.

The next time Uncle Clarence came up to our house he handed me a neatly wrapped small box and said, "This is from Esta, which she purchased for a favorite nephew." I was so surprised I hardly knew how to express my appreciation. When I opened the package, there was a beautiful pen and pencil set. I was not expecting that! It was a gift I have always cherished. That exchange led me to regard her as a very dear aunt. The pen set often reminded me of Aunt Esta and how even a small kind deed can make a lasting warm memory.

Closer Than a Neighbor

Aunt Ola, Pop's youngest sister, and her husband, Roy Kincaid, were our closest neighbors. They lived just across the railroad south of us. They often let us children ride with them to church services whenever there happened to be one in the neighborhood or at Hosmer. Uncle Roy frequently visited our house and was always very friendly to us children. He was one of the few people in the neighborhood who owned a car.

When there was bad weather, Uncle Roy allowed their daughter, Jessie, to drive her brother, Eldon, to school. On those days, the children of our family were allowed to ride with them. On one rainy day, she failed to negotiate a turn in the road and ran into an embankment. Fortunately, no one was seriously hurt. Lelah got a bad bump on her head and a small cut that caused some bleeding. She was taken to a neighbor's house to treat her injury and stop the bleeding. From there we continued on to school.

Eldon was born with a stub leg that had a small foot protruding toward the back. His knee was fitted into a pad on top of a peg leg, which was made by Uncle Roy. As he grew older, Uncle Roy would have to add an extension to the peg leg or make him a new one. When Eldon was about 14 years of age, he was sent to Indianapolis where the foot was removed and he was fitted with an artificial leg.

Eldon did not like to join in our work projects. When it was time for him to go home, Aunt Ola would stand in her back door facing our house and call for Eldon loud enough for all of us to hear. Eldon would then hasten down the road and across the tracks toward home.

Aunt Ola was a good Christian woman who expressed her faith in the Lord and was faithful to attend any revival service close to home. She often invited any of us children who would like to go along. After I got a driver's license, I frequently invited her to church where some of us would be attending.

Grandpa Harry Parker

We hardly knew anything about our maternal grandparents until Grandpa Harry Parker, Mom's dad, came to stay with us in the mid 1930s. He had lived near Richland City, Indiana, much of his life; it is where he was born and raised. It is there he married Grace Gilliland, Mom's mother, who died when Mom was a little girl.

The earliest memory I have of Grandpa Parker was when he lived in Rockport, Indiana...by then he was divorced from his third wife (Mable Fortune). I was 10 or 12 years old when he came to live with us. I am not sure why he came to our house, but it was in the latter years of the Great Depression days when many people were out of work. Grandpa made a little money delivering papers, distributing leaflets for places of business, and other small jobs. He always wanted to look like a businessperson, so he carried a battery of pencils in his shirt or coat pocket. That could have been his means of earning a little income. In desperation, he was looking for ways to make a living. Perhaps he was just happy to have a place he could call home. We tried to make him feel welcome and he seemed to appreciate the comforts of our good home and busy life.

Mom fixed up the outdoor room, where Uncle Casper had lived, so Grandpa Parker could have some privacy. He joined the family for meals and much of his daytime activity. Grandpa enjoyed playing indoor games with us children and he was especially fond of checkers. He really just liked to play if he could win. So as the older children would get more proficient at checkers and start to win, he'd start choosing his opponents to be the younger children because they hadn't yet become skilled at the game. Grandpa Parker was even willing to help with the chores around the house. When it came time to do outdoor chores, now that was different story. He did join us in the outdoor work but not very willingly. He would especially complain if one of us were doing something else or excused from a particular job. His peculiar ways livened up our house and we really enjoyed having him stay with us.

He remained living with us a few years, but when the economy started getting better Grandpa returned to his familiar territory in Rockport. We were sad to see him leave. Occasionally Mom corresponded with him by letter. Evidently, the places where he used to make deliveries were glad to have him back to deliver papers again. He was keeping busy and making enough to provide a necessary income.

We received word one day that Grandpa had been in an accident. He had been distributing handbills along the main street in town...he got careless and failed to watch for traffic. He stepped out into the street from between parked cars and was struck by an oncoming car, which knocked him into the path of a light delivery truck. Grandpa was badly injured and taken to the hospital, but did not survive through the night.

Our family traveled to Rockport for his funeral and we five brothers served as pallbearers along with one of his friends. Grandpa was buried east of Richland City next to Grace, my mom's mother, and his parents, Mr. and Mrs. William Parker.

Losing a Family Friend

Down a dirt road, a half mile south of the Willis School, lived a secluded distant relative named Roy Willis. My memories of him are his occasional visits to our house. It seemed like he always had some business matters and other things to talk about with Pop. He seemed to be a business minded person and it was believed that he had gained an inheritance somewhere along the way such that he did not have to worry about the depression years as much as other people.

He and Pop did have a business arrangement of sorts, as he had loaned Pop the necessary cash with which to build our home. I was never aware of the amount of the loan and I am not sure anyone else knew about it. Evidently, there was an agreement between Pop and Roy that the money from the sale of a calf or some pigs would be applied to the loan. I doubt if there was a written agreement because many such arrangements were made with a handshake. However, it is likely that each of them kept record of the amounts applied to the loan.

When it was time to sell a calf or some pigs, Roy would bring his car with a makeshift rack fixed on the back to take the animals to market. It was sort of sad to see those small animals being taken away. I thought we ought to keep them around longer, but I understood the time to sell them was Pop's decision. We would say goodbye to our small animals and would not see Roy's old vehicle again until the next season. He only drove it on special occasions. Any other time he would visit, he walked up the path beside the canal that led to our house from Uncle Clarence's house.

Another connection we had with Roy Willis was the times that Pop would take us there in the wagon to plant some vegetables in the rich soil near his house. Pop would use the team of horses to plow and prepare a large area of the ground for planting. Most of our family joined in the planting of things Roy wanted in his garden. Roy was not exactly disabled but he was not physically able to do much of that kind of work.

Burglary and crime was almost unheard of in our community or even in nearby towns. Therefore, most people seldom locked their doors and some people lived alone without any fear of intruders. So it was, that Roy lived alone in his out-of-the-way place with hardly a worry of any harm. It was commonly believed that Roy was well off and probably kept his money hid about his place. Many people did not trust the banks during the depression years.

One of the neighbors grew concerned about Roy because they had not seen him for a few days. When the neighbor went to his house, they found he had been shot in the head. There was evidence someone had ransacked his place, as if looking for his hidden money.

Authorities claimed the burglary and murder had taken place two or three days before he was found. I do not know of any investigation was ever made in connection with that case. Randal, Uncle Edmund's son was arrested on suspicion but was released for lack of evidence. No one ever believed Randal was guilty. We were very sad to lose a good friend of the family.

Casper Capers

His real name was Jasper M. Willis. There were several men who had been named Jasper Willis in the Clark's Station area over the years, so maybe to avoid confusion he went by Casper. We called him Uncle Casper, but we did not know that he really was a relative. His grandfather George (nickname Duck) was a brother to Maxwell (my great great grandfather). Jasper's (Casper's) father, Hayden, was a cousin to my great grandfather Jasper. Jasper was four years older than Hayden, so it is conceivable that Uncle Casper was named after my great grandfather Jasper. Uncle Casper was seven years older than my grandpa Beverly. Unfortunately our family does not have any recorded stories about Uncle Casper's family, his activities with my grandfather's family, or how he came to be intertwined with our family.

115

My first memory of Uncle Casper was when I was very young. He lived by himself in an old log cabin that was built long before our time. It was located a half mile up the railroad from our house. Ten feet from his cabin was an open dug well without any curb and only covered with some boards. We were cautioned to stay away from the well. No other special word was needed! We did not want to fall into that well.

Farming Casper's Land

Pop farmed some of Casper's acreage in addition to the limited tillable ground on Grandma's place. Corn was the primary crop that was grown on his place. The acreage near home was used mostly for hay, wheat, and pasture with some for additional corn, which was much needed for our livestock. Each year Pop would plant an acre of soup beans at Casper's farm. When the beans matured for harvest, we would pull the vines and stomp out the beans in a sack then pour beans from one container to another letting the wind blow out the trash and chaff. At harvest time one year we had a large wagon with hay racks loaded with bean vines, which were hauled to Grandma's barn. A hayrack is a frame made to fit on top of the wagon bed with boards extending out each side and back to make a wide platform for hauling hay.

That year Pop had in mind to use John Malott's new invention to hull the beans. Otherwise, we would have had a lot of stomping to do. John Malott was a neighbor who was always trying to build and invent something. He had built a small threshing machine and agreed to bring it down to the barn with his old tractor and experiment with his newly built contraption to hull our beans. While he was up on the platform feeding the bean vines into the thresher, a gear or something caught his pant leg and tore his britches off. Fortunately, he was able to keep from being pulled into the machine. There he stood in his shorts! The women folks, who had come to watch the process, were embarrassed and quickly went to the house.

Grandma sent out another pair of trousers for him and the bean hulling continued. Despite the potential hazard of losing ones clothing while using the homemade machine, it provided a practical way to shell the beans and we ended up with three bushels of navy beans–enough to share with relatives. We kids picked up beans that were thrown out on the ground by the machine and Mom made each of us a beanbag to toss as a game.

The Sorghum Mill

Another important crop was sorghum cane. Casper had raised sorghum cane for several years, so Pop reserved some space on Casper's farm for growing sorghum cane for our family. Uncle Casper had a sorghum mill on his place and when the cane was ripe, it was sorghum making time. Uncle Casper helped Pop to make several gallons of sorghum from the cane that Pop grew. There was enough for our use and some left over that could be sold. In addition, several people would bring their cane to Pop to make sorghum for them. Pop would not refuse to make sorghum for anyone. If they could not afford to pay him, he would accept a share of the sorghum for payment. He gained a reputation of making the best sorghum that could be found.

As kids, we thought of sorghum making time as a highlight of the season and the sorghum foam as a real treat. However, it was not all fun! Sometimes we had to help strip the leaves from the cane stalks, feed the mill, and carry away the excess pummy (the term we used for the crushed stalks the mill ejected).

Pop was very skilled at knowing how to build the furnace and set it all up for cooking sorghum. He used five vats to separate the sorghum into stages as it cooked from one stage to another. Another crucial step was knowing just how to keep the fire the right temperature and not allowing it to get too hot as to scorch the juice. He knew just when the juice needed to be dipped from one vat to the next, which he judged from the texture of the liquid. Most important was the timing required to take the finished sorghum from the last vat (which was also the coolest) without letting it overcook. Foam taken from the vats was saved in buckets to supplement feed for the hogs. We kids watched eagerly for the foam to be skimmed off the finishing vat. That was our candy!! The Sorghum in the last vat had to be watched closely. After it had cooked just the right amount of time, it was dipped into jugs or buckets. It is possible that Pop had been making sorghum since he was young. Maybe Casper or Grandpa Beverly taught him the art.

When I was about eight or nine I had to take my turn at feeding the iron rollers that squeezed the cane juice from the stalks. I would stand back far enough to avoid letting my hand get close to those rollers. One day when Wesley was feeding the mill, he let out a loud scream. Pop's instinct told him that Wesley had a hand headed for the rollers. He immediately yelled, "Whoa!" at the horse hitched to the mill. Fortunately, the horse pulling the long arm, which turned the rollers, was the one that would respond instantly to the command and he stopped! Wesley's hand was caught but had not been pulled into the rollers. That was a fair warning to hold those stalks at a distance without getting close to the rollers.

Whenever we were working at Uncle Casper's place, Mom would have some of us children help her carry a basket lunch up the railroad to his house. There under two big oak trees she would spread a sheet and set out the food for lunch, which included a pan of biscuits for everyone to enjoy.

Cooking vats

The sorghum mill in full operation at the Casper Willis farm. Pop operated the cooking vats. Making sorghum molasses was an important project toward the end of summer, when the cane was ripe.
[A.E. Willis illustration]

Casper's Calamity

Eventually Pop discontinued farming and no longer made use of the sorghum mill. Old Uncle Casper continued to live by himself in his log cabin for a few years (he always seemed like an old person to me). Since we were his nearest neighbors, he frequently walked down the railroad to visit us. It was probably the only time he would have a good meal. He was not in good health and one time when he arrived, he was not feeling well. After he left for home that evening Mom was much concerned about him and asked Pop to check on him to see if he made it home. Pop found him where he had fallen beside the railroad tracks in pain and unable to move. Pop got him to his feet and brought him back to our house where he spent the night. He stayed with us that night and never did return to his old log cabin. That is how Uncle Casper became a member of our family.

Uncle Casper had three sons and a daughter with comfortable homes, but they did not intend to take care of him. When Pop realized he would be an indefinite resident at our house, he decided to build a special room for him. Since our house was limited on bedroom space, Pop and Wesley built a fair sized room onto the side of the cellar house. It was furnished with a bed, table, chairs, and a stove. Casper would come into the house to eat with us or one of us would carry a plate of food to him.

Casper did not want to be a burden on our family and was always working at something around the house to compensate for his care even though it was not expected of him. He would make garden, clear fence rows, cut small trees for wood, grub weeds, and anything he could find to do. I often volunteered to help him with his projects.

Woodcutter

When people start getting older, they find there are

benefits to having youngsters nearby. Their youthful energy can be harnessed in helpful ways. That was the case with Uncle Casper. He often called upon me, and I became his favorite helper. That turned out to be a good for me because I actually learned a lot about him and from him.

Anytime Uncle Casper had a project he wanted to work on, he would ask, "James, would you help me [on thus and so]?" One of those requests was, "James, I want to cut some wood today." We went down to the end of the garden where we did our wood cutting. Using a crosscut saw, he on one end and I on the other, we would drag the saw back and forth on the logs to make firewood. Some were big logs that Pop and Imel had previously hauled down from the woods on Grandma's place or wherever there might be fallen trees.

After we sawed for a while, Uncle Casper would get tired and need to rest. While he was resting I would split the chunks of wood we had cut and he would tell tales of his adventures in life. After he rested a while, then he would go back to working with me cutting more logs. If Emory Fowler were there, as he often came over to enjoy Casper's company, they would sit and spin their stories back and forth. I would continue with the wood splitting and listen to them while I worked.

By the end of summer, we would have two cords of wood cut and stacked up near the house, where it would be handy for use in the kitchen cook stove, the living room fireplace, or the big wood and coal heating stove in the dining room. Morris and Orace Wayne were willing to help haul the wood to the house in our little red wagon.

Casper and I worked at many projects during his few years of living with us. I enjoyed working with him, because he was so agreeable and was always looking for constructive things to do. He would tell stories of his childhood and sometimes tell of things he read in the Bible.

Uncle Casper (left), my wood cutting partner.
On the right is Emory Fowler, a neighbor and daily visitor
who would spin tales with Casper.

A Fishy Story

On one occasion, Uncle Casper called to me, "James, I believe if we'll take some dough balls and set a trotline in the canal we'll catch a big fish. Some big fish swim in this shallow end of the canal." (A trotline is a line stretched across the canal.) He continued, "I'll have Inez make us some dough balls. You and I can go put out the lines and bait them with the dough balls." Enthusiastically, he explained his plan, "We'll put the trot line on the shallow end where we might catch the big fish." I had little faith in his particular project, because the really big fish seldom came into the shallow water. Rather than dampen his spirit, I just went along with his plans.

Mom made the dough balls for us, then Uncle Casper and I took them along with the trotlines down to the canal. We were successful in getting the lines across the canal with the hooks hanging with leads. Then we began baiting all the hooks with our dough balls on both lines. Suddenly there was a big splash out in the water! Uncle Casper was so excited and exclaimed, "Oh, that must've been a big one out there. Let's hurry and get this other line baited so we can catch him." Within a few minutes, there was another big splash! Uncle Casper was really excited about those fish flouncing in the water. He exclaimed, "There's another one!" However, I was suspicious, knowing my mischievous brothers. I suspected Morris and Orace Wayne were throwing things from behind some bushes having fun at our expense. Of course, they would have learned why Mom was making dough balls for us and began planning for a little fun.

Then a clod came sailing through the air at a time when Uncle Casper looked up. He said with disgust, "Oh, that's those dang boys up there throwing clods". "Hey!" I yelled at them to appease and support Uncle Casper, "Stop throwing clods! You'll scare the fish away." Eventually our efforts were rewarded with a few fish and maybe a turtle, but we never did catch the big buffalo. We boys often played tricks on Casper and he might get aggravated at our mischievousness, but in certain ways he liked for us to be around. If we were gone for any length of time, he would ask Mom, "Inez, where's the boys?" Later, Mom told us how Uncle Casper was curious about our absence.

Casper's Bible

Our "star boarder" would often sit around in some secluded place to practice telling stories to himself, so he could tell them to visitors. Sometimes he would stop and have a big laugh about his story. We young boys liked to sneak up and listen to his stories. When he was not working at something or telling his stories we would find him in his room reading the Bible or a newspaper. Uncle Casper was very knowledgeable of both the old and new testaments of the Bible. Many were aware he was an avid reader of the Bible and knew much of it by memory.

One summer a minister by the name of Porter was holding a *brush arbor meeting* just across the railroad tracks from our house. He knew Casper was a long time reader of the Bible and thought the local people attending the meeting might be encouraged or inspired by Casper's gifted memorization of it. Mr. Porter inquired if Casper would come over one evening and speak to the people...to talk about the Bible or quote some of his favorite scriptures.

He finally agreed to go and Mom dressed him up the best she could with a white shirt and clean trousers. It was a special occasion and we children went along. He stood before those anxious people and quoted scripture from both the old and new testament for about 30 minutes without stopping. It was truly an inspiration to all those present. I was real proud of my wood-cutting partner standing up there confidently quoting scripture without even looking at the Bible. I was inspired to want to read the Bible for myself.

Uncle Casper lived to be 83 years old. He died of natural causes in the room addition that Pop built for him. Two of his sons, Harley and Riley, were at his bedside at the time of his death. At that time, we were still too poor to afford a tombstone and his children did not offer to buy one, so Pop made a concrete marker for his gravesite. He was buried in the Old Union Cemetery just one mile north of our home.

(standing L-R) Esta, Clarence, Ola, and Floyd
Seated - Mae and her husband Lawrence
This is Pop and his siblings as I remember them from my youth. All of my
uncles and aunts, their growing children, and our family lived within two
miles of the area where they were born. Aunt Mae and Uncle Lawrence
moved to St. Louis with their family.

Seated in front - Grandma Belle (R) with her sister, Tempe
(Back L-R) unknown, Tom and Ethyl Abell, Milt Willis
Floyd (my dad) is sitting on the ground - far left

Chapter 7

EARLY SCHOOL YEARS IN RURAL INDIANA

Train up a child in the way he should go: and
when he is old, he will not depart from it. (Proverbs 22:6)

Expanding World

In the fall of 1930, I started school at a little one-room schoolhouse that was one mile from home. Only four students (me, another boy and two girls) started in the first grade at the Willis School that year. The school was built on a one-acre plot of ground several years earlier and named Willis School because it was largely a Willis settlement. At the time I began school, most of the students had the last name of Willis or were closely related to a Willis. I'm not exactly sure when the school was built, but as early as 1893 the Willis School was mentioned in the local newspaper called the Petersburg Pike County Democrat. My father, as well as my aunts and uncles, all had attended that one-room school. It was in that same little school, where all seven of us children completed the first through eighth grades of our education.

Many events that happened at school remain a vivid memory. The beginning of school that first year was an exciting adventure and yet, I went with some fear of what could happen. I had heard stories about the teacher using a large whip on disobedient students. Of course, I intended to try to do what was expected of me, but suppose I made a mistake or something happened that I could not help, then what?

Sure enough, when I got to school there were long switches laid across some nails above the chalkboard...up front where all could see them. I well knew they were there to be used, and I did not like to think of that. They spoke louder than any words from the teacher.

From the start, I rather liked learning the words that told

the stories about the pictures in my reader. I was required to take my reader book home with me each night to practice reading the next lesson. Marybelle was my home tutor and she would make me read each page repeatedly until I knew every word on them. But I *really* liked to count and put numbers together to make addition and subtraction problems.

Warner Ammerman

Warner Ammerman was my first grade teacher. The eighth grade kids all sat in desks on one side of the room. The succeeding rows of desks were smaller for lower grade students until the last row of quite small desks were for first and second grade pupils. On my third day of school, a very exciting and scary thing happened. There was some very loud arguing and hateful yelling in the eighth grade row on the far side of the room from me. When I looked up, Mr. Ammerman and Stanton Nance, a cousin to me, were shouting at each other. Stanton was a big heavy boy in the eighth grade. Mr. Ammerman was also a big person. All of a sudden, Mr. Ammerman shoved Stanton backward and he fell flat on his back with a loud thud. Stanton got up from the floor and stomped out of the schoolhouse saying some ugly words as he left.

He never came back to school after that. I do not know if he quit school (which would have been acceptable at that time) or if he transferred to Beckville, a neighboring country school. I soon learned to like Mr. Ammerman as a teacher because he was good to us if we tried to get our lessons and would live by his strict rules.

One day in the hustle of getting ready for school, while I was yet in first grade, I forgot my speller book and left it at home. When it came time for spelling lesson, I had no spelling book with which to study my words. Mr. Ammerman asked, "James, where is your spelling book?" I replied very timidly, "I forgot to bring it with me to school." I wondered what he would do. He very calmly said, "Just for that, you will have to study from your sister's eighth grade book."

I was disturbed at the thought of having to learn those big words in Marybelle's lessons. I didn't know that when you got your spelling book in first grade, you would use it all the way through the eighth grade because the words for every grade were in the same book. That was a relief to me, and I went home bragging I had studied words from Marybelle's spelling book.

During the pleasant days of fall and when the delightful days of spring were appearing, Mr. Ammerman would dismiss us first grade children an hour early in the afternoon. I loved walking home from school by myself. My favorite route was to go past John and Polly's beautiful flowers, up the Wertz Hill and across his field, through Grandma's locust trees, then diagonally across Wyatt's field to our house. I truly enjoyed the walk home all by myself. There were ditches to cross and paths through the thicket of trees. I could imagine I was driving a toy car or a cart along the paths and over the ditches as I made my way home. When I would come to a log that was in way, I wondered how I would get "my car" across.

Three of us who started in the first grade that year completed all our first grade books early in the school term. Mr. Ammerman let the us continue into the second grade books and we finished them by the end of the school year. We passed the second grade examination test and were allowed to go into the third grade for our second year of school. In later years I thought that was not a wise decision, because in upper grades and through high school I always felt the other students were a little ahead of me.

The Willis School

The school had no modern plumbing facilities or electricity. A large coal-heating stove sat near the center of the room for heating. The large windows on the north side of the room furnished our only light. Drinking water was carried from a pump 200 yards down a hill off the official schoolyard. A small area just inside the entrance of the school was a place to hang our coats on a hook, a shelf for lunch buckets, and a location for the water tank dispenser. Each child was supposed to have their own drinking cup.

The enrollment consisted of a total of 20 to 25 students in all eight grades. There were rows of wooden seats and desks with wrought iron fittings, which were fastened securely to the floor. Each grade was called to the front for special instruction, when it was time for their class, where they sat on the *recitation bench* in front of the teacher's desk.

In the classroom, there was no such thing as foul play or disobedience. We did not talk; we did not whisper; we did not get out of our seat without permission. Each student did his/her own lessons. The supply of hickory switches that lay above the chalkboard were a grim reminder of strict regulations.

Class-time was strictly for the business of learning, but recess was fun and games. In good weather, children would come running out of the school and down the steps for a time to play. It was often a continuation of previous games. Many times even the teacher entered into our games and activities.

Recess Ruckus

Some children would run to the ball diamond to play, while hop-scotch would be of interest to others. In the spring, there was usually a season of playing marbles and mumble peg by the boys. Jump rope was always enjoyed by all ages. Then there were a variety of circle games, such as tag and drop the handkerchief, which provided plenty of excitement. We all liked handy-over (throwing the ball over the schoolhouse to the other team). Other outdoor games consisted of tag, fox and geese, and improvised activities. What we played varied with the season of the year. Softball was the most important outdoor game. Sometimes we would go to another school on Friday for a competitive game of softball or another school would come to our school for a game. All boys and most girls became very good ball players.

There were different games for indoor play during inclement weather. A very popular and rowdy game for indoors was upset-the-fruit basket. That game started with several kids seated on and around the recitation bench. An "it" person called out names to exchange seats and sometimes everyone had to get a different seat. During the exchange the "it" person tried to grab one of the seats. Anyone left without a seat became "it"! Other indoor activities were guessing games, board games, drawing, and chalkboard activity. There was never a dull moment during recess!

Frances Vaughn

Lelah started first grade the next year. We had been playmates from the very beginning and she had been my first teacher by instructing me how to talk. I was happy to have her going to school with us. There were four from our family in Willis School that year...Marybelle, Wesley, Lelah, and me.

Frances Vaughn became the teacher at Willis School that year and I was in the third grade. By then I could read simple children's stories and soon learned to work out the pronunciation and meaning of unfamiliar words.

Miss Frances started something that really motivated many of the students, including myself, to enjoy reading. She would bring a selection of good books, which had interesting stories, from the Petersburg Library and sign them out to us. She appointed an older student as the librarian to keep record of the books we selected. After a few weeks Miss Frances returned all those books and brought back different ones. Although, sometimes she brought some of the same books that we especially liked. One of the first books I selected was a story about two Dutch children, who were twins. I could hardly stop reading the book long enough to work on my school lessons. It was a fascinating story about life and conditions in

Holland. I learned more about the country from that story than I would have learned from a geography book. From that time on, reading became an enjoyable hobby. However, there were so many other activities at school and at home that reading was only a sideline most of the time.

Miss Frances was a Christian and would read a Bible story to us some mornings. She also held a Bible verse contest each Monday morning, to see how many Bible verses each student could recite from memory. Doreen Gray, an eighth grade girl, usually won. I often wondered how she could remember so many verses. I did well to memorize just one verse.

I remember Miss Frances as a good teacher who brought out the best in her students. We were also quite fond of the parties she would have for us on special days like Thanksgiving, Christmas, Valentine's Day, and Easter.

Everyone liked Miss Frances very much. She was my teacher through the third and fourth grades. Her kindness and interesting ways made learning fun, especially in math...which I liked best. At the end of her second year she bid us farewell. She explained that she would not be our teacher any longer as it was her last year of teaching at Willis School. That left us sad and in great suspense as to who our teacher would be for the next year. She invited parents to bring baskets of food for a picnic on the last day of school.

Lelah was permitted to complete all the first and second grade lessons during her first of school, just as I had done the previous year. She would go into the third grade the next year and be just one grade behind me for the remainder of our elementary and high school years.

Journey to School

Mom and Pop believed our education was very important and we could only stay home if we were seriously sick, which was a rare occasion. Any sickness required one to stay in bed all day! That was the cure for a possible faked sickness. No one wanted to spend the day in bed! Therefore, it was not in our vocabulary to stay home from school.

Even if the weather was bad (rain, snow, or freezing), we still went to school. The walk was a little difficult when the road was muddy or if there had been a heavy snow. We liked the snow when it had drifted to make deep places for us to jump into. We knew that when we got to school there would be a hot stove in the middle of the room waiting for us to get warm and dry. It was enjoyable to arrive home, after the cold winter walk, to a warm house, a home cooked meal, and family fellowship of love.

The routine one-mile walk to and from school was usually a pleasant time of the day especially when the weather was good. During good weather two other alternate shortcut routes across some fields shaved a little off the distance. We might run, play, jump, or just socialize...but sometimes we invented playful and exciting adventures along the way.

The Broomsage Fire

On one such occasion in the spring, when the weather was very nice with a good breeze, Wesley thought he would create a little excitement. I believe there were six of us in the group that day. It was Wesley, myself, Lelah, and Morris from our family. Then there was Agatha and Arbutus from Uncle Edmund's family. Elden Kincaid, another cousin, might have been along because sometimes he went to the Willis School with us. Wesley stepped up a small bank into a field and brought back a handful of dry broomsage (a tall grass-like weed that looks like broom straw and is very flammable). We were not supposed to carry matches, especially to school, but Wesley was always a little brazen to violate the rules. In addition, of course, no one was going to tell on him. He struck a match and set fire to the handful of broomsage in the middle of the dirt road. That seemed very harmless, so a few of the others of us went up and got another handful of the dry stuff to make the fire a little bigger. Wesley announced, "Don't anyone get any more. We need to let this burn up then we can head toward home."

About that time, one of the girls picked up a handful of the broomsage that was burning on one end and tossed it up the bank into the field before anyone could stop her. The wind caught the flame quickly and a fire began to spread rapidly. We were all very scared and instead of attempting to extinguish the fire we ran ahead up the road past the field of dry grass to the top of the hill. Then looking out across the field, we could see the fire racing across it. Someone suggested maybe we should have tried to put it out. But it was too late and perhaps it was better we never attempted that.

The nearest neighbors were at least a half-mile away, but as many as saw the smoke and fire came to help put it out. They worked into the night and finally managed to contain the flames before they reached John Malott's house, which was in a corner of the field. The fire had scorched practically the entire field. We children never said a word about our part in the starting of that fire. I imagine Wesley had cautioned us to never say anything about it, maybe even with strong warning of what might happen to us. We respected his word because he was the oldest one in the group. Our ability to keep that secret was due partly to loyalty to each other, and the regret for the trouble it caused all the neighbors. We were very sorry for what had happened and felt ashamed of the damage we caused. We knew there would be some severe punishment if our parents ever found out. None of us ever talked about it at home, at school, at play, or anywhere–not even among ourselves. It surely was a well kept secret.

The Costly Disaster

During those early school years, we were quite poor and it was difficult for Pop and Mom to manage all the needs of our family. At times Pop worked in the coal mine during the winter months to supplement the family income. One evening when Pop had come home from working at the mine, Henry Malott was there with his truck and asked Pop to crank it for him to get it started (many old vehicles had to be started that way). If the motor started, the crank would slip out of its socket and hang loose. But if the motor backfired, it caused the motor to turn backwards, then the crank would also fly backwards. Pop was not aware a kickback could happen, so he was not prepared for that possibility. When Pop tried to crank the motor, it backfired...the crank flew backward, struck his arm, and broke it. Someone took him to the doctor, but Henry would not pay the doctor bill.

Wesley and Pop with broken arm ca1930

I remember Pop wearing his arm in a sling when we came home from school that day. He had to wear the sling for several weeks because the bone was broken below the elbow. Pop had been working at the coal mine at the time and that put him out of work. He could not work shoveling coal with a broken arm. Without an income our hard times were going to get even more difficult.

Since there was no government program for the unemployed or any such thing as insurance benefits in those days, we all had to help in any way we could. Imel was about 14 years old and he had to do the spring plowing that year.

Mom had an old pedal type Singer sewing machine, which she used to make a lot of our clothes. She always bought material to make shirts for the boys of the family and dresses for the girls. She usually managed to buy each boy one or two pairs of overalls and one pair of shoes if we needed them. They had to last us through the entire school year. However, when it came time to start school in the fall, there was no money to buy clothes or other things needed for school. Pop did not want to ask for any help, but Mom decided to talk the township trustee to seek help to get the children some clothes for school.

Mom dressed up the best she could and had me to dress up with clean overalls to go with her. I was without a shirt and barefoot, but I had my hair clean and combed nicely. We walked the four miles to town to see the trustee at the courthouse. While waiting outside his office, we heard a woman and the trustee arguing and talking very hateful in loud voices, storming at each other. When the woman came out with her son, we had an idea what caused the problem. Her boy had on ragged clothes, was dirty, and had matted hair. The woman had on a very pitiful looking outfit and brought her boy unkempt, as if their appearance would persuade the trustee of their dire need.

When we entered the office, the trustee complimented Mom on her dress and on my cleanliness. He had sent the woman home to clean up herself and her boy before coming back to ask for assistance. He said anyone could have a bar of soap to wash and clean up, and comb their hair. The trustee again complimented Mom on bringing me in looking neat and clean, with freshly washed overalls, even though I was barefoot and had no shirt. Perhaps we made a good impression because of the contrast between the shoddiness of the pair before us and the neatness of our appearance. It may have caused him to have a good attitude toward us. He granted mom a credit account at a store to buy material, shoes, and other needs for us to start school. We went directly to the store and got as many school supplies as the credit voucher allowed. Mom was so happy to have the new material that she began making our shirts the very next day.

She was able to make Lelah two dresses and each of us boys two shirts. She bought two shades of blue cloth for our shirts, which made them look much nicer than our usual drab gray ones. All the other kids at school admired our attractive new shirts.

Angels Ever Watching

The Wertz deep shaft coal mine was along our route to school. Uncle Roy worked there, at the scales, weighing loads of coal. We would stop, when he was not busy, and let him weigh us on the scales. Within a few years the mine discontinued operation.

It was during my third or fourth grade, after the mine closed, that we stopped and went up to the shaft to look down inside. We liked to pitch rocks down in the hole to hear them splash in the water. There was no guardrail around the pit, so some kids would scoot up close on their belly to see the rock hit the water. The shaft was a great hole in the ground that had been used to lift the coal to the surface. It was about 15 feet down to the surface of the water and the pit was cluttered with broken timbers fallen from the deteriorated shaft.

That was a very dangerous thing we did. It makes me shudder to think about what could have happened if one of us had slipped on some loose slack and fell into the pit. Angels were surely watching over us! We only did that one or two times because our parents warned us not to go near the mine. Eventually Mr. Wertz had the pit filled to avoid such danger.

The Days of the Hickory Stick

In the fall of 1932, we arrived at school filled with much anxiety to learn who would be our new teacher. It would be my fourth year in school and I was entering the fifth grade. Charley Miley, who lived only one mile west and south of our home, was at the school waiting for us when we got there. Mr. Miley was a very stern disciplinarian and was going to be our new teacher. He was known to have used a switch on 17 boys at one school for playing keeps in marbles. We played marbles many times but were not allowed to keep any marbles that we won from the circle. In the end each boy got back all of his own marbles.

Mr. Miley had a habit of chewing his tongue, especially in times of anxiety or frustration. He was a strict teacher and kept switches of different lengths above the chalkboard. They had distinct qualities, from being stiff and inflexible to thin and pliable. Perhaps he had a way of choosing a particular switch as being most effective for a particular infraction.

Sometimes Mr. Miley would throw an eraser or a piece of chalk to hit a student who was turned around in their seat or was doing something wrong. It was quite a strain to keep from laughing at him whether he missed his target or not. It made the situation even more funny because he would be frustrated and chew his tongue, but we dared not let him see us laughing. If he marched back to a student with one of those keen switches, everyone knew he had become so angry that he was going to use it on the unlucky kid.

He had perfect attention from the students except when he wasn't looking. Even then we had to be very careful, because it was said that teachers and parents had eyes in the back of their heads. Indeed, they seemed to sense what we children were doing even without looking. We all knew the consequences of getting caught at horseplay in the classroom.

Mr. Miley was not usually stern with the girls and he treated them better than the boys. One of the boys received a

138

severe and merciless treatment on his backside for making comments about Mr. Miley's preferential treatment of girls. The boy's dad came to the school the next day and challenged Mr. Miley to come out for a fight. Mr Miley would not go out and take his punishment or be challenged.

Yet, there was one girl Mr. Miley did not seem to like. Olivia Hale was kind of a tomboy, playing mostly the games the boys played and being quite mischievous at times. When she was in trouble or had done something wrong, Mr. Miley would call her to the front of the room (which was customary when there was a problem) and question her. Whether out of humiliation, shame, or maybe even fear...Olivia would not talk. He would give her a switch on her back, but she would only drop her head with a stony gaze toward the floor.

I think Mr. Miley would have listened to the girl and excused her if she would have explained what was going on. However, she would remain stubbornly silent with head bowed. He would try to raise her head but could not budge it. He would hit her a few times with a switch and still she would not talk, holding her head down. Tears would roll down her cheeks as Mr. Miley repeatedly used the switch on her legs and back, in an attempt to get her to talk. It was unmerciful treatment and we all wished Olivia would just say something! Finally, he would give up or get tired from the ordeal and let Olivia return to her seat. She would lay her head on the desk humiliated, sobbing, and hurting over the ordeal.

I had Mr. Miley for a teacher through the fifth, sixth, and seventh grades. At the end of each year he would have a little speech for his captive audience. In his annual dissertation, he included some thoughts about the uncertainty of life. He would say, "I come to the end of another year. I always wonder if I will still be living next year at this time." When the next school year came, Mr. Miley would still be there. He retired after several years of teaching and lived to be 90 years old.

During those years I spent many nights with Grandma. In her living room was her bed and a small table where I could work my lessons. During the evenings, I often sat at that table working long lists of math problems and wondered why the teacher had us do so many after we already knew how to work them. I know now, having been a teacher, how important that practice was.

Special Memories of Grandma

Pop did not want Grandma staying by herself. I stayed at Grandma's house when Arba was away working and had to be gone for a few days. Even when he was just going to be gone until late in the night, Arba would ask me, "James, will you go up and spend the night with Ma (as he called her)?" Of course, I was always happy to go. It was a delight to stay with Grandma. She was a very special person to me.

She was truly a saintly grandmother and I felt like I was her pet grandchild. When I stayed with her I brought in coal and wood, drew water from the well, gathered eggs, fed the chickens, and kept the fire going in the grated fireplace. When we went to bed and she always wanted my knees pressing in her lower back to comfort her pain. I regret I did not know how to express my love for her, but yet, as I reflect back I realize that as a child I was showing love to her by eagerly and willingly helping her the way I did.

Grandma never ran out of stories to tell of her life and things in general. She liked to tell of the trips she and Grandpa Beverly made in their buggy with their fine horses when they were young. She also told of the hard work on their farm and the struggles to raise a large family. Sometimes she would tell about their young children who died at an early age and the sad time it was for her and Beverly. Their faith in God had seen them through all their trials and successes of life.

In the evening when I worked my math problems, I liked listening to Grandma talk. I would stop between problems to chat with her and ask questions or I would take time out to fix the fire and let her look at my schoolwork. She always had complimentary words of encouragement. She also told about her school days when she was a child. I wish I had written down her stories, because most of our conversations did not leave a lasting memory on my young mind.

Most women in those days were experts at cooking and preparing meals, no matter how simple they may have been! Grandma was no exception. She would get up before me and go to the kitchen to prepare breakfast. By the time I got up, I could smell the brewing of coffee. She would have a pan of buttermilk biscuits, eggs, bacon or ham, and gravy for us to eat. If it was a school day, she would fix my lunch and the other kids would come past on the way to school and I would join them.

After school, as we came to Grandma's house on the way home, she would meet us with a cold biscuit or maybe a cookie. Sometimes Uncle Edmund's girls would walk across the field with us to Grandma's place just to get the treat of a biscuit. I would go ahead home with my siblings for supper even if I was to return and spend the night with Grandma. Occasionally I felt it was unfair to the other children that I was the one who got to stay with Grandma the most.

In April of 1934 Grandma became very sick with a fever. My Mom and some other women were there with her when the doctor came. Some of the other kids and I were out in the yard and were told to not be noisy out there because Grandma was very sick. Later that evening, Grandma had a high fever and died of what they called a "common illness".

Grandma had meant so much to us. It was a great loss and a sad time when she died. Many people, in addition to her relatives, came to mourn her passing. Pop was named administrator of her estate and continued to farm her place and take care of the property until it could be sold. He wanted to buy her homestead, but the depression times made it impossible. Pop rented the house during the time he was waiting for an appraisal and required legal procedures for the sale of the property. The estate sale was widely advertised in order that it might be a successful auction.

When the auction date finally arrived a fairly large crowd of people showed up and it appeared that the auction would be a big success. I was one of the spectators and anxious to see an auction for the first time.

The auctioneer talked up the value of the 40-acre estate first, then called for a starting bid of $2000. Nothing but silence. He kept coming down in price calling for a bid while he continued talking up the value of the property. He finally came to $1000 and explained that was the appraised value, which would be a cheap price. Still, no bid! Evidently most of the people were spectators with no money to buy. From out in the crowd Joe Hurst, the community store owner, called out, "I bid $666.67." Joe knew the property had to sell for at least two-thirds of the appraised value. The auctioneer tried to get a counter bid to no avail. After a few attempts, he announced, "Sold!". That valuable homestead with a good house, a solid barn, and other outbuildings on 40 acres of nice farmland sold to Joe Hurst for $666.67!

The remaining property to be sold was the seven acres adjoining our home and the seven acres adjoining Aunt Ola's place. Those two plots were appraised at $300 as one plot of 14 acres. The auctioneer proceeded to get someone to bid on that 14-acre parcel. Pop could not bid on the properties because he was the administrator. He made an agreement ahead of time with Uncle Roy to buy the two plots, then they would divide it. Uncle Roy was the only bidder and he bought the parcel for $200. Pop paid him $100 and was happy to own the seven acres adjoining our home, which was used for pasture and small crops for several years.

Onward to School

One of our short cuts to school from Grandma's, was to go across the field to Uncle Edmund's house. A big persimmon tree stood along the path. It supplied an abundance of persimmons, but we dared not eat them until after a good frost, because they were very bitter. After a few heavy frosts they would become tasty and sweet. The persimmons were a real treat to eat while passing to and from school. Three or four of Uncle Edmund's girls, who were school age, would join us on the remainder of the way to school.

At school it was the same routine–classes began at 8:30, a short recess at 10, one hour for lunch and play at noon, a short recess at 2:30, and dismissal at 4. The last hour seemed to be the longest part of the day.

I excelled in math, but had to work hard to make decent grades in other subjects. Sometimes Mr. Miley would have me to help others with their math or illustrate a problem on the chalkboard. A few times he had me go to the chalkboard and show Wesley how to solve a problem. At the time I thought that was great. However, in later years I realized that was not a prudent decision of Mr. Miley to make. It would have been better for me to help Wesley at his seat rather than in front of the whole school.

Mr. Miley would get excited about our ball games and chew his tongue, which was a habit of his when he got excited or angry. He was very good at taking us to play games at other schools on Fridays when the weather was nice. His 1930 Chevrolet would hold several kids. Another parent from the neighborhood might bring a car to haul several more. Almost all the students could pile into two vehicles, especially if one was a pickup truck. If there were some children who could not go on the outing, Mr. Miley would have an adult from the neighborhood come and stay at the school with them until we returned.

Industrious Mom

The Works Project Administration (WPA) was a government sponsored program established under President Roosevelt in 1935. It was for the purpose of creating jobs and getting folks back to work, as an effort to get the county out of severe depression. One of the projects in our community was to rebuild the two dirt roads south of our home across the railroad.

One was up Beckville Hill, then east to the Line Road. The other was from Aunt Ola's house going due east to the Line Road. Several men had started working on those roads using only shovels, axes, wheelbarrows, horses, and wagons in the early spring of 1936 before school was out.

By the time we were out of school for summer vacation, several of the men were working fairly near to our home. Mom saw an opportunity to sell our extra supply of milk to the hungry and thirsty workers. Seeing us children free from schoolwork and needing something constructive to do, she decided to capitalize on her built-in work force.

Our two cows supplied six to eight gallons of milk each day—more than we could use. We kept the milk in the cellar where it would remain fresh and cool. It would serve as a perfect refreshment and source of nutrition for thirsty men.

Each morning we would fill 30 to 40 pint jars with milk (or as many as we could carry in two washtubs), with cool wholesome milk. During the workers' lunch hour we would carry the tubs, with a little cold water in the bottom, down the road and over the railroad tracks to the construction. The tubs were so heavy we would have to stop and rest a few times before getting to where the men were working. The milk was sold to the men for 5 cents per jar. We did not mind the work because we were earning money for the family, while making the men happy. The men were anxious to see us coming and greeted us eagerly with their 5 cents. Pop was one of the workers and I think he felt proud of his little peddlers.

Mom decided to extend our product line and increase sales by making four or five pies each day for us to peddle along with the milk. We sold the pie at 10 cents per slice, but we did not furnish a plate or fork. It was not considered unmannerly or unsanitary at that time to hold a piece of pie in your hand to eat it. Those pies really created some excitement!

The men would see us coming and some would run to meet us, because they knew we would sell out and they might miss a chance to get any. It didn't make any difference what kind of pie it was. The men heartily enjoyed those treats!

As we returned to go back home, we would pass the men and collect the empty jars. We always returned home with an empty tub, empty jars, empty pie plates and a pocket full of coins! Then the jars had to be washed so that we could be ready for the next day.

All the money we collected was given to Mom as a supplement to the household income. Our reward was the happy men and a good supper at the end of day. Some might think that little enterprise was unfair to us children, but we did not think so! We were proud to be contributing to the needs of the family. On Pop's payday we got a treat at the store! We look back on that time with a sense of accomplishment and thank God for the experience.

In addition to Mom's regular chores at home she was industrious in finding ways to supplement the family income. For a few years she was a representative for C. I. Togstad Company of Kokomo, Indiana, distributing various home cooking products. I walked with her to distant neighbors to take orders and then to deliver the products after they arrived in the mail. The best of her products was a can of extra special coconut pie filling. Sometimes we children would sneak into the cupboard and eat some of it right from the can.

The amount of work and endurance required of a mother in those days is beyond description. Everything required more effort and labor than it does today. Mothers did not have washing machines...they *were* the washing machines on laundry days. The stove did not turn on with a knob, a fire had to be built in it. Cooking a meal was an orchestrated event, demanding time and preparation of everything by hand. Food did not appear out of a box or come frozen, ready to be heated and served in 15 minutes. They even made their own home remedies and cleansing agents. Mom's day began before sun-up and ended late at night.

Mom had to be an early riser, getting up at four o'clock many mornings, especially during school days and when Pop was working. Each morning her day began by preparing breakfast for the family. During the weekdays she also prepared eight lunches (nine when we had a boarder).

The kitchen noises would awaken me, and I would get up to see if I could be of help. She would beckon me to go back to bed and sleep some more, but I could not leave her working alone. At least I could be company and keep the fires going. I could help pack the lunches and keep the water bucket full. During the wintertime, I could punch up the fires in the grate and the heating stove to warm up the house. I took great satisfaction in being helpful in any possible way.

I remember Mom as being a very industrious and energetic woman who found ways to overcome the adversities the Great Depression placed on her family. I never heard her grumble over circumstances, she simply tried to find ways to make our lives better. In her arms we found love; in her presence, the joy of life. Through her optimism we learned to improvise.

A Beautiful Young Teacher

During eighth grade (my last year at Willis School), we had a young teacher, Miss Hester Haugget. It was her first year of teaching and for transportation she had bought a brand new 1937 Ford.

At recess Miss Hester, as we called her, enthusiastically entered the games as we played. She even taught us some new games to play as a group. Sometimes she would extend our recess time because she was enjoying the time with us. However, when recess was over playtime stopped and she maintained an orderly classroom. We had all learned to be respectful to our elders and especially to teachers. So no one tried to give her a hard time just because she was new at teaching.

There were four students in the eighth grade and Lelah was the only student in the seventh grade most of the year until the arrival of Clarence Hilborn, the son of Pop's cousin Everett. He came to school later in the year and was put in the seventh grade with Lelah. He had been sent to the reformatory at Pendleton, Indiana, for a few years. It was not because of a crime but because his stepmother did not want him. He had associated with a lot of bad characters in the reformatory. That was a serious misfortune for Clarence. He was not interested in learning and was a problem for the teacher. However, he played fair and got along well with the other children. He was just mischievous and disruptive in the classroom. He was not a mean boy, he just wanted to get attention and have fun.

Clarence was so disruptive during class time that Miss Hester decided she had to give him the "hickory stick rule" (it was actually a switch from any convenient tree), which was a common form of discipline. She sent all the children out to play and took Clarence to the vestibule with the switch. He started yelling very loud before she even touched him. It was just a fun time for him, because the switch was not big and Miss Hester could not strike him hard enough to hurt.

Miss Hester felt so embarrassed because she thought the neighbors could hear him yelling. After the whipping, Clarence would come out to sit on the steps and laugh so hard that tears would roll down his cheeks. Miss Hester would go sit at her desk feeling terrible. We all laughed at Clarence but felt sorry for Miss Hester. Actually, Clarence did things on purpose to get a whipping.

Finally, Clarence was expelled from school. Yet he became a great helper in the neighborhood doing odd jobs for people. Clarence grew up and got a good job in Evansville, got married, and ended up having a good family life.

One Saturday Miss Hester took the eighth grade students on a trip to Vincennes in her new 1937 Ford. Since Lelah was alone in the seventh grade, she took her along with us. That seemed like a long trip and was the first time we had ever been to a *big* city. The trip to Vincennes was the first time I ever remembered going out of Pike County. Even though my family had traveled to Rockport, Indiana, when I was younger, I was too young to remember those trips.

That was a very exciting trip to visit the historical places in the first Capitol of Indiana. It was an important celebration for me since I was graduating from the eighth grade.

I would be starting to Petersburg High School the next year but I was not really looking forward to it. I knew it would not be like our good times at the Willis School. The future filled me with trepidation. I would be starting the ninth grade in a completely new and strange environment.

During her year as teacher we always had parties on special days. At the end of the year Miss Hester planned a picnic for the whole school. Some mothers, including my mom, brought food to contribute and we ate in a nice grassy area under the big hickory trees down by the water pump.

I believe Miss Hester came to love us as much as we loved her. The time of parting was a sad time for all us. Miss Hester felt sad because it was her last year at the Willis School. After only teaching one year, she was having to leave the country children who had become like a family to her.

Some 60 years later I had the chance to meet Miss Hester again. By then, she was no longer Miss Hester by name. She had become Mrs. Hester Collins and she was still the wonderful woman that I had known in my early years of school. We shared some thoughts about the year when she was my teacher at Willis School. She was pleased that I had become a teacher and was contributing to the education of other children.

Willis School (1936 - 1937)
Grades One - Eight
(L-R) Back row: Hester Haugget (teacher), James Willis, Hilda Mae Willis, Ralph Church, Lelah Willis. Middle row: Heloise Perry, Alvin Church, Grace Perry, Donald Church, Phillip Porter, Elizabeth Ammerman, Morris Willis, Ruth Ann Ammerman. Front row: Mabel Porter, Ron/Ronnie Porter (preschool), Tommy Porter, Gene Willis, Marie Ready, Orace Wayne Willis, Alvin Porter, Gardner Willis, Sylvester Porter

Chapter 8

HIGH SCHOOL YEARS

But whoso looketh into the perfect law of liberty, and continueth therein, he being not a forgetful hearer, but a doer of the work, this man shall be blessed in his deed. (James 1:25)

Getting Started

A successful journey always takes you forward. It was coming time to start back to school in the autumn of 1937 and I was facing a strange new world. The last carefree days of summer were ending and it was time to prepare for high school. Even the word *high school* has a connotation of higher learning for which I did not feel prepared. I was leaving behind the familiarity and comfort of the Willis School where just about everyone was family. I was stepping into the unknown, with strange rules and unfamiliar people. Anxiety was high and anticipation was even greater.

I heard of a student work program at the Petersburg High School where needy students could work part time for 15 cents per hour. It sounded like a good opportunity to make some spending money for necessary books and supplies. At that time, the average wage for working men was one or two dollars per day. I thought I would be making good money for just being 13 years old.

A few weeks before school was to start, Mom walked with me the four miles to the Petersburg school to inquire about the work program. We still had no automobile at that time. Mom was always an instigator of getting things done and thought I ought not approach the authorities by myself. The principal, Mr. Manhart, enrolled me in the program and asked me to report for work on the following Monday to help get things ready before classes were to begin. Then after the school started, I would get an hour of work each school day.

151

I walked to school on Monday and got there very early. Two other boys and I were given the job of pulling grass and weeds. One boy quit after the first day! He did not like that kind of work. It was hot and tiring work, but I didn't mind because I was used to it. The other boy, Travis, and I worked for 10 days at pulling grass, various cleaning jobs, and other things to get the school ready for the first day of classes.

Then Mr. Manhart called me in one day to inform me that he had learned the required age was 16 years old to qualify for the work program. I was only 13! I was very disappointed, but I was paid for the time I had worked, which amounted to $12. It was the most money I had earned in my life. I saved the money to use for necessary expenses throughout the whole year. I was happy I could buy my own necessities without having to ask my parents for money.

Rigors of the First Year

Two weeks later, in the month of September, I began the new experience of attending high school. I had to walk four miles to and from school, which took about an hour each way. The schools in Pike County did not furnish students transportation at that time.

There were 96 students in my freshman class when I started to high school. It was reported to be the largest freshman class that had ever started there. We were divided into three sections. I liked the idea of going to different rooms for each subject. That was better than sitting in one room and at one desk all day as we had in the elementary school.

I enjoyed English class under Mr. Johnson, because I liked figuring out the parts of speech in a sentence. But I was a slow reader when we began to study literature during the second semester.

A man by the name of General Sanders taught the biology class and he made it very interesting. When we were studying birds, he would imitate the call or whistle of many of them. He tried not to let it show, but he took a special interest in me because he and Pop were good friends. Mr. Sanders would come to our house and visit my dad occasionally.

The social studies classes were always difficult for a slow reader like me. Endlessly, we had to remember dates, places, people, and events that meant very little to me.

There was some anxiety about starting algebra. Someone had said we would be using letters for numbers. I had never heard of such a thing. Math had never been anything other than numbers, but I thought to myself, "I know if it's a form of math, I can get it if others can. With determination to pay close attention to the instructions by Mr. Weathers, I should be able to learn algebra." Mr. Weathers proved to be my best teacher. Could it have been because math was my favorite subject?

Bob Willis sat right behind me in algebra class. Bob was a distant cousin. He was the grandson of Uncle Casper, who was living with us at the time. Uncle Casper and my Grandfather Beverly were second cousins. Bob and I were the two top students in the class and Mr. Weathers sometimes called on one of us to illustrate a problem to the class. The two of us always made the same grade on a test or on homework—usually a perfect score. Toward the end of the year, Mr. Weathers announced to the class, "We have a situation over toward the back of the classroom. There are two Willis boys sitting back there close together who always make the same grade on every test and every homework assignment. If one has an incorrect problem, the other does also. How can that happen?"

He knew neither of us needed to copy nor wanted to let anyone copy from us. He was just teasing the class! After letting the class think on it for a minute he clarified the accusation by explaining, "However, Jim and Bob never miss the same problem. If they miss anything at all, they miss different problems. They are both capable students without having to cheat!" Needless to say Bob and I earned top grades in the class!

At the end of the year, we were supposed to attend a promotion and award ceremony in the gym one evening. I had perfect attendance that year and wanted to be there to get my reward. Rather than walk all the way home then back again for the program, I just stayed at school and loafed around.

When giving the attendance awards, a teacher read the names as the certificates were given, but she did not call my name! After the program I questioned her, "Did I have a perfect attendance award? I was told to be here for the program if I wanted to receive my award."

She looked among her papers and answered, "Yes, here it is! Your certificate got stuck here and I failed to see it!" I received the attendance award but I was disappointed. I had sacrificed to earn that certificate more than any other student. I felt slighted when I did not get the proper recognition for my perfect attendance. I thought about it on my walk home that night. Those hurt feelings stayed with me for a long time.

Transportation

During my first year of high school I usually walked to school by myself and seldom caught a ride except in bad weather or when I knew of someone who was going that way. Melvin Cockerham, a senior, and I were the only students from our neighborhood going to the Petersburg High School that year. He lived one mile further south from our home, but we seldom walked together going to school. However, we usually walked home together. After school, if we could get to the courthouse in time, Frank Amos would let us ride with him in his open-top Model A Ford (on the days he was working).

Regardless of the weather or whether I had a ride, I went to school every day. One day a cold sleeting rain was facing me all the way to town. I was always dressed for the weather, but that was a difficult walk and there were no cars on the road to offer a ride. A boy who sat across the isle from me in our home room had a serious complaint that morning. He turned to me and said, "I had to walk nine blocks through this sleet this morning." I replied, "You were lucky. I had to walk four miles." He returned, "Wow! If I would have that far to walk, I would not be here today!" I thought about my younger three siblings who got up after me and walked the mile to the Willis School through the same miserable weather that morning.

During the summers, while school was out, it was sometimes possible to earn money by working for farmers in tomato fields, tending crops, or other odd jobs. That let us have a little money of our own to spend as we saw fit. Pop had reduced his amount of farming considerably because of the public works program and we were not needed much at home except for some chores.

When school started the next year, five more students from our community were beginning high school...including Lelah. Two of them were Arthur and Paul Elmore, grandsons of Charley H. Miley. Mr. Miley had been our teacher at Willis School and the two boys lived with him. The older boy had a license to drive and was allowed to drive his granddad's 1930 Chevrolet car to school. The other four of us paid him 5 cents each day to ride with him. Gasoline was only 15 cents per gallon, so that more than paid his driving expenses.

Math classes were about the same as the previous year, except we had geometry instead of algebra in our sophomore year. Geometry was not nearly as interesting but I still excelled in it. Another big change was taking physics instead of biology. Those subjects were equally interesting, but physics was more challenging. World history was somewhat interesting but the memorization of dates, people, etc took away the fun of the subject.

I did not earn a perfect attendance that year because I developed boils in places that made it painful for me to sit down. To my disappointment, the boils caused me to miss seven days of school. Lelah brought home some of my books, but I did not feel like studying because I was in so much discomfort.

During the following summer, the state was building a new highway south of Petersburg that would go all the way to Evansville. It was really exciting to think we were getting a concrete road to Petersburg. While they were building the grade for the road, the three of us younger boys liked to go watch the big equipment in operation. Sometimes there would be scrap lumber, buckets, and things we could salvage. We valued those items because they could be useful around home.

By fall the highway grade was completed but it was left as a dirt road through the winter. They had to wait until the next summer for appropriate weather to pour the concrete surface. The dirt grade was good traveling most of the time, but it became an almost impassable mud road in rainy weather and in the winter when the snow melted.

The Jitney Wagon

When school started in the fall of 1939, my junior year, there were 10 students on "cousin road" (in our immediate community) attending Petersburg High School. Imel got a contract with the township trustee to haul students from our neighborhood area to school in his 1934 Chevy pickup truck. Imel built a wooden canopy over the back of his pickup truck and he built benches on each side for us to sit on. We called it the "Jitney Wagon".

Imel was teaching in a one-room elementary school about 4 miles northeast of Petersburg, so he would deliver us to school and then go on to his teaching job. Then after he dismissed the students from his school, he would come back past the high school and pick up his passengers.

There was no heat in the back of the truck, so we had to dress warm in the winter months. The canopy had no doors or covering over the back opening, but we were accustomed to enduring the cold weather. When it was cold, we would let the girls sit toward the front of the canopy away from the cold air at the open back. In nice weather we would scramble to get a seat near the tailgate.

Riding back and forth to school in the jitney wagon was fun. We told jokes, teased one another, as well as sang familiar songs. We knew several songs of the day and sang them repeatedly until we almost got tired of hearing them. Sometimes we would make up a new song to break the monotony.

Imel's contract was during the year before they poured concrete for the new highway. Imel drove on the dirt highway when the weather was good, but when it became muddy we had to detour east of home two miles, then go north on Line Road.

It was two miles out of the way and 20 minutes longer. Sometimes Imel did not have time to take us to school without being late to work. On those days, he would drive his 1934 Plymouth directly to his school and I would drive the bus route. Imel had taught me to drive the previous year. I had passed a driver's test with a state policeman that summer and received a driver's license.

It was an exciting year because more of my neighborhood friends were attending school with me. I took advanced Algebra as an elective, again with Mr. Weathers. I was so focused on math that my other lessons were neglected. That caused my other grades to go down. I had to take American History that year. The teacher, Miss Solmon, was the same teacher for World History, which I had taken the previous year. She knew history well, but I had a difficult time following her instructions.

It was the first year Lelah and I were privileged to take a class together. Even though she was a grade behind me, we both signed up for Latin as an elective course. We liked to work our lessons together at home. That was a real advantage for us because Miss Bryant, the teacher, was very strict and demanded we do our lessons each day. Although she was strict, Miss Bryant was kind and interesting. She was one of the best teachers in our school.

Some of the bigger boys were inclined to be disruptive

in some classes, but not in Miss Bryant's class. She was a little teacher with plenty of spunk. She had been known to slap a student almost out of their seat for being disrespectful. The students in her class did not whisper or offer any trouble whatsoever! Lelah and I enjoyed her class and decided we wanted to take second year Latin the next year.

The end of that school year, Imel's contract to haul students in his "hackney" (another nickname for the improvised bus) was terminated. The next year the township trustee would be hiring a driver with a regular school bus.

That summer it was very exciting to see the concrete being laid for the new highway. Again, we boys watched the project when it was close to our home. More dramatic was when they finally opened the new highway and I was able to drive our old 1929 Model A Ford on it.

It was around that time Imel put his Chevrolet truck with the canopy to good use in another way. He and Rachel had started going to the Church of God in Petersburg, which Imel had attended during his high school years. He invited us kids to go to church with them. We were eager to hop in the back of his truck and ride along. It was not long before he had several teenagers going with them. Since the church did not have a resident preacher, Reverend Hillenburg and his wife would drive 60 miles from Bedford every Sunday to conduct the morning and evening services. It was the first time that we had ever attended church regularly. We realized that church was a good place to learn about the ways of God and His teachings.

Old Enough to Work

A few weeks before school started, I drove to the high school to sign up for the student work program. I was entering my senior year and at 16, I finally met the age requirement for the work program. By then, the principal knew me and had no problem letting me begin work a week before school started. After school began, I was assigned a room to sweep each morning instead of going to the early home-room period.

That was my job every day and regardless how long or how little time it took me to sweep it, I was paid for one hour of work. As soon as I got to school, I spent 20 or 30 minutes sweeping my assigned room. The pay was 15 cents per hour and I had earned $6 before school started. During school I was paid 75 cents each week. I saved almost every bit of it, because I knew there would be extra expenses during my senior year. I was hoping I could save enough money for graduation expenses, because I did not want to be a financial burden to the family. I do not know how they would have been able to come up the money anyway.

That year, for the first time in the history of our community, we rode a regular school bus. The trustee hired Mr. Jay Cockerham, to drive the bus. Mr. Cockerham brought his son and the Miley boys (who lived close to him). Then he picked up students in my neighborhood and others en route that were going to high school. Children from our neighborhood would gather at our house, because they all lived across the railroad on dirt roads where the bus would not go. The bus was more like a truck with a school bus body tacked on, but it was more comfortable than Imel's pickup truck. Over 20 students rode the bus and I was the only one in the senior class.

The Church of God

Imel continued to drive a group of children to the Church of God each week for Sunday school. I developed a sense of spiritual calling as I attended church with Imel and Rachel on Sunday and Wednesday evening services. That fall a new preacher, Rev. Harold Stiff and his wife, arrived to pastor the church. They really acted on faith, because our church attendance was so small there was not enough money to pay him a sufficient salary to be a full-time pastor. Rev. H. Stiff was not deterred. He took a job in a war factory in Evansville until the church could afford to pay him a salary.

Rev. H. Stiff was a young dynamic preacher and willing to do whatever it took to make the Church of God successful. Harold Stiff had worked as a taxi driver in Chicago and had been a driver for Al Capone. He had experienced some rough times before becoming a Christian. He grew up in the Catholic Church but found a Bible one day and turned to the Lord believing God had something better for his life.

The congregation began to grow under his ministry and dedicated leadership. He appointed a new Board of Trustees and restructured the Sunday school and church services. Every Saturday he spent most of the day visiting homes in the city of Petersburg. During each month, he would try to visit as many homes as possible in the city and the surrounding areas. As a result of his visitations and outgoing personality, the church experienced an astonishing growth in numbers. Within four months, all the seats were filled during the Sunday morning services.

Rev. H. Stiff held a revival meeting at the church in January of 1941. I attended every night with Imel and Rachel. During the revival I committed my life to Jesus and vowed to live a Christian life thereafter. My life took on a whole new meaning and it resulted in a lifetime commitment to Christ. The next day at school, as I looked at classmates, I thought every one of them ought to have the same experience.

As I continued through my senior year, everything at school seemed more enjoyable (even the job of cleaning the room each morning). I felt God had given a purpose to my subjects, my job, social life, even my activities, and my future. Church attendance definitely became fulfilling and more meaningful.

I tried to concentrate more on my schoolwork because I wanted to meet the requirements for college–if there would be an open door for me to attend. Lelah and I were in the second year of Latin together. We had a new teacher, Mrs. Rocky, who was not very strict and allowed too many disruptions. We did not enjoy the class under her as we had with Miss Bryant.

One senior girl and I were the two top students in Mr. Coleman's Solid Geometry II class. Mr. Coleman did very little teaching. We were just given assignments in the textbook and expected to learn the *proof* of problems as we progressed. Our grades were based on the number of theorems and/or propositions (solutions) we could prove at the chalkboard. On the last day of classes, I was prepared to make one more *proof* so I could be ahead of the girl and get the top grade in the class. Later, I thought it had been a little selfish of me to feel like I had to get the edge and claim the top grade for myself. I should have been content to share the honors of the top grade with her and come out even.

My first exposure to the study of United States government was in civics class during my senior year. It was taught by the school superintendent, Mr. J.B. Lease, who was a very knowledgeable teacher and tried to make the subject interesting. He demanded very strict attention–similar to Miss Bryant. All of the approximately 80 seniors were in one classroom. A great deal of what he taught seemed new to me and a little confusing. I realized I needed a further study of our government, which I did later in a college class.

For the first time during my years of high school attendance I engaged in competitive sports. My lack of experience in basketball did not offer me any opportunity in that sport. The distance from school made it difficult to participate in practice after school. However, I decided to try out for the track team because I liked to run. I scored fairly well in different running events of track meets but never set any records.

Graduation

My biggest expense as a senior was to buy a graduation suit. I ordered a teal green suit from the Montgomery Ward catalog for $16.95. It was a large sum for me to spend. It would have bought 100 gallons of gasoline or 165 loaves of bread. My savings gave me enough money for the suit and a few other items I needed. After all my expenses, I still had about $15 left in my savings at the end of the year.

Four good years of important studies were behind me with some excellent grades and a few average grades in subjects of lesser interest. However, I earned enough credits for graduation and I qualified for a state college entrance.

My graduation date was April 20, 1941, just three days before I became 17 years of age. I was indeed happy to receive my high school diploma. I knew it would open the door to future opportunities–especially college.

James high school graduation 1941

Career Minded

Upon graduating from Petersburg High School, I was wondering what should I do next. Several things came in the mail to solicit my decision. Most of the mailings were from branches of the military and various colleges. Many of them seemed adventurous and interesting, but I thought it would be best to attend one of the state colleges where the tuition would be less expensive.

I thought of continuing my studies at some university or college toward a career that attracted my interest. Through the college mailings I learned that Purdue University was an agriculture and engineering school. Purdue had a School of Forestry in the agriculture department that seemed appealing.

However, there was a real problem. We were a poor family and there was no money for college expenses. Life was enjoyable at home with the family regardless of the limited resources for any luxuries, but it was time to be thinking of a career. The feeling for adventure or change was not a rebellious attitude just to get away from home. Quite the contrary–the love of family and home was more likely to hold me back from making a decision to leave. That was the hard part!

Like many graduates, I just did not know what would make an interesting career choice. Farm life was appealing but it was hard work with little pay as we knew it. Although, it was about the only work experience I had. I thought there seemed to be little future in the field of agriculture and I could not understand how a college degree in agriculture would help someone be a better farmer.

The more I thought about it though, learning about the life of a forest ranger really sounded intriguing and adventuresome. I thought I could enjoy that kind of life. I was an outdoor person and already knew many kinds of trees and their uses. Finally, I decided going to the Purdue Forestry School was what I would like to do. I knew if I expected to go to college, it was necessary for me to find a summer job to at least earn enough funds to enroll. I was told there would be part-time jobs available at the university.

Visit with Arba

Cousin Arba had worked in Connersville, Indiana, for several years along with some other men from Pike County who had found good jobs there. He thought it would be easy for me to find a job in Connersville, so he invited me to come and stay with him while looking for employment. When Pop was in his early teens and was still living at home with his mother, he became kind of a father image to Arba, which caused the children in our family to feel a little closer to Arba rather than just another cousin.

Arba was brought up by his Christian grandmother and taught the right way to live a good life. Unfortunately, in his teen years he began drinking some with other boys and living a wayward life. Other than that, he was a good honest man and hard worker. He had kept a good job in Connersville for several years.

Because of our close family relationship, I eagerly decided to accept his invitation to visit him in Connersville and check out the opportunity that he had made sound so appealing. Early one morning I left home to hitchhike to Connersville in hopes of finding a job. Catching rides along the roads was easy in those days when cars traveled slower and violence was unheard of.

The average speed on highways was about 40 miles per hour. I was on the road about eight hours and traveled 190 miles. I found Arba's mobile home according to the instructions he had given me and waited there about an hour for him to come home from work.

Arba had lived in a boarding house with other men who were also factory workers. Recently though, he had bought a small mobile home where he lived by himself. He wanted me to stay with him so I could save the expense of room and board elsewhere.

Arba introduced me to a few potential employers and told me of some prospective places to inquire about a job, but I soon became seriously disappointed. Employers were not interested in hiring a 17-year-old boy who would probably soon be drafted into the military.

On the first Saturday of my visit we went to Renfro Valley in Kentucky with two other men from Pike County. It was my first time of being out of the state of Indiana. One of the men drove his 1938 Chevrolet so the four of us could travel comfortably. We went to see the Saturday night Renfro Valley Barn Dance show. That live radio show was comparable to the Grand Ole Opry at Nashville, Tennessee. It consisted of country music and singing mingled with some square dancing.

I thoroughly enjoyed the show. It was fascinating to see the program that we had been hearing on the radio at home regularly. It was a good clean entertaining show with no obscenity or vulgarity. We spent the night in a motel room and returned to Connersville the next morning. I enjoyed the friendly fellowship of my companions and the wholesome conversations along the way. There was no vulgar talk nor alcoholic drinking of any kind on the whole trip. It was an exhilarating trip! Arba even paid for all my expenses.

On Sunday evening after we returned, Arba went with me to a Nazarene Church service because he knew I liked to go to church. He knew I read the Bible almost daily while at his place. Arba was not a regular church person, so I thought it commendable of him not only to honor my wishes to attend church but also to go with me.

Arba had a 1936 Terraplane pickup truck that needed to be painted. One day he asked, "James, would you paint my truck for me if I buy some paint?" I replied, "I've done some painting but never did paint a vehicle. But I'll try my luck at if you want me to." I thought he expected me to use a sprayer. He bought two quarts of gloss black paint for cars and a good hand brush. I brush painted the whole truck and even though I left a few visible brush marks, I made it look much better.

Arba had a drinking buddy, Jack, who visited a time or two. I did not appreciate his visits and Arba tried to discourage them while I was there. Arba took me to a movie one evening and picked up Jack to go along. They carried a bottle of liquor with them and both were drinking during the evening. On the way home Jack was driving, as Arba had drank too much, until Jack stated, "It looks like I'm seeing two roads and I can't tell which one to take." Arba had him stop and let me drive the remainder of the way home. I was an experienced driver by then, so I knew I could safely drive us home.

I did most of the cooking while I was staying with Arba. One day I even tried my luck at making an apple pie. We enjoyed every bit of it. I spent two interesting weeks with Arba in his house trailer but did not find a job. Considerable time was spent just walking around observing the town, the factories, and businesses. I asked about a job at some places, but actually I was not very experienced in the art of seeking a job in such a city. I thought those people simply did not know how lucky they would be to have a hard worker and honest person like me to work for them, but I did not know how to tell them that. Anyway, the Lord knew what was best and I still had faith in earning money for college somewhere...somehow.

On the second weekend, Arba and Jack took me back home to Clark's Station in his newly painted pickup. They did not take a liquor bottle with them, therefore it was a safe trip. Upon arriving home, he called attention to the newly painted truck to my family, and of course, everyone had to admire the excellent paint job. I was not especially proud of it but at least for my first auto paint job it did look fairly good.

1936 Terraplane

Arba and James

Even though the trip to Connersville was an entertaining and an educational adventure, I thanked God for His guidance and a safe return home. The Lord was surely with me even by closing the doors to finding a job there. I did not have any occasion to visit Arba again while he lived there.

England was still at war with Germany and Hitler was trying to conquer all of Europe. President Roosevelt was considering drafting boys 18 years old and over to build up the U.S. military for national defense and possible involvement in the war. The newspapers and radio were full of news about the world in turmoil. It was the subject that most people talked about. I was not interested in going to war, but the next year I would be the right age for the draft. I just had to accept it.

Before Arba returned home he offered to take our family to visit our relatives in St. Louis in his truck, which had a canopy on the back. It was the first time my younger siblings had ever been beyond the border of Indiana. Arba and Jack took turns driving and Pop rode in the cab with them. Mom and the rest of us rode in the back. Arba had an accident in St. Louis, which smashed up one side of the front fender of his beautifully painted pickup, but it was still driveable. No one was seriously hurt, except Mom got bumped in the mouth causing some bleeding. She was taken care of at the scene.

After a long police investigation, we continued on our way to Aunt Mae's house. We spent several days with her and with her daughter, Ruby. It was a fun trip and it was good to spend time with our relatives. The visit to the city was fascinating but it did not seem better than living in our good country home. We wondered about the boring life those people lived without any fun things to do like we had back home.

Upon returning from our trip, Imel and Gerald offered me a job with their painting projects in Princeton (a town not far from where we lived). As a helper, I did some scraping, cleaning, and painting of the lower areas. It freed them for the upper and more important sections. I worked with them the rest of the summer, saving what I made for college. The job paid 25 cents per hour and I was able to save over $100 before college started that fall.

It was a blessing in several ways...that I was unable to find employment in Connersville. First, it would probably not have been good for me to have been with Arba and live in that environment during that summer. Perhaps the Lord was protecting me from harm or other undesirable situations. By going back home, the Lord blessed me with not only the opportunity to work together with Imel and Gerald, which was enjoyable, but mostly it was a blessing to be ready with the funds needed to start college that fall.

Chapter 9

BOILERMAKERS AND BEYOND

Then I saw that wisdom excelleth folly,
as far as light excelleth darkness. (Ecclesiastes 2:13)

College Enrollment

Imel took me the 150 miles to Purdue University in Lafayette, Indiana, to see about getting enrolled in the first semester and register for the School of Forestry. The campus was beautiful and there were many buildings scattered over the whole sprawling campus. I began to wonder how I would find my way around to the buildings where my classes would be.

At the time of registration, I had sufficient funds to pay for the first semester tuition of $72 plus enough for books and other small expenses. I needed funds to pay for housing and other living expenses. The office of student employment and housing informed us that the manager of the Varsity Apartments was looking for a student to work part time in exchange for rent. We immediately went to the apartment building to inquire about the job.

The manager, Mr. Pierce, was very pleased with my application because of my painting experience. He hired me on the spot and asked me to start as soon as possible because he had some rooms to paint before school began. He and I painted rooms for two weeks before the beginning of classes.

Throughout the school year I helped with occasional jobs around the apartments and assisted tenants with moving in or out. I always tried to make myself available for the moving jobs, as I was usually rewarded with a lucrative tip.

In addition, Mr. Pierce would occasionally ask me to sit in his apartment to answer service calls while he had to be out for any extended length of time. It gave me an opportunity to do some schoolwork in a quiet environment. The position was a real blessing because it provided me with free rent for the entire first year of school.

These pictures are of the Varsity Apartments, where I worked and lived during my first semester at Purdue University. Photo taken in the summer of 2014, when I made an excursion to Lafayette, Indiana.

I was excited to be on my own in a wholesome atmosphere at the university and become a part of the Purdue Boilermakers. The apartment was very close to the campus, and it was a pleasure to walk through the beautiful well-kept grounds with the stately red brick university buildings. I was too busy to think about things back home or get homesick.

I shared a two-room apartment with four other fellows. We had one large sleeping room for all of us and another large room where we each of had a shelf and desk. One of my roommates was a rich boy from Italy named Dara Seckban. He had a new 1942 DeSoto automobile, made by Chrysler. He had me drive it for him a few times. Another was Charles Ember, who was a farmer. He and I could relate to one another with our farming experiences and intentionally confuse the others with some terms and names of things we mentioned. The other roommate was Tom Houchens who was very friendly and considerate, although he seemed to be a know-it-all at times. It was a friendly arrangement and we good-naturedly shared the facilities without any conflict.

First Year Studies

During the first year, the schedule was fairly well dictated with only one elective (entomology or botany). All freshmen students took the basic required courses. Biology was one of them and even though I enjoyed the course, it used up considerable study time. The one class I did not enjoy was speech. I was too shy and felt awkward when speaking before groups, but still I managed to get a passing grade. Introductory Forestry was a non-credit required course for forestry students. I thought it was a very interesting class. I also took advanced algebra in first semester and trigonometry the second semester. Those two math courses were also required for forestry students. Naturally, those were my favorite subjects.

All male students were required to take the Reserve Officer Training Course (ROTC) and were furnished a regular military uniform and shoes. The ROTC class was a field artillery training course and met two times each week. During class we were taught military rules and instructions on use of artillery weapons. We were required to wear our uniform to ROTC class, and then, because we did not have opportunity to change between classes, it was necessary to wear it all day.

I had not begun to shave yet and had a little whisker growth on my face. During the second day of class, the sergeant gave me orders, "Willis, get that fuzz off your face before the next class." I went that evening and invested in shaving equipment for the first time in my life.

Activity on the campus was alive with students going to various buildings for classes. I wondered why all those students were so friendly to a country kid like me. I learned that many of them, like me, came from the country. There were often friendly greetings with other students while walking across campus and it was easy to make friends. Being away from home, many of those country kids were as eager as I was to have companionship.

One of the forestry students invited me to his room one day. He was wearing a cross hanging from a chain around his neck that I had not noticed before. I asked him the meaning of it and he replied, "I wear it all the time so if I get killed, the priest can pray me into heaven." I had never heard of such a thing and gave him a little sermon. I explained to him that was not possible, because a priest could not pray anyone into heaven. I told him he needed to pray for himself and accept salvation while he is living in order to go to heaven. I do not think he accepted my belief any more than I accepted the meaning of his cross. However, we remained friends as long as we were at Purdue.

Part-Time Jobs

It soon became clear that I needed to get another part-time job in order to have money for additional expenses. Upon checking with the student employment office, I learned there was a job at a restaurant conveniently located near the apartment building where I was living. They were hiring a few students at the regular student rate of 25 cents per hour. I applied for the position and was hired even though I lacked any restaurant experience. My job there was to clear away the dishes and clean the table when people were finished eating.

Surprisingly, that job turned out to be very disturbing to me. It was not because the work was hard–for I was merely busing tables–rather, the conspicuous waste of food offended me. I was a farm boy from a poor home where food was never wasted. I was astonished at the fancy restaurant with, what seemed to me, astronomical prices. To further my distress, when I went to work and cleared those tables, I watched perfectly good food being thrown into the garbage. Workers were not permitted to make any use of the untouched food. Instead, we had to pay full price for anything we wanted to eat. With their exorbitant prices, it was not a place where I could afford to eat. Food for one meal cost more than I made in a day!

At home, we did not waste anything, especially food. The seeming disregard for the philosophy of "waste not, want not" continued to grate on my ingrained set of principles and values. But I needed the job and by working there about two hours each day it was a way of making enough money for my basic needs.

After enduring that unpleasant job for a short while, Mr. Pierce approached me with an opportunity to work for a locker plant. He said, "Jim, Mr. Gould owns a locker plant just one block from here and he is looking for someone for evening part-time work. Would you be interested?" I replied, "Yes, Mr. Pierce, I think I would like about anything better than the restaurant job." He explained that the locker plant was a meat processing business. Mr. Pierce felt confident to have already given me a good recommendation, because he knew I was honest, dependable, and a good worker. He gave me directions to the plant, which was located just one block from my apartment, and told me to speak with Tom Gould.

Mr. Pierce further explained, "I have spoken to Mr. Gould and he's expecting you to come see him." I considered it an added blessing and a reward for being a faithful worker. Mr. Pierce had my interest in mind and I think he knew the restaurant was not really to my liking.

I went just as soon as possible to see about the new job. I introduced myself to Mr. Gould and he met me in a very friendly manner. He said, "Mr. Pierce says you might be interested in a part-time job." I replied, "Yes, he told me that you were expecting me." He continued, "This is an evening job and I would need you here for about three hours each evening to help put up orders which would involve some meat cutting." Then he asked, "Have you had any experience like that?"

I replied, "Well, I have helped my dad butcher hogs. I've skinned rabbits, cleaned fish, and helped my mom dress chickens. Does that qualify?" He laughed about that and said, "That's good enough to suit me. If you can be here tomorrow about 7 pm, the evening worker is George. He'll show you what to do. And from now on you can just call me Tom." I think I was actually hired before I got there thanks to Mr. Pierce's recommendation.

It was an evening job that paid the same wage of 25 cents per hour but it gave me more hours and fit better with my class schedule. I worked from three to four hours every evening and on Saturday, after my morning class. In those days, many colleges had Saturday classes and we were required to take at least one. I scheduled the earliest class available, so I could report for work as soon as possible. By earning $6 to $8 each week, I could easily save enough for my second semester tuition, which had increased to a phenomenal cost of $74. The extra $2 was for a lab fee.

The new job proved to be an excellent move and very interesting. The meat-cutting manager of the processing room trained me to be a meat cutter. I learned the process of cutting slabs of meat into steaks, grinding hamburger, and slicing bacon. My responsibilities also included filling orders for restaurants, campus student housing and walk-in customers.

After filling orders on Tuesday nights, we usually had to wait for the delivery truck to arrive from Chicago, which brought a supply of pork and beef quarters along with containers of other meat products. On those nights, it would be 11 o'clock or midnight before we finished unloading and could go home. We even got paid for our time waiting on the truck. When orders were slack on Saturday, one or two of us would have to work in the walk-in freezer to organize and arrange the frozen supplies. On those days we had to be prepared with coat, cap, and gloves for that task.

Another benefit of the job was I could buy lunch meat and cheese, for making sandwiches, at a discounted price. Additionally, I had learned a new skill and trade in the process. Mr. Gould was very pleased with my work and attitude and would, upon occasion, give me a small package of some goodies to take home as an extra bonus. That job proved to be a real blessing to me. I believe it was a result of my faith in the Lord and trusting that He would provide for my needs.

After six weeks of school, I had been away from home for eight weeks. It was the longest I had ever been away and I was getting homesick. However, in order to get home after Saturday class and return for Monday class didn't give much time for the trip, which was 150 miles each way. My only way to go home was to hitchhike, which meant I had to get out on the road, hold out my thumb, and hope someone would give me a ride down the road. I decided to try it even if I was late getting back on Sunday.

One Saturday, Mr. Gould gave me permission to be off work. So, as soon as my class was over at nine o'clock that morning, I wasted no time getting out of town to catch a ride. Many people were willing to pick up students who were dressed respectably and I made it home by about four o'clock that evening.

There was one bit of sad news for me. In the summer

before leaving for college, I had raised fifteen ducklings. When I left, I still kept them pinned up to keep them from going to the canal, because if the little ones got out on the canal, it was the turtles' delight to get hold of a tiny foot and pull the duckling down for a feast. While I was gone my flock of ducks had been turned loose and most had not survived. However, it was a joyful time to get back home and see all the family. By noon on Sunday, I was back catching rides to Lafayette, and I made it back to my apartment by 6 pm.

After that refreshing trip home, I returned to attending classes with enthusiasm and eager to be back at the locker plant each evening. After a few weeks, I had a fairly regular routine established. I was up early so I could stop at the small restaurant across the street for a cheap breakfast and then ahead to my eight o'clock class. Between classes I would use the time to study. I would have a late lunch somewhere, if time permitted, then back to my room for some more studying before needing to be at the locker plant by 7 pm. After the success of my first trip to Petersburg, I made trips home about every four or five weeks.

All of the new life at Purdue was an exciting adventure for me. There was so much that had happened during just the first semester! College life was an interesting experience, even though I had to work part time. Yet, I really think the work made it more rewarding.

Pearl Harbor Attacked

One Sunday afternoon I was watching the office when Mr. Pierce and his wife returned from their Sunday afternoon drive. He asked me, "Jim have you heard the news?" I replied, "No, I've been busy studying and haven't turned on the radio." (There was no such thing as television at that time.) He announced, "Japan bombed Pearl Harbor this morning."

The day after the assault, President Franklin D. Roosevelt asked Congress to declare war on Japan; they approved with just one dissenting vote. Three days later, Japanese allies, Germany and Italy also declared war on the United States. Once again, Congress reciprocated. More than two years into the international conflict, America had finally joined World War II.

The bombing of Pearl Harbor was completely unexpected on that fateful day of December 7, 1941. It is recorded in history as a *Day of Infamy* for the world to remember. Those events gave me reason to believe that in the near future I would be called up and my college work interrupted. However, I planned to remain in school until that time.

By working so many hours, it was difficult to find enough time to study. Nevertheless, I got through the first year with good grades and excelled in trigonometry the second semester. My previous success in algebra and geometry played an important factor in my joy of trigonometry. We had an outstanding teacher, who expected us to come to class with completed lessons, tools, and our books–ready to learn.

Toward the end of the school year, in the spring of 1942, all students in the School of Forestry were offered an opportunity to apply for summer employment with the National Forest Service. The job paid 70 cents per hour, which was more than most labor jobs at 50 cents an hour. I eagerly signed up and waited for my assignment. I soon received word that I was to report to a firefighting camp in Missoula, Montana, on June 15. That was only two weeks after school was out, so I only had about one week to go home and prepare to travel west. I was feeling the anticipation of yet another adventure.

Developments of the War

Up to that time we had been hearing of some serious things happening in the war. News did not travel as fast as it does today, often we did not get information about the developments as they took place. We heard that the Japanese were making advances in the pacific. Eventually, we learned about the severity of the Japanese attacks.

Map of Bataan Death March

In the later part of December 1941, the Japanese invaded the Philippines. The United States and Philippine soldiers tried to resist the invasion, but had neither sufficient manpower, training, nor equipment to hold out against the Japanese. They were defeated by the Japanese. The survivors were taken as prisoners and forced into what became known as the Bataan Death March. The Japanese were very cruel and inhumane, treating them like animals.

Over 5,000 prisoners died or were killed on that march. Hundreds of others died as Japanese POW's by starvation, disease, or punishment. For that war crime, some Japanese leaders were tried and executed after the war.

A recent high school survey revealed that less than 10 percent of the students had ever heard of those atrocities. I believe those events and those of the holocaust should be required reading in all history classes of our schools.

Montana Forestry Adventure

After my last day of classes for the semester, I gathered my few belongings and hitchhiked home to prepare for my journey to Montana. The only preparation needed was to assemble some needed things in a traveling bag and study some road maps to determine the best route to take.

Public transportation was rather expensive, so I decided to hitchhike the 2,000 miles to Missoula, Montana. Mom and Pop thought it was too much for me to hitchhike that far, but I had no doubts about it. I left home on a Monday morning with one small travel bag and $50 in my pocket. I had some interesting experiences meeting people along the way, especially the ones who gave me rides. One guy picked me up in the evening, he drove all night and then took me to his home for breakfast. After we finished eating, he drove me out to the edge of town where I could catch the next ride.

Another night I had a very frightening experience. A man had let me off at a "road house" far out in the country. It was late in the evening with very little traffic. I had been waiting beside the road for two hours for a ride, then three guys came staggering out of the "road house" and offered to give me a ride. Against my better judgment, I got in the car even though I thought they had been drinking. I thought maybe they could at least get me to the next town or to a place where there was more traffic and I could get a different ride.

After they took off, I realized my error. All of them were very drunk and the driver was going dangerously fast. Suddenly, I saw we were on a collision course, approaching an old Model-T Ford creeping slowly along. I yelled at the driver, "There's a car in front of you!" He swerved to miss the old slow moving car and almost lost control. We finally came to a stop...sitting crossways on a long bridge that crossed over a river. I grabbed my hand bag, jumped out, and ran back to the old Model-T to ask the driver if I could ride ahead into the next town with him.

The man acted really scared! I then realized how it could have looked like a hold up or something! A car speeding past him; blocking his way; then one of the passengers running back toward him! I quickly explained, "That is a drunk driver! He almost rear-ended your car and would have caused a bad wreck if I had not been along to yell at him. I think that I saved the lives of some of us." Then I asked, "May I ride to the next town with you?" He replied, "Climb in young man, you're welcome!"

The driver of the Chevy got his car straightened around on the bridge and drove away. I rode with the man in the old open top Ford the short distance into the next town where I got a $2 room for the night.

I arrived in Missoula, with no other special incidents, on Friday at noon and reported immediately to the National Forest Headquarters as instructed. After getting signed in, I had time to shop for logging boots and other recommended supplies. I had left home with $50 and spent about $30 during the five-day trip. That left me enough cash to buy the required work clothes.

Some other college guys, from various colleges all over the country, had also arrived at the Forestry office. Late in the afternoon a forest ranger took us 40 miles, in the back of a truck, to a camp that was nine miles north of the little town of Huson. Appropriately, it was named *Nine Mile Camp*. It was a forest firefighting camp deep in the wilderness of western Montana.

The Ranger Station and barn (below) at the Ninemile Remount Depot
Photos taken in the summer of 2014
The buildings are just as I remember them in 1942

I found a tame mule that let me pet him,
while visiting the Remount Depot in 2014

Nine Mile Camp entrance - photo taken summer 2014

The foundation and concrete slab remains of the washroom.
It is the only evidence of the location of the barracks - 70 years later.

Nine Mile Camp - photo taken ca1930s

Mess Hall - photo taken ca1930s

It was very cold in the barracks when we got there, even though it was in the middle of June, we built a fire in the stove that was in the middle of the room. There were 100 guys that arrived at the camp from different colleges around the United States. We were divided into four crews, with twenty-five in each group, living in four separate barracks.

Life was unusual and stimulating at the forest camp. Our supervisor warned us not to feed the bears and to be especially cautious if we saw a bear with cubs. We were taught methods of fighting forest fires. Each crew had two men assigned to run the crosscut saw, for cutting trees or logs. Several aspired for that assignment, so the foreman had each one demonstrate their abilities. I was quite experienced with the saw and gave others some pointers on the correct technique. The foreman observed my level of proficiency and put me on the opposite end from the men being tested. Needless to say, I was assigned to the crosscut job. When fighting fires, I enjoyed running the saw more than digging trenches or other jobs.

Cross-cut saws used for training and fighting the fires

We worked at making hay for the mules. Some of us had a chance to drive the old antique trucks while helping with that task. Nine Mile Camp was near the mountain in the background.

Mules ran wild on the open range. Occasionally some were rounded up and brought to the forest ranger's ranch for training. One day while I was working in the hay field at the ranch, I saw they were training the wild mules. It was a new experience for me and interesting to watch. However, knowing the nature of mules, I was not surprised at their capers.

The mules were not pleased with the affair and threw some fits that left no doubt about their displeasure of being controlled. They were trained for use in mule trains to carry supplies into the forests. A mule train consists of 9 or 10 mules all in single file with a lead strap to each and led by a man on a saddle horse. Mule trains were always taken with us to all fire locations.

The mules can carry over 200 pounds apiece. Some work solely as pack mules and can't be ridden under saddle. Others can be ridden under saddle and these are called *ridin' mules*. Guides often argue about which ones are which.

One day our crew climbed to the top of a 4000 feet high peak to help condition us for hiking in the mountains and to get us accustomed to high altitudes.

One night at about midnight the whole crew was called out to prepare for a long trip to a fire in Yellowstone National Park, where two separate fires were burning. The kitchen had made sack lunches for us to have something to eat on the way. We loaded on the back of camp trucks and were taken to Missoula. There we boarded Greyhound buses for the trip to Yellowstone National Park.

We traveled all night and arrived at Yellowstone the next morning. There, open-top park sightseeing buses were waiting to take us to the area of the fire. I thought they would rush us there as fast as possible. However, they claimed we could not do much with the fire until later in the evening or early in the morning. So the buses drove past the tourist attractions and places of interest along the way and even stopped occasionally for us to take pictures.

After the buses delivered us to the place where we unloaded to get to the fire, we hiked some distance through the forest. We arrived at the fire in the afternoon followed by the mule train carrying supplies.

Immediately we began work on the fire trenches. When it became dark, it was time to bed down in our sleeping bags at a safe distance from the fire.

The camp leader woke us up early each morning at four o'clock. After washing in ice-cold water from the mountain stream, we had breakfast at the field kitchen. Then we filed out, following the leader to where we would work at controlling the smoldering fire. That was the usual procedure when out on a fire. Our fire fighting crew of 100 ambitious guys had that fire under control in four days. I do not know where the mules had been kept, but they were there ready to carry supplies out. We packed up our sleeping bags and hiked out to the road where it looked like we were back to civilization.

The park service brought a convoy of sightseeing buses again, and took us around the southern part of the park past many interesting spots along the way to another fire on the east side of the park. After unloading from the buses, trucks took us through the forest for three miles. Then we hiked another three miles to the area of the fire. A mule train carried supplies to our campsite again. It took three days to get that fire under control. The remnants of both fires were left for the park service mop-up crews.

We returned to civilization again, where the park buses were waiting to pick us up. We were given another tour past more fascinating sights and delivered to a hotel at the north entrance of the park. There we got to clean up, have a good meal, and sleep in a nice bed. It was like a luxury hotel to us and a special treat after living in the wilderness for over a week. What a blessing to our exhausted crew!

Early the next morning we boarded a train to take us back to Missoula. It was a relaxing ride with a good lunch served, while watching the beautiful mountain scenery along the way. As the train approached Missoula, we could see a fire on a mountain slope some distance to the east of us. Although we were anxious to get back to camp, we figured that fire would be our next destination. Sure enough! The forest service had trucks waiting there with the tools we would need and they took us to the fire area. We immediately started digging a trench hoping to stop the fire before morning. Fortunately, a rain came during the early hours of the morning and quenched the fire. We were weary, wet, and cold, but glad the fire was out and were ready to be taken back to Nine Mile Camp. They let us rest all the next day and have the day off with pay.

My summer at Nine Mile Forest Camp was a memorable experience in outdoor living, working, and spending time with other young men my age, who had a common interest in working with nature and getting an education. However, not many of the guys were inclined to spiritual matters. There were no chapel services, opportunities for a formal worship, or Bible studies. During the evening, after our day's activity, I would often slip away among the trees that surrounded the camp area. I would find a log to sit on and read a portion of the scripture. Then I would kneel and give thanks to God for His many blessings and pray for the well-being of my family back home. On Sunday mornings, I provided my own worship services among the trees...as had become my custom.

On one such occasion, the Lord impressed on me that my family might be in need of some money. Times were still difficult at home because the family depended on the meager income Pop made working for the WPA. I kept up frequent correspondence with the family, so the next day I put a 10-dollar bill in with my letter. I learned later that my family was working in the potato patch when the letter arrived. The money was much needed and a blessing to them. I learned that when Mom received the money, she immediately sent someone to the grocery store to get some food items for lunch.

Some of us decided to build a dam across a nearby creek, using large rocks from the bottom of the creek, to make a swimming pool. The water was cold, coming from up in the mountains, but it was refreshing to take a dip after a day of work in the field making hay or hiking in the forest. There was a wash-house for us to do laundry, but some of us took our laundry to the creek. Our white things began to look rather dingy by the end of the summer.

On one occasion some boys decided to catch a bear that kept getting into the kitchen garbage can each evening. I wondered what they thought they would do if they caught the bear. They borrowed a rope and fixed a lasso around the top of the garbage can, then hid in a building close by, waiting for the bear to make his regular evening visit. When the bear got his body half way down in the barrel, they pulled the rope. The rope slid over the bear's head, but only caught one front leg. However, they had the bear! He was jumping, growling, and throwing a fit trying to get loose. The whole camp was watching that fine sport at a distance! After a while, the boys began to wonder how they would get the rope off the bear.

The boys did not want to let the bear go with their rope because they would have to pay for it, so they held on. The bear got a little slack in the rope, climbed up a large post and stood there with all four feet on top of the post. It was a stand off between the bear and the rope holders. Finally, the bear got the rope off his foot and ran into the forest.

Our days at Nine Mile Camp were always filled with interesting activities. Watching the parachute exercises was one of them. When in the open field, we could see the smoke jumpers practice parachuting from their plane. On one occasion we saw a guy fall halfway to the ground before his chute opened! We had feared we were watching a man fall to his death.

The camp was operated by the Civilian Conservation Corps (CCC) boys. Many of the boys working there had been dismissed because the government began closing some CCC camp operations. That caused a shortage of help to care for the large sugar beet crop. All the boys from our forest camp went to the rescue of the beet farm for two or three days. It was an unpleasant task of crawling down between the rows pulling small weeds. Then every row had to be cultivated with a hoe. Our 100 boys put the beet crop in good shape within two days.

It was a big accomplishment and the field looked great.

By the end of our assignment with the forest service, we were all were ready to get back to civilization and make ready for school. Of course our ultimate goal was to prepare for a vocation in life. That exciting summer work confirmed I had made the right choice of a career in forestry.

The job ended late in August giving us just enough time to make it back for the beginning of classes. Two of the guys at the camp were from Purdue. One of them was driving back to Chicago. His name was Bill, and he offered me and the other classmate a ride with him for $10 each to share expenses.

We took turns driving but I did not trust the driving of the other boy, Don Creekbaum. One night Don was driving and Bill was sleeping in the back seat, I stayed awake to help watch the road. All the roads and highways were narrow with only two lanes and not so safe. Sometime late in the night our car started crossing the center line heading toward an oncoming truck. Glancing over, I saw Creekbaum was sleeping at the wheel! I quickly reached over, grabbed the steering wheel, and jerked the car back to our lane–just in time to miss the truck as it sailed past us with the horn blaring! Creekbaum snapped awake when I grabbed the wheel out of his hands, just in time to glimpse the terrifying sight of the truck just barely missing us. If I had been sleeping, none of us would have lived to tell the story.

When we reached Chicago, Bill took me out to the edge of town where I could easily catch a ride to continue my journey down Highway 41 to get home. It was a happy reunion to see my family again. There was even a little time to spend with my family before returning to school. It was easy to fall right in with the others doing usual farm work and chores until it was necessary to take my leave to return to Purdue.

The summer at Nine Mile National Forest Camp was one of the most exciting adventures of my life as a result of having enrolled in the School of Forestry at Purdue University.

Back to the Boilermakers

My income from the forestry job made it possible to pay for my next semester of school and still have quite a bit of money left over to use for some clothing and other school needs. Coming home with almost $500 in my pocket made me feel as if I were almost rich.

While I was home I attended the Petersburg Church of God and I learned that Roy Kline, a man who was friendly to our church, had a small house trailer he was selling for $150. I bought the trailer, thinking it would provide a better living arrangement for me at Purdue. I could be free from having to work for my rent, which would give me more time to study. I looked forward to having my own place without having interruptions, additionally it would be more quiet and peaceful by not having to be housed with other students.

After buying the trailer, I still had enough of my summer earnings left for getting started back to school. I made a trip to Lafayette in our family's 1934 Plymouth to get registered for school and look for a place to park the trailer. I also inquired about my job at the meat locker plant. Tom Gould, the owner, was glad to have me return to work and even gave me a five-cent raise, making my wage 30 cents per hour.

I returned home and Imel pulled the trailer to Lafayette for me with his 1941 pickup truck. Morris, Orace Wayne, and Eugene Willis (a friend from school) went along to help set the trailer and have a little adventure. I took my old bicycle along to use for transportation because my trailer was going to be about a half mile from campus. My bicycle was an old 28-inch *clincher wheel*, which was a good riding bike.

The house trailer made living at Purdue quite different. It was an easy ride on my bike to and from my destinations on campus and my job at the meat locker. Most of my days were spent on campus at the library when not in class. That put me closer to the locker plant when it was time to report for evening work. When I arrived at the trailer in the evening, or whenever there was time during the day, it was great to have a quiet place to study and prepare my meals. I had an electric cooking stove, which made it possible for me to cook the special cuts of meat that Mr. Gould occasionally gave to me. During the winter days, I could turn on the electric heater when I arrived to the trailer. It didn't take long for it to get cozy and warm. I enjoyed living in the trailer much better than living in the apartment.

Taken in front of my house trailer at Purdue
(I am pulling a string to take self photo)

By the end of the fall semester, the war department began drafting 18-year-old boys into the army as more and more soldiers were needed. I did not want to pay the next semester tuition, with the high likelihood I would soon be drafted and lose the money I had paid. College students were being deferred, but it was unknown how long that would last. Therefore, at the end of that semester I used the family's Plymouth to pull my trailer back home, where I sold it for almost the amount that I had paid for it. I decided to do some farm work with Imel and help around our home or possibly find some part-time jobs until I was drafted.

Chapter 10

A SEASON OF FARMING

To every thing there is a season, and a time
to every purpose under the heaven: (Ecclesiastes 3:1)

Farmers Needed

There was not exactly a food shortage in America, but various government programs were enacted to keep the nation fed while the war placed greater demands on agricultural resources. A couple of bold measures were put in place to ensure there was enough food for our people at home, our soldiers abroad, and for our allies, whose citizens were desperately needing food. One important plan was a nationwide rationing system and another was draft deferment for men and boys operating farms.

The government began urging farmers to increase production of crops and livestock in anticipation of a need for larger quantities of food for the military buildup. A deferment from the military draft was granted to all young men working on productive farms. That was a wise decision! If a farmer lost his helpers, it would definitely cut back on his production and he might even have to quit farming.

We soon learned the government was deferring anyone who was engaged in qualified farming operations. Agriculture activities were considered critical to the success of the war effort and the government pushed for larger, more economical farms that could produce greater yields using less labor.

Everyone had food stamps allowing them to buy limited amounts of meat, sugar, butter, cheese, flour, and other staples that were among the rationed food items. Gasoline, tires, and nylon also were rationed as well as many other things. However, fuel was not rationed for farmers, so they were able to buy as much as they needed for the operation of their farm machinery.

Upon learning of the possible deferment, Imel and I decided to expand his meager farming activities and call it a partnership, in order to qualify for a draft postponement. I registered as a farm worker and applied for the deferment. Imel registered with the draft board as a farmer and also as a conscious objector. That required a letter from his minister stating his beliefs and objections to killing anyone...even in war.

Not much farm production can be accomplished with just a team of horses, so Imel purchased a new Oliver tractor. It was an essential piece of equipment for plowing any sizable piece of ground, because using the slow moving horses would take too long. Imel drove the tractor home from Petersburg, where he bought it. Of course we all had to inspect the modern piece of equipment with admiration. It was soon put to the test to see how it would perform pulling a set of two bottom plows.

Imel on his first tractor, a new Oliver
Photo taken by the Willis home 1942

The Oliver was a row-crop tractor and came with a set of two row cultivators for use in the corn fields. That was a relatively new thing for that era and of course it saved a lot of time from having to use a horse drawn cultivator.

The tractor was not a large one but it served our purpose

quite well. Many farmers still farmed with horses and some of them were anxious to hire us to plow their ground with the tractor. We could get it done faster and save their horses for other work. Our first custom work with the Oliver was plowing a 40-acre field that paid us $3 per acre. The man was very happy to get it done so much quicker than it would have been with his team. He could then work the ground and plant his crop with the horses.

Morris Willis on the right. Janet (Imel's daughter) on Ol' Tom in the center. Photo taken at the old Harvey home near Union, Indiana in 1943. Tom was a very good pet, as well as a sturdy work horse. Imel's Oliver tractor is in the background.

A few other farmers learned of our business and were eager to have us plow their fields rather than using their horses. The custom plowing that we did with the Oliver tractor, over two years time, almost paid for it. When plowing a large field, we kept the tractor going nearly 24 hours a day by each of us working five to six hour shifts.

For labor, our brothers, Morris and Orace Wayne were our primary hired hands in the partnership. They were not quite old enough for the draft and too young to apply for jobs in the war factories. They loved to help us keep the Oliver going. Sometimes we had to hire additional workers for our bigger jobs. Our farming operations were scattered here and there, and we lacked proper techniques for a large-scale venture, as a result we did not make much money. Nevertheless, we were able to pay expenses and keep a little operating capital. More importantly, we were making the quota that met the draft board's requirements for continued draft deferment.

Farmall tractor which looks just like the one Imel bought

In the spring of 1943, Imel got a bargain on a used Farmall tractor he bought at an auction. It had steel wheels with lugs and had to be driven home for the ten miles on back roads to avoid the highway. The tractor did not look too pretty, but it sure was a stout farm tractor and was a great help with our large amount of plowing. It relieved the Oliver for cultivating and other needs. Several acres of soybeans were planted that year. We knew that it would be necessary to hire someone to combine the soybeans unless we could find a good used combine.

The Highway Mowing

The horse drawn mower is what we used for cutting hay and mowing the right-of-way by the highway. It was hard work for the teams and the drivers.

During the summer of 1943 a contract was given to us for mowing 10 miles of right-of-way along Highway 57 south of Petersburg. Used mowers would be easy to find where farmers were no longer in the hay business. There were always farmers around who had quit and were anxious to sell their equipment. In those days, there was no such thing as the modern tractor mower like we see today. We used teams of horses to pull the old sickle-type mowing machines.

We had one good team of horses named Tom and Baldy. At least another animal was needed to work with Kate, a crippled mule that had been in the family for a few years, and another mower. That would give us two teams with which to pull the mowers.

We bargained for another mule that a man was anxious to sell because he could not keep the mule fenced in. He was a gentle mule and willing to work, but he would not stay in the pasture. We called him Dillard because we considered him to be like an outlaw. He was always running away from home but only went far enough to find some good pasture. He was neither wild nor mean. Any of us could walk right up to him wherever he was and lead him back home. He was one of the best work animals we had.

After crops were planted most of the cultivating would be done with the tractor, then the teams would be freed up for highway mowing. We soon realized mowing was slow-paced work, and a third team and mower was needed. Imel knew of a horse trader at Oakland City where he found two more horses.

He found a strong horse, named King, he thought might work well with his best horse, Tom. The horse trader had another strong horse, a healthy mare named Dolly, that was not trained to work. We knew enough about horses that Imel was willing to take her at a bargain price.

It was fascinating to watch Dolly being trained to work with another horse. At first she flinched at the feel of the harness, but reluctantly accepted it. She was led out to the wagon where King was already hitched. The two back wheels were chained so they would not roll, but would slide. That would make the wagon harder to pull. One person held Dolly in place beside King, while Imel held the reins and a third person carefully hitched her to the wagon.

They turned her loose and she was ready to run! She even tried to gallop part of the time, but King was able to keep them going in the proper direction and held them in check. She was ready to slow down after a few rounds through the field. Both horses were tired and needed a rest. She caught her breath, then wanted to go again.

Imel let them run for a bit but was soon able to slow them down to a walk. After that tiring episode we could hitch Dolly to a mowing machine, but we could not get her in difficult places or she would just stop. If she thought a load was too heavy she would balk!

Mowing was really hard work, especially for the horses, and tiring for the person riding the mower. The highway had some very difficult places to mow. Those poor creatures were surely tired after pulling the mower all day.

We were getting along so well and doing such good work, the state supervisor offered us a 10-mile extension further south. It was really difficult for highway department to find people willing to take the job, so Imel accepted it and began to look for a fourth team.

General Sanders, my biology teacher in high school and a close friend to Pop, was instrumental in getting us one last contract. He was involved in politics and had some influence with the state highway officials. The mowing job was very profitable, so we were glad when our range was once again extended to almost 15 miles south of Oakland City, to a village called Buckskin. Thus, the farthest distance from home to the end of where we mowed was about 30 miles.

When our mowing took us farther from home, toward Oakland City and beyond, we rented barn space closer to our mowing area where we could keep the teams at night. That gave everyone a little extra rest each day.

Imel found two more horses for a fourth team. One of those horses was white and stood out from the others. We then needed more harness, thus he bought a new set. The new harness was used on the best team.

Tom was really the best horse of all. We could work him any place or with any of the other animals. He was sure footed and would watch carefully where he walked. If he sidled away from something, you knew he saw something in the way or some kind of danger. King was a very stout horse and was teamed with Tom for a while, but we switched the horses around to team them up according to the best performance.

A man by the name of Ben Hayes was hired to help with the mowing. We let him drive the best team most of the time. He was especially proud of the new set of harness. I was mowing with him one day using the small team of mules. We stopped at a Mr. Hawse's house to get a drink of water, and he came out to meet us. He began to admire the new harness on Ben Hayes' fine team and very adamantly exclaimed, "It's a nice set of harness, but I don't like the hames!"

It was an excellent set of hames topped with brass knobs. They were secured on a beautiful set of black collars with new collar pads that came with the harness. His crude remark made Ben angry who sharply retorted, "Well, I do! I like it all! Thanks for the water. We'll be moving on with our job." Ben never wanted to stop at the Mr. Hawse's house for water again. I could not figure why Mr. Hawse was so rude or why he did not like every part of that beautiful harness set.

The White Elephant

We learned of a retired farmer who had a pull-type Farmall combine stored in his barn which he claimed had been used very little. Imel manged to find the money to buy it. After we got it home, we cleaned off the dust and dirt that had accumulated during storage, then the combine looked like new. Imel used it that summer to combine a couple of wheat fields for other farmers and it performed excellently. The income from that custom work partially paid for the combine.

We planted mainly crops of corn and soybeans, but we also grew sufficient hay for our animals. We did not attempt to buy any land of our own. Instead we rented ground, sometimes through arrangements in which a share of the crop would go to the landowner. The International Farmall tractor, the Oliver, and the horse teams enabled us to expand our operation as we found other parcels of land to rent.

One of our soybean fields was near the home of Grester Amos, where he also had a large field of beans. He spoke to us about harvesting his beans using our combine. Instead of exchanging money, we made an agreement to share labor and equipment. Since our Oliver tractor was being used to cultivate our fields, Grester used his tractor to pull our combine in both his and our fields while I operated the combine.

Grester and I noticed the combine was throwing beans out with the trash. I tried every setting possible attempting to get better performance from the combine, but I never could get it set so that all the beans were collected in the hopper. We had no way of knowing how many were thrown back onto the field. We continued combining both fields of beans even with the faulty equipment because we could not afford to hire the work done. We decided our good looking combine was not practical for our use in harvesting soybeans, so we put it up for sale.

I used Imel's truck to haul our soybeans to the market and collected the money. When I got home, for some reason no vehicle was available for me to deliver Grester's share of the money. I looked up and there were the mules looking like they wanted attention. I put the bridle on our favorite mule, Dillard and hopped on his back to deliver the money to Grester, whose home was about two miles away.

When I got there, I tied Dillard to a post and walked back in the field and climbed a fence to get where Grester was working. He was pleased to receive his pay for the beans and, as I left, he thanked me for making the special effort to get it to him. Dillard and I made our way back home. When I dismounted from my steed, I suddenly noticed my billfold was missing!

It gave me a sinking feeling to think I had lost the billfold with our share of the money, which was over $300, still in it! I got right back on Dillard to go look for the billfold. Dillard didn't know why were going again, but he seemed to like it. I made him go real slow, allowing me to look carefully as we followed our tracks all the way back to the Line Road and down to Grester's house. No luck!! I tied Dillard again and retraced my steps through the field. What a relief I had when I saw the billfold lying in the grass where I had climbed the fence. I made sure the $300 was secure in my pocket all the way home. That was equivalent to three to four thousand dollars in today's money.

After the harvest, Imel was ready to sell the combine. Evidently it needed repairs we were not equipped to make. The man who had Imel combine his wheat had seen the excellent performance of the machine and was eager to buy it at a discount price. He thought it would be no problem to make the adjustments necessary for it to combine beans. For one whole year we kept seeing the combine sit idle in his barnyard as if it was not being used. Imel decided to stop and talk to him about it. The man expressed his regret in buying it. He said, "It is impossible for me to get it adjusted to combine anything without throwing most of the harvest out on the ground. It's nothing but a big *white elephant* to me. I have to mark it off as a bad investment."

Corn Husking Days

Several acres of corn had been planted during the spring of 1943 and there was an abundant crop to be harvested that fall. There was no rush to harvest the corn except we were anxious to get it sold. With our other work of mowing and hay baling, the corn shucking could be done in between jobs or when we were not so busy. The corn could just hang on the stalk into the winter months if necessary.

When the corn was ready, the corn stalks would be cut and placed in shocks. Then the corn would be pulled from the stalk at a later time. Few farmers in our area had a corn picker and it would have been counterproductive for us to hire our corn picked.

When it was corn husking time, two or three of us would take a wagon with a team to the cornfield. We would let the horses pull the wagon (without a driver) down through the field while we picked the corn, shucked it, and pitched the ears into the wagon. It was slow going!! Three of us could usually shuck two wagon loads of corn in a day. We filled our corn crib for winter feed. We sold some to a local man to feed his hogs and the rest was sold to Wyatt's elevator in Petersburg. Some of the corn stalks were used for fodder (roughage feed) for the animals during the winter.

Hay Baling

Another job good for our business was baling hay, because many farmers needed that work done. Sometimes a bargain was struck with the farmer to harvest the hay *on shares*. That is...we would mow, rake, and bale in exchange for half of the hay. On those occasions, we could then sell our share and make nice profit.

That was before the advent of the modern baler, pulled by a tractor through the field, that picks up the hay and spits out bales. Ours was the old stationary baler that was parked in the field and we hauled the hay from shocks or windrows over to it.

At the baler, it took one person to feed the hay into it. We even hired an experienced man named Jasper Beck, from Hosmer, for that job. It took someone with quick hands and a feel for the machine, as the baler did not automatically block and tie the bales. Two other fellows also worked at the baler, one to feed the wires through the blocks and the other to tie the wires securely as the hay was pressed into bales.

Several workers were needed when baling in the field. In addition to the three at the baler, four to six others were needed to get the hay to the machine. At the end of the day the bales needed to be covered or hauled to shelter to protect them from the weather.

Morris and Orace Wayne were our good and faithful helpers during baling time. Other boys we hired to help with the hay included Gene and Gardner Willis (they were brothers), Fred Leighty, Monroe and Bob Catt (they were brothers), and others from the neighborhood. There was no *boss* because everyone knew what had to be done and we worked together as a team. Usually! All except the day Monroe created an issue while working in the field, whereby he and Morris got into an argument. Monroe was sent home, because Morris fired him on the spot. It was really an ambitious crew of workers with no slackers. It was no place for a trouble maker.

There were times, the farmers would have the hay

already stored in their barn loft and would hire us to bale directly from the barn. In those situations, the baler would be set below the barn loft opening and some of us would pitch the hay from the loft onto the platform of the baler. The man feeding the baler and the two men tying the bales took care of all the ground work.

During the summer of 1944, the most successful of our hay baling jobs came from Mr. Hightower's farm near Oakland City. He had over 100 acres, which was mostly in hay. He observed us mowing the highway past his farm and he talked to Imel about working his hay fields on shares. He was no longer able to tend his farm and needed help. He even talked of letting us farm his whole place with other crops the next year.

Mr. Hightower had a big team of Clydesdale horses to work his farm. He said they really needed to be worked and he had not even been able to harness them up lately. He told Imel we were welcome to use them to mow the hay, pull the wagons, and whatever we needed. Imel did use the Clydesdales to cut the hay, but we preferred to use our own horses to pull wagons.

There is an old expression that goes "make hay while the sun shines". How well we knew the meaning of this saying because hay-making is during the hottest time of the season and has to be done when the sun is shining. We worked some scorching days, during the summer of 1944, in Mr. Hightower's hay fields.

We liked to take as much baled hay as possible to the shelter of the barn each evening. One evening I had the flighty team of Dolly and the white horse pulling a large wagon load of hay, which weighed over a ton, to the barn. As we were going up an incline, a wheel dropped into a six-inch dip. Dolly stopped! The other horse tried to go, but Dolly balked. They see-sawed back and forth but just would not continue pulling the load. I had to unhitch them from the wagon and bring the small mules, Kate and Dillard, to hitch to the wagon. They buckled down and took the heavy load on up the hill and to the barn. Kate was gentle, reliable, and worked anywhere we needed her. Dillard was also a willing worker at any task.

Orace Wayne rode Dillard in the mule race at the Princeton County Fair and easily came out the winner. We had the same trouble as the previous owner of keeping Dillard in the pasture. If he could get his head under the fence anywhere, he would crawl through. One night he crawled under the fence for the last time! He wandered up onto the highway and the next morning we found him dead beside the road. He had been hit by a vehicle–most likely a truck. That left Kate without a teammate. However, fate was on its way and Kate would not need a mate. The time was near that our farming operation would be interrupted whereby we would not be needing the horses, mules, and equipment.

After some negotiations, Imel arranged for us to farm Mr. Hightower's land the next year. For the past two years we had struggled with the difficulty of having our operations scattered in different directions. It appeared the Lord had blessed us with the opportunity to be more successful with our business by having it centrally located on one big farm. We looked forward to the next year being mostly in one place. However, the Lord works in mysterious ways!

Call to Duty

In the middle of August 1944, I received a notification that my deferment was discontinued. The war was consuming material and men at an enormous rate, therefore greater numbers of single boys were being called to action. I was ordered to report for a physical examination. Later that month, I made an *all expense paid* trip to Indianapolis for a physical examination to see if I qualified for military service. I continued helping with farm work until I received notice to appear for another *free ride* to the military induction center.

It was early in September when I received my induction notice. I had two weeks before departing and the remaining hay baling and fall harvest would be left in the hands of Imel and his helpers. I knew they could handle it but I felt like I was deserting them. Yet it was out of my control.

Imel proceeded to make big plans for the Hightower land in the coming spring. He used the owner's Clydesdale team to spread manure on the fields, thus everything would be ready for spring planting.

However, the farming business was totally shut down when Imel received his notice that winter to report for military duty. He had a big auction to sell off all our equipment and livestock. It was the end of our farming partnership, but not the end of our partnership in other ventures.

We look back on our enterprise with fond memories and a sense of accomplishment. We were accustomed to hard work and we did make enough to keep the operation going while providing wages to those we hired, as well as providing food for many hungry folk. If these achievements were a measure of our success, then ours was a business that flourished.

Chapter 11

MY MILITARY YEARS

The Lord is my strength and my shield; my heart trusted in Him, and I am helped: therefore my heart greatly rejoiceth; and with my song I will praise Him. (Psalms 28:7)

The Military Odyssey

In my book, *The Odyssey of a Purple Heart Vet*, a more complete account is given about my service as a soldier during World War II. Although my time in the army was relatively short, the experience left the most profound impression in my mind and had a greater impact than any other event in my life. I feel my memoirs would be incomplete without including a brief account of my time in the military. This is an abbreviated version, yet I include additional details not mentioned before.

Tour of Duty

During those few weeks before time to leave home to be inducted into the army, my thoughts were troubled about what lay ahead of me. The War in Germany was still going strong. Also, there was news of the United States losing men in battles in the Philippines and other islands in the Pacific. I would have no choice where the army would send me.

On the morning of my departure, September 14, 1944, I was up early getting ready to go. Mom would not let me leave without breakfast. It was a solemn time, especially for Mom, knowing I was leaving for some unknown destination and probably to a dangerous area. She could not hold back the tears as she gave me a hug before I left. I did not dread to leave but I was much grieved for the anguish Mom felt. One of my brothers drove me to Petersburg. I joined several other guys who had gathered there waiting for the bus. The group included

213

a cousin, some school mates, and other familiar men of the community. Finally, a Greyhound bus arrived, with other men who were from the Princeton area, to take us to Indianapolis, Indiana.

It was not a peacetime army that we were entering. The war was consuming men at an alarming rate. Only the military planners knew what armies were on the move, where our battle lines were holding, and what requirements were necessary for a strategy to win a war being fought on two fronts. Their greatest need was for foot soldiers because they always incur the greatest number of casualties. As we rode on the bus toward our unknown future in the military, I'm sure many were wondering about what would happen to us and whether we would even return home.

Our induction ceremony took place in Indianapolis. In that same afternoon those of us who had newly become part of the U.S. Army were then driven to Camp Atterbury, about 40 miles away. During our week of processing at the camp we were outfitted with an entire wardrobe of combat boots (also called clobber boots), hats, army green fatigues, and tan dress uniforms. We learned very little, other than how to wear our uniforms and how to salute officers. Although, I did learn how to peel potatoes the army way!

After our processing at Camp Atterbury, we were transferred by troop train to Camp Blanding, Florida, for 15 weeks of basic infantry training. I was soon assigned to a group of selected men to receive extra training in combat engineering techniques. Those of us in that group had some college or other advanced schooling.

PVT James Willis holding his M-1 rifle
Taken in front of his hut at Camp Blanding, Florida

Upon leaving Camp Blanding, my orders were to ship out for battle from Seattle, Washington. I had a 20-day furlough, so I went home first. Then I continued on to my final destination of Seattle via Chicago and Fort Ord, California. I was among thousands of soldiers being sent to various places in the Pacific Theater of the war.

We were confined to the base in Seattle. After a few days, orders were given to pack up and get ready to leave. During the darkness of night we were taken to the waterfront, in the back of canvas covered army trucks, where we got a glimpse of the giant gray transport ships waiting for us. And so it was, for the first time in my life I found myself aboard a ship and out at sea. While it was definitely not a cruise ship, the lumbering transport did get us safely to our first port of call, Hawaii, in five days.

It had been about three years since Japan bombed Pearl Harbor. As our ship steamed into the harbor, the evidence of Japan's treachery was still strikingly visible. Moving slowly to avoid submerged hulks and sunken wreckage, it took longer than usual for our ship to make way to her assigned berth.

From our ship, we stumbled down the gangway. Our sea legs protested, as the change from the constant swaying of the ship to rock solid land made walking slightly awkward.

From the base at Pearl Harbor we were loaded aboard a miniature train. The train seemed so little to me as I was used to seeing the mighty steam locomotives pulling long lines of rail cars along the Wabash-Erie Canal at home. We were crammed into the little open-topped cattle cars with no room to sit during our journey. The small steam engine struggled to pull the heavily loaded cars filled with standing soldiers to a camp in the upper hills of the island.

The base camp for the training facility was nestled in a lush green jungle, far too scenic and beautiful to be an army base. It definitely did not look like a war training zone. From there we marched to other areas in the hills learning how to fight and survive in jungle warfare.

When it was time for us to leave, the little train took us back down the mountain where several hundred of us boarded two transport ships for a destination unknown to us. The ships were crowded with soldiers and sailors. It was on that voyage I made an acquaintance with a particular soldier that would become a lifelong friend.

A Lifelong Friend

In the war, all soldiers were friends because all were in the army together for a common cause. None appeared any better than his mates; we all dressed alike and received the same treatment. We were all prone to the same tongue lashings from our sergeants and endured the rigors of military life. However, there were differences of opinions and dispositions.

One morning at breakfast I met Herbert Weithorn and as we talked, we wondered if we had been at the same camp in Hawaii. We learned that we both had come from common backgrounds and believed in putting our faith in God to return us home. We spent most of the remaining four days on the ship walking the decks and spending time together. We developed quite a bond of fellowship. If we survived the war, we were determined to make contact with each other again or if only one of us made it home, he would contact the other one's family.

Both ships docked at the island of Saipan, where we spent three weeks preparing for our advance to a battle area. Herbert and I were temporarily separated as the men were shuffled to different camps on the island, but we soon found each other and explored the island during our off-duty time.

Six troop transport ships were waiting in the harbor of Saipan when it was time for us to leave. Several army trucks arrived at the dock during the night, loaded with hundreds of soldiers. We were transferred to the ships and assigned sleeping bunks below deck. It was an eerie feeling to think of the possibility of an enemy torpedo sinking our ship and all of us going to the bottom of the sea.

I supposed Herbert had been on one of those army trucks that brought us to the docks and was on one of the six ships, but I had no idea if we would ever see each other again. I thought we were no doubt separated for good.

Amazingly, the next morning Herb (Herbert) and I found each other again! We ate our meals together, explored the decks of the ship, and spent most of our time together while waiting to depart. It was enjoyable to have his friendship and the Christian fellowship.

For reasons known only to the military leaders, we sat anchored in Saipan harbor for several days. Then one night, the ship started creaking and shuddering as we moved out into the ocean swells. We were underway to somewhere in the pacific.

The six troop ships sailed in a convoy, protected by several escort ships of various types. Those smaller ships were far different from the big troop transports. They were fast and powerfully gunned with low profiles to make them difficult to spot from afar. The Navy was determined to get us safely to our destination.

Battle of Okinawa

After a few days at sea, we reached Okinawa just before sunset. Herb and I doubted we would be together after we landed. That was confirmed when we debarked over the side of the ship on rope ladders into small landing craft late in the night. Herbert was nowhere to be found in my landing boat. When we got ashore, we marched inland for about an hour then stopped to set up our tents. For three days we lived in that virtual tent city...a sea of two-man tents.

When the orders came for us to move out, we packed up our tents and assembled to hear a message and prayer by a Chaplain. He tried to offer encouraging words and admonished us to have faith in God for our destiny. He did not try to hide the truth of our danger, but frankly said that some of us would not return. I still remember his words, "If a bullet has your name on it, please be prepared to meet your maker." I have often said, "The bullet with my name on it, saved my life!"

We started marching south, straight into the heart of the bloodiest battle of the Pacific. Thousands of us were marched into the hills of Okinawa through thick sticky mud, passing dead Japanese bodies along the way. We were to be assigned as casualty replacements for the various combat units fighting on the Shuri Line (the Japanese defense line).

I was assigned to Company C of the 77th Infantry Division. To my surprise, Herbert arrived with some other guys and amazingly they were being assigned to my platoon! There we were together again...able to share the same foxhole and fight side by side. I never slept any during the first night in the foxhole because of flares lighting the sky and constant noise of artillery firing overhead all night long. Foxholes were not very comfortable, but after that first night I could lay on the hard ground and sleep soundly when it was my turn to rest.

While on the front line, as we advanced, army tanks rumbled up along with us to fire on a mountain or hillside... always attempting to fire into any cave opening and other hiding places for the Japanese. Mortar crews and artillery were continually firing over us into the enemy territory. All of that was a great help in subduing the Japanese and destroying their hideouts. But it was the foot soldier who had to go in and finally take possession of the area.

Early one morning, B Company came through our lines making an advance on the next hill. That hill was a major obstacle in getting to Shuri Hill and taking Shuri Castle, which was the assigned mission of the 77th Division.

Later that afternoon, our captain began calling on volunteers to go with him to rescue the wounded from those who had advanced on ahead of us. Reluctantly, I raised my hand. While we were standing around a tank that was to protect us during our assault, something slammed into my left shoulder with such force it spun me around and knocked me to the ground. I realized I had been shot and motioned to the medic seated some 20 feet away. Everyone was in their foxholes to keep out of the line of fire–so was the medic. He called for me to come to him. I attempted to crawl but discovered it was impossible because of the pain in my injured shoulder, so I jumped to my feet and ran to him.

When the medic removed my back pack and fatigue jacket, I noticed blood oozing out of the wound faster than I liked to see. I told the medic I would hold my finger on the hole in front to stop the bleeding while he took care of the wound on the back side.

The bullet that struck me to the ground may have actually saved my life. The American army was making so many assaults on the hills, that the ground was strewn with bodies...friend and foe. The flying bullets did not discriminate. I was a casualty but thankful to the Lord my life was spared. My time of fighting was over, at least until I recovered.

After getting a temporary patch on my wounds the medic said, "Take that path over there and keep going. You will find a road that will take you to a field aid station not far away."

I soon came upon a soldier with a leg wound who was having a hard time. I let him take hold of my right shoulder to serve as a crutch for him. We stopped at a mortar station to rest a while. The men manning the station gave us all the water from their canteens.

Soon after we found the road, a tank loaded with other wounded men came along. The driver stopped and called to us, "Climb on if you can find room!" The men on board started pulling us up onto the tank. We were delivered to a field aid station and from there I was taken by jeep ambulance to a field hospital.

Some time in the wee hours of the night, a doctor came to my stretcher and said, "It's your turn. We are taking you to a table." I said, "Doctor, I'm resting good and in no pain. Take some of these other fellows that are in worse condition." He said, "No, it's your turn. We're taking you now."

I woke up the next day with an arm and body cast. I was soon sent to a hospital in Guam and there had an opportunity to send a letter home telling about my injury. It was the first time I had been able to write to my family for several weeks and I knew they would be worried about me.

Through a series of travels and hospitals, I finally reached a hospital in Nashville, Tennessee. There were hundreds of soldiers there who were not seriously injured and were expected to serve again. We were expecting to return to the Pacific for the invasion of Japan. News of the atom bomb and the surrender of Japan was a relief to us. We no longer had to be concerned about that dreaded mission.

Surrender of Japan

Upon the surrender of Japan, the war was over and there was much celebration throughout our country. Soon thereafter men were being mustered out of the military. Those who had served the longest time were being discharged first. I would serve several more months in follow-up duties before being eligible for discharge.

Reassignment to duty

I was sent to an army rehabilitation and replacement center at an army base in San Antonio, Texas, for reassignment to duty. I was able to make contact with my friend, Herbert Weithorn, who had been wounded in the hand and left Okinawa two days after me. He was there at the same army base in San Antonio for rehabilitation of his hand injury.

Herbert taught me some interesting things about Texas by giving a grand tour of his family farm and the small nearby town of McGregor. He also invited me to a large outdoor Texas barbeque. My short stay at the base in San Antonio allowed me to meet many other guys who had a variety of experiences to tell about, which included one soldier who had survived the horrible Bataan Death March in the Philippines.

I was beginning to like the area and was hoping to get

assigned to duty at that base. However, that did not happen. Rather, my orders were to travel with three other soldiers by train all the way across the southern states to Fort Bragg, North Carolina. We were assigned to the Army Ground Forces at Fort Bragg.

I was a little excited about being sent to a new place I knew nothing about. Yet, I had some reservations when I considered what kind of assignment it might be. I wondered if it would be the same kind of military and marching maneuvers experienced during basic training.

An army truck was at the train station at Fayetteville, North Carolina, to take us the remaining 10 miles to Fort Bragg. The next morning revealed unpleasant scenery of white sand, scrubby trees and regular old army barracks. What an unpleasant place to have to stay for the next 6 to 8 months–so I thought! I was eventually assigned to the postal station of the Army Ground Forces department on the base. That was a fun job working for the post office. I received a double promotion from PFC to sergeant while working in the postal department.

I received my discharge from the army at Camp Atterbury on June 26, 1946. I had traveled many miles and been places during those 21 months. I had been in the last battle of World War II on Okinawa where I witnessed situations and tragedies beyond the ability to describe in words.

Service with Honor

We can passively read about the loss of lives, giving little thought of the seriousness of the numbers or the individuals who died. Many men on the navy ships suffered terrible burns or went to the bottom of the sea with their ship. Winston Churchill once stated, the Battle of Okinawa was "among the most intense and famous in military history."

Tens of thousands of men gave of themselves during World War II, with a great number coming back injured or crippled for life. There were numerous who did not come home to their families, but paid the supreme price with their lives for the victory and freedom of our country.

Occasionally, someone will thank me when they see my Purple Heart license plate or otherwise learn of my service in the war. I accept the recognition graciously but I do not want to elaborate so as to appear boastful. I am glad I was able to serve in the army to protect our country. The ones who did not return are the ones deserving the honors and must never be forgotten!

Sgt. James B. Willis, Company C
77th Infantry Division, U.S. Army
Purple Heart Veteran of World War II
Wounded on Okinawa June 17, 1945

Chapter 12

THE BAREFOOT BRIDE

Whoso findeth a wife findeth a good thing,
and obtaineth favor of the Lord. (Proverbs 18:22)

The Mystery of Romance

Now sit back, relax, and enjoy this next section! I consider this the most important and best part of my story. In fact, a large book could be written to cover it completely. The Lord works in mysterious ways, and many things happen through the providence of God. In this part of my life, he clearly led the way.

Church services in the army chapels were designed to accommodate military personnel of different faiths and were more formal than I preferred as a place to attend church. I began to look for a church more to my liking in Fayetteville, even though it was a 10-mile trip from Fort Bragg.

Afternoon Pastime

There was a regular 24-hour bus service to and from Fort Bragg. On weekends I went to town as often as I could just to get away from the boredom of the camp. Every Sunday, if I was not on duty, I would go to Fayetteville for morning and evening church services. At other times I would loaf about, find interesting sights, do some window shopping, etc. The farm and hardware stores were favorite places to browse even if I had no intention of buying anything.

I visited several historical spots around Fayetteville including the famous Market House in the center of town. It was built on the ruins of the old Statehouse and served as a town market until 1906. It had the infamous reputation of having been a place where slaves were bought and sold at auction during the days of slavery. The Market House served as the Town Hall until 1907. Later it was furnished with park benches and the second floor was used for a library. At the time I was stationed at Ft. Bragg, it was a place for loafing or lounging on the benches. Also, farmers brought their produce to sell there. Presently, the Market House Museum occupies the second floor.

The Market House

The Cape Fear River Bridge was one of my favorite places to loaf during pleasant weather. Looking each direction from the bridge gave a nice view of trees lining the riverbank reminding me of the countryside of my home. I might see some boats cruising by or a pile of debris floating down the river. Usually some people would be fishing from the bridge or the river bank. Occasionally I would witness a small catch and compliment the person.

Cape River Bridge

I seldom found any of the guys at camp interested in my type of afternoon entertainment. However, I was introduced to another enjoyable pastime. One of the guys from the base invited me to go with him to the roller skating rink in town. Ice skating had been a favorite sport when growing up at home, but I had never tried to roller skate. I was game to try it and went along with him. The experience was vastly different than skating on ice. I took a few spills in the process of learning to control the roller skates and managed to get the hang of it. Skating was a fun activity and I went several times, but it was more enjoyable to take a stroll out to the river bridge.

Sometimes I went to town on Friday or Saturday and spent the night at the USO Club. The United Serviceman's Organization (USO) had service centers all over the world. They provided places for soldiers to go where they could find wholesome entertainment, something to eat, a place to relax, and stay the night. Spending my free time in Fayetteville was more interesting than being on the base. Bed space at the USO was limited, so I would usually just slip off my shoes and sleep on one of the couches.

One morning, after spending the night at the USO, I woke up to find my 10-dollar Florsheim shoes were gone and an old pair sitting in their place. They looked as if they had been on a march across the USA. I didn't want to go to church with such worn-out looking shoes, so as soon as possible I went shopping and found a nice pair of dress shoes for $5. I did not want to spend $10 on another pair of shoes.

Fayetteville Church of God

I found a Church of God, which I thought was of the same denomination as I had attended when I was home. I soon learned it was a Pentecostal Church of God, with a different type of worship service than my home church. Nevertheless, I really enjoyed the sincerity and spiritual atmosphere of the congregation. Every Sunday I went there for church service and sometimes stayed in town to attend the evening service. Those people did not "quench the Spirit"! Harvey Turlington, the preacher, would stamp his foot and preach an inspiring and meaningful sermon loud enough to keep the congregation awake–and some of the neighbors, too.

The church had a special communion service during a midweek service that I attended. They also practiced foot washing and I was glad to take part in that as it had been practiced in my home church.

A Special Acquaintance

It was at the Church of God in Fayetteville, North Carolina, where I met a girl that would set me on a new path in life. How we met is as significant as where, and it is probable the timing of it was the most critical element of all. I have an important question to ask the reader...I certainly had many at the time, being the shy country lad that I was. But I am getting ahead of myself. First I must tell you how she stole my heart.

While my prime interest was the worship service at church, I also happened to observe the few young ladies in attendance. I suppose they would also notice a new, young fellow coming to their church, especially one that was in military uniform. In those days, military personnel were required to be in full dress uniform anytime they were off base. Maybe the sparkle of my medals drew their attention.

I thought *one* of the girls at church was more attractive than all the others. One Sunday I invited a soldier friend, named Ruffo, to church with me. After church he confirmed my opinion. On the way back to camp Ruffo described which girl he thought was the prettiest and indicated he would like to get acquainted with her. He described the very girl I had been watching! I never let on how I felt about her because I was backward about such things. Ruffo was a handsome guy with an outgoing personality who could quickly make friends and win the admiration of girls. I never invited him back to church with me again!

The Little Address Book

The church had a good Sunday school class for young people, which I usually attended. While in that class one Sunday, some of the girls began asking my name and wanted to know more about me. One of them asked, "Do you have an address book in which we could write our name?" I did carry a small address book and it was passed around for any to write in as they pleased. Of course, that tickled me even though the boys in the class probably resented it. While my little address book was being passed around, I watched out of the corner of my eye to see if the pretty girl signed it. To my delight she was writing a little more than just her name. I could hardly wait for the chance to read her note, and this is what it said, "Berline Barefoot, I work at Roses 5 &10 store. Stop by sometime."

After I got my address book back, I was pleasantly distracted as I studied her name and her short message. I admit I gave little attention to the Sunday school lesson that day!

Some might think it was a little too forward or out of order for Berline to write that short invitation. However, it let me know she would welcome my visit at the store and that she would like to learn more about me. I was certainly interested in learning more about her! If she had not written that message, I might never have had the courage to seek her attention or even talk to her.

Over the next few days, more and more of my thoughts were filled with the pretty girl named Berline. I liked that name! I had never heard of the name Barefoot and it intrigued me. I did not realize our common ancestral homeland until many years later when I learned that Barefoot was an English surname.

Now let me ask the question...if you were a young unattached guy, away from home, with plenty of spare time on the weekends, kind of lonely, and longing for wholesome companionship...then a beautiful Christian girl writes you an encouraging message, what would you do? You would probably do just as I did!

The first opportunity I had to get away from camp, I made straightway for Rose's 5 & 10 store. A five and dime store, as they were often called, was a place where many small items could be bought for 5 or 10 cents. They usually had a snack bar with a soda fountain. Most every town of any size had such stores in those days.

I found the store and I anxiously wondered if she would be working. As casually as I could, I sauntered in as though I were shopping for something. I looked through the store and there she was! Such a beautiful girl; my heart made a little flip. I wanted to take her into my arms right then and there, but that would have to wait. We visited a few minutes then I asked her if I could walk her home when she got off work. She allowed that would be nice, but told me I could only walk with her part way. She was not ready for her dad to know of our acquaintance.

When she was able to leave work, we joined the bustle of other folk on their way home. After we reached a certain point, I stopped and she walked on ahead. How long do you suppose I stood and watched her? From that time on, we began to see each other as often as the opportunity provided. We did not sit together during church, but afterward, I would walk her part of the way home.

Berline 1945

Father's Concern

One day after church, Magdeline (Berline's cousin) invited me to walk the two of them to Berline's house for lunch. I was happy to accept even though I was treading on risky ground, but after all–I was invited! As often happens, the bad actions of a few military men in town had marred the reputation of all army guys, and I was well aware of the possible prejudices against me. However, I was fairly well accepted at the Barefoot house, especially by Berline's two younger brothers, Oscar and James. We had a good Southern-style lunch, which I enjoyed immensely. I sensed some questioning eyes at the end of the table where the master of the house sat, and not much conversation came from that end! Berline's mother and dad were friendly, but her dad kept his distance. I was one of those Yankee soldiers of ill repute giving attention to his daughter.

Their home was a humble three-room dwelling on a back street. It was comparable to my homeplace and I felt at ease. It was obvious Berline's family lived on limited means, similar to my own home situation. Yet I was impressed with the cleanliness and how things were well kept. It indicated they took pride in their modest dwelling.

Thereafter, Berline and I began making more convenient times to meet, and her father soon knew of our close attraction. We went to church regularly, afterwards we would meet and I would walk her home. We sat in the porch swing at her house, walked in the park, visited her grandmother, or whatever we could do to spend time together. I took her to a different church for revival service one evening. On the way home, I got brave enough to hold her hand! We considered that our first date!

I learned later she was scared her father would see us holding hands. It was clear to me Berline was more than a little fearful her dad might be spying on us. He had done some bizarre things around home that caused his family to be afraid of him. At the time, I did not know the extent of her fears nor what caused her to feel that way. Since then, I have come to realize he was thinking just as any father does. He was a smart man and knew our relationship could become serious. Most men who have a beautiful young daughter think no boy is good enough or worthy of his daughter. Isn't that the truth!

One Saturday I was strolling by the old Market Place, passing the time until Berline got off work, when Mr. Barefoot *just happened* to be there. Mr. Barefoot greeted me in a friendly manner and made it seem as though our meeting was purely by accident. Of course, I appreciated the cordial attitude, but I soon realized he seemed to have an ulterior motive to his conversation. I was suspicious it was not a chance meeting as I had first thought!

After the friendly greeting and a few casual words, Mr. Barefoot began to talk seriously. His tone was kind, serious, and thoughtful with no harsh words or any indication of malice toward me. He gave me the impression of playing a Good Samaritan, out to rescue me with some sound advice. Mr. Barefoot explained that Berline was quite a problem girl. He also described his wife as being uncooperative and perhaps being the instigator of conflict. I thought, "How can that be? Mrs. Barefoot seems to be a wonderful Christian woman!"

Mr. Barefoot spent an hour with me elaborating on what a terrible wife and daughter he had to live with. He claimed that Melissa, Berline's mother, was very temperamental and hateful toward him. According to him, Melissa had raised Berline to be just like her. Mr. Barefoot said he had lived with that grouchy and spiteful woman for many years. He complained of having both of them against him, because his only daughter was a little trouble maker demon–just like her mother. He may not have used those exact words but that was my interpretation of his diatribe. He proceeded to give details of some of their awful conflicts. All of it was the fault of his wife and daughter. I could have thought, "*Is he trying to get me to take one of them off his hands?*"

It seemed like Mr. Barefoot was warning me as to what an awful mess I would be getting into if I had to live with such torment. But I knew his real motive! I realized his motive was to turn me against Berline! He was smart enough to know we were spending a good deal of time together and where that could lead. It was more than he wanted and he was advising me in a subtle way to break my relationship with her before it got serious.

Little did he know we were already quite seriously in

love with each other. Being a good soldier, I listened and tried to understand all that Mr. Barefoot was telling me. I thought, *"How could God allow such a beautiful creation–this lovely girl–be a demon?"* Berline seemed earnest about her life with God. She was attentive in Sunday school and to the preaching of the Word of God, so it appeared she was faithful and serious regarding church. In her life, as I had seen, she was diligent and wanted to do what was right. It did not make sense what her father was saying to me.

While Mr. Barefoot never showed any hostility toward me, he did not trust me either. First, because I was a soldier; second, because I was a Northern Yankee. For him, those old Southern feelings of mistrust against the Yankees of the North were still alive and well–120 years after the Civil War. Perhaps my carefree behavior did not foster his trust. I found no fault with his use of psychology in an attempt to protect his daughter, as Berline would be the first of his children to "leave the nest".

Anyway, it was too late for him to be giving such advice–the love bug had already bit! Contrary to his efforts, I could hardly wait to excuse myself and go be with the "awful" girl that he had been characterizing as God's mistaken creation. Love usually tends to resist any reasonably sound advice, whether it is good or bad.

Continued Courtship

As I became more of a household fixture in the Barefoot home, Berline sometimes invited me to join their family dinners. One of the first times I ate with them, I made a serious blunder in table etiquette, which no doubt, further reduced my suitability in the eyes of Mr. Barefoot. On the occasion of that visit, the family was gathered around the table eating in the quiet dignity Mr. Barefoot demanded during mealtimes. Meals at my home were usually more relaxed and social affairs; we were a large family and we sat enjoying both food and talk with gusto. The Barefoot table was more subdued and, dare I say, more mannerly.

At one point during the meal, Oscar asked for a biscuit. I, being the closest one to the plate of biscuits, took one and tossed it to him! There was a small gasp from someone and a sudden quiet as nervous eyes turned to the head of the table. Mr. Barefoot didn't say anything, nor did he have to...for me to know that I had made a grave error. After the meal, Berline cautioned me not to throw food at the table.

One Saturday afternoon, several family members and neighbors had gathered on the front porch of their house talking and relaxing as was customary in those times. I sat by the doorway into the house, in an inconspicuous place. I was just sort of listening to their Southern talk, in their slow Southern way, discussing things that were important or interesting to them. Berline passed by me with a smile, on her way to the kitchen for something. While nobody was paying me any particular attention, I slipped into the house. She looked up when I entered the kitchen, I took her hand and motioned to her to come with me out the back door. We stepped outside and I saw there was nobody around (just as I had hoped)! I turned to her and, taking her in my arms, I kissed her. We did not dare linger even though we would have liked to. It was our first kiss!

Orders for Discharge

At the end of May 1946, I got a short leave and went home for a visit. At the end of my leave Morris drove me back to Fort Bragg in his nice 1942 Chevrolet accompanied by Gerald Gene Gray (Marybelle's son), our 13-year-old nephew. We stopped in town so I could see Berline and introduce them to my girlfriend. That night they drove me out to the base and dropped me off at my barracks. Then they immediately headed on back to Indiana.

Upon my return to the barracks, the first thing I heard from the guys was, "Willis, you're getting discharged! You start mustering out tomorrow." I also learned a few other guys would be leaving with me the next day. We were being sent to Camp Atterbury, Indiana, where we would receive our final discharge.

That was great news, but I had mixed feelings. I was not ready to leave Berline behind. It was time for some serious strategy and hasty plans had to be made. I had to tell Berline about my orders, but there was no way I could get a base pass to go into town that night, and little chance I could in the morning before leaving. I was in turmoil! It was extremely important to see Berline before I left Fort Bragg. What I wanted to say to her could not be said on the phone or in a letter. I knew what I had to do!

Early the next morning before breakfast, for the first and only time I went AWOL (Absent Without Leave) to find Berline. I was risking punishment if I got caught, then I planned my dash into town...calculating the minutes it would take me to make the trip without being missed. My hope was to catch her at work. From the bus stop, I hurried straight to the 5 and 10 store. She was there! I told her about my discharge orders and asked her if we could go somewhere to talk. She quickly told her supervisor and checked out.

As we walked to one of our favorite places, it was clear Berline was upset about my leaving. Finally, she could no longer hold back the tears and began to cry, saying, "I'll never see you again." It broke my heart to see her so distraught. I gave her my handkerchief to wipe her tears. Then, with my heart pounding, I asked her, "If I come back will you marry me?" She did not hesitate with the reply, "Yes!"

Maybe her answer should have been enough for me, but I didn't want her to feel pressured by the emotional distress of my departure. Also, I felt some reservations because she was still young; although she would be 16 in November, she was not of age to make her own decision. I wondered if we should wait a year or two to correspond and think things over before getting married. She did not want to wait any longer than necessary. She just wanted me to return as soon as possible! I promised I would and wrapped my arms around her.

We held each other with joy for the decision we had made. However, my time was short and reluctantly we parted so I could return to base. I walked her back to the road and she went toward home rather than back to the store. She told me later it was emotionally impossible for her to return to the store. Lightheaded with happiness, yet in anguish; it was not easy to leave her that day. We had given a serious promise to each other and a solemn commitment to God.

I made haste to return to Ft. Bragg, because I knew they would be looking for me. When I got back to the barracks, the guys immediately began asking, "Willis, where have you been? The office has been calling for you to make arrangements for your travel to Indiana." I hurried over to the administration office where I learned there were three soldiers traveling with me. I was the highest-ranking soldier in the group, therefore, I was in charge of carrying our travel papers and meal vouchers for the trip. An army vehicle was detailed (ordered out) to take us to the train station in Fayetteville later that day. As we boarded the train, I could not help but feel reluctant to leave without Berline, but I had no choice. However, I trusted the Lord that if it was His will, I would return for her very soon.

We arrived at Camp Atterbury the next day, and it took two days for all the mustering out details to be administered. At last, I was once again a free man! The army furnished me transportation to Indianapolis. As soon as I arrived there, I went to an auto dealer to look for a car to buy. The pay for our service was $50 per month and I was able to save $900. From my military savings and mustering out pay, I purchased a 1939 Buick.

The car was in good condition. It had been driven little during the war years, mainly because of the rationing of gasoline, oil, tires and other parts necessary for operating an automobile. The car rode nicely and I enjoyed the drive home to Petersburg.

1939 Buick - this is like the one I bought on my way home after I was discharged from the army

Foremost on my mind was to make plans to return to North Carolina. When I got home, it wasn't long before I told my family I was going back to Fayetteville to marry Berline. I am sure members of my family wondered why I wanted to go so far from home to find a bride. However, they seemed supportive of my plans.

On the third day home, my plans came crashing down when I received a heartbreaking letter from Berline. She told me in the letter, among other things, that she did not love me anymore and said I should not come back to Fayetteville for her! Devastated by the shocking turn of events, I struggled to understand the words she had clearly written! What had happened? I was so disturbed that I felt like immediately making a trip to Fayetteville to find out what had gone wrong. Needless to say, I spent a sleepless night wrestling with my heartache and broken dreams. The next day I received another letter from Berline, which she had secretly written after she had sent the first one. It explained everything. She wrote that her dad had set her down and made her write the previous letter. What she had written was not true. She begged me to understand and return to get her as soon as possible because she loved me very much.

Returning for the Bride

My 1939 Buick was running fine, but it was using oil as if there had been considerable wear on the engine. Morris and I decided it would be best to overhaul the engine and install new rings before we made the long trip. We spent two days completing the task. The engine did not seem to run as smooth as it did before our repair job. However, we were confident the Buick was ready for the trip.

I left for North Carolina filled with trepidation about what to expect. Morris made the trip with me, and we arrived on July 1. We were not exactly sure what kind of situation we would be facing, but we felt we were ready for anything. Later, I learned my life could have been in danger, because her father was intensely angry and upset that I had returned. God surely sent Morris along to be a shield of protection. Berline and I later pondered, "Did the presence of Morris deflect an immediate hostile confrontation?"

Our arrival at the Barefoot home was not welcomed by everyone. Mr. Barefoot was sullen and bothered to see me around again, but at least he stayed out of our presence most of the time. He really acted kind of terrible at times. Still, I thought I should talk to him and Mrs. Barefoot about our plans. I wanted to have their blessings on our marriage, if it were possible. I was glad that I made the effort because after we talked, Mr. Barefoot's attitude changed. He realized we were determined to get married.

There were some preparations we needed to make even though it would not be an elaborate wedding. We went to town and bought a simulated diamond wedding ring for a staggering price of $14.99. Berline bought a few items of nice clothing for the occasion. I had taken along my high school graduation suit, white shirt, and a colorful tie in anticipation of the wedding.

Our big plans were to get married on July 4, so on the 3rd we went to the courthouse to get our license and to the health department for the required blood tests. Then we had to wait 24 hours for the test results before we could get married. However, a setback was in store for us...the Health Department was closed on the 4th of July holiday. Since we could not get our blood test results as planned, we had to wait until the following day to get married.

We had an interesting Fourth of July together. Morris and I went to the Barefoot home that morning to pick up Berline. We drove around, seeing the interesting sites in Fayetteville and then had lunch. During the afternoon, we rode out to the country so I could show Morris some of the farming practices in the South, which were very different from what we did in Indiana. We watched fireworks in the evening, but the best part of the day was being with my wife-to-be.

The next morning, Berline needed time to get herself ready for the big moment. Early in the afternoon, we went to pick up Berline and her parents, but Mr. Barefoot refused to go. On the afternoon of July 5, 1946, Berline Mae Barefoot became Mrs. James B. Willis. We exchanged our lifetime vows, to each other and before God, in the minister's home. It was the same minister who had married Berline's mother and dad. There was no big fanfare, fancy arrangements, reception, or celebration—just a simple sacred ceremony. Moreover, we would not have had it any other way.

After the wedding, we drove around town until the evening. There was no curfew or family restriction for Berline any longer! She belonged to me!! We could not afford a *honeymoon*, as people think of today. Our honeymoon would be our trip to Indiana.

Indiana Newlyweds

My car was giving some trouble due to the "expert" mechanic work by Morris and me. We thought we had done a good job, but our inexperience was proving otherwise. Even though it had been using a little oil, we should have left it alone and just kept an eye on the oil level. After we arrived to

Fayetteville, Morris adjusted the rod bearings and it seemed to be running all right. He thought he had the car fixed and ready for the return to Indiana.

Berline spent the evening of our wedding day packing her few belongings in preparation for the trip. We spent the night at her house and she seemed very anxious to leave the next day. At the time, I did not quite understand why she wanted to get started so soon. Not that I objected; I knew of no reason we should delay our leaving. So, early the next morning we bid farewell to Berline's family and started the 800-mile trek to Indiana.

It was a beautiful summer drive through the mountains. We stopped at Chimney Rock in North Carolina and a few other sights along the way. Most of the highways on the route to North Carolina had only two lanes with winding switchbacks through the Cumberland Mountains. Some of those roads were quite dangerous and nothing like the wide, smooth freeways that now exist for travel. Morris was a good driver and I let him drive until he got tired. We took turns driving through the night so we could get home the next day. The night driving also had the advantage of being cooler than during the hot daylight hours. Cars did not have air conditioning in those days, so we rode with the windows down to enjoy the breeze.

Berline had never seen the mountains and she was fascinated by them. Morris and I joked that the mountains grew from little hills and she believed us. We really did not know how the mountains were formed, we thought we were being cute with our joke. Later though, we learned that our *joke* was somewhat the truth, because mountains do grow and change over time. When we were about 50 miles from home, the Buick started running rough and the engine began sounding bad. We made it as far as Montgomery, Indiana, then the car would go no further. We almost made it! We were on Highway 50, with just twenty-five miles to go. We called Imel to bring his pickup truck and pull the car the rest of the way home. What a climax to our honeymoon celebration!

My family was eager to meet the beautiful *Southern Belle* that I had brought home as my wife. Berline felt a little awkward when meeting them but they soon got acquainted. The accent of her lovely voice characterized her as uniquely different from us Northerners. This endearing trait captivated my heart and has always been an attribute I adore.

I am thankful that through my service in the military God led me to the most important thing in my life, Berline. Otherwise, I might not have ever known such wonderful things can be found in the South.

Chapter 14

STARTING A NEW LIFE

Therefore shall a man leave his father and his mother,
and shall cleave unto his wife:
and they shall be one flesh. (Genesis 2:24)

A Place to Live

Imel had married a young woman from Princeton named Rachel and they already had established a home at Clark's Station by the time Berline and I got married. Imel invited Berline and I to move into a spare room of their house because we did not yet have a place to live. We accepted his offer and began talking about going back to college that fall. I decided to attend Indiana University (IU) in Bloomington, Indiana, with Imel instead of going back to Purdue.

Imel asked us if we would be interested in sharing a house with them in Bloomington, as it would save us all money. We made a trip to Bloomington to check on the possibility of housing near the college. Renting a place was so limited and expensive that it seemed impossible to find living quarters for both our families. Imel was a good thinker and accustomed to finding solutions to difficult situations. He said, "We can solve this housing accommodation problem by building a house for ourselves. I'll look for a lot or space where we can build a house. Then we'll employ our brothers to help us build it."

A suitable lot was found on South Fess Street 10 blocks south of the campus. Imel began drawing plans for a small two-story house. The downstairs would have two bedrooms, a living room, and kitchen. Additionally, the upstairs would have two rooms for the children. We began preparing the material needed for the construction.

We hauled lumber and other building supplies from

Petersburg to Imel's house where we setup a workshop in his backyard. Imel had a mold for making concrete blocks, so we started making blocks for the foundation. A batch of about 50 blocks could be made at one time, then they had to cure for two days before being removed from the mold. During those two days we would cut the lumber for the framework and prepared other items before taking them to Bloomington.

We were ready to start construction by August 1. We had about 30 days in which to build the house, because September 1 was our deadline to be finished. We wanted to be moved in and not be concerned with working on the house when classes began.

A brother-in-law to Imel, Roy Fowler, had a large truck with which we hauled the building supplies, blocks, and precut lumber to the construction site. We took food, bedding, and camping equipment with us so we could stay on the property all week. Morris and Orace Wayne willingly went along to help us in any way they could. We had the blocks laid and the frame constructed in two weeks. Weekdays we batched and slept in the back of the truck, then on Saturday afternoon, we returned to Petersburg to get more materials. Roy went along and helped the first week, but after that he just let us use his truck.

Working with my three brothers on that project was a lot of fun. It reminded me of the enjoyment we had shared when farming together a few years before. We knew the strengths and weaknesses of the each other, which enabled us to work in harmony. By the end of the third week we had the house enclosed, which included the doors and windows installed. A neighbor commented, "I never did see a house go up so fast."

In addition to Roy's truck, Morris drove his car each week which provided enough room for the workers traveling to the job site. It also provided a better vehicle for running small errands. We took turns driving the truck back to Petersburg and on the third week, it fell my lot to drive it.

As I was leaving Bloomington, the brakes quit working. That was not going to stop me from getting back to see my love. I drove the entire 80 miles home without any brakes. It was a stick shift, therefore I could use the gears to slow and stop. It was necessary to start gearing down well before a known stop and turn off the engine if there was a need to completely stop. It was tricky business to drive that way and a great relief to make the final stop in Imel's driveway.

It was a difficult time for Berline, as it was so early in our marriage. She was so far from the things she was familiar with and her people. Living in a strange environment with people she hardly knew, she was very lonely while I was gone. I felt badly having to leave Berline alone and being separated for several days each week.

Once we had the house enclosed, Imel and I felt we could do the inside work. I was glad because Berline could finally go along with us and we could camp inside the unfinished house. She was a great help in many ways by cleaning, picking up things, and getting the house ready. She also proved to be good with a hammer and helped with some of the finish work. We continued with our routine of camping in Bloomington during the week and return to Petersburg for the weekend. We would load up Roy's truck with additional materials, including furniture, and drive to Bloomington on Monday morning.

It was a race against time to have the house completely finished by September 1. We were really pushing it and we almost had it ready, but we could see we were just not going to make it. Fortunately, the university delayed the start of school by two weeks. There was an overload of student enrollment and they needed extra time for preparing the classrooms. That was a great relief! It gave us ample time for completing some unfinished areas and put the finishing touches to the house.

Finally, it was moving day. Roy's truck was again used for moving all the furniture to the new home. Rachel and their three children (Janet, Sandra, and Anita) arrived with some additional items of theirs plus our belongings. One bedroom of the house was a temporary residence for Berline and me, which was sufficient for our bedroom set and what little other items we had at that time.

It was good timing. The house was finished and we were moved in just as school enrollment began. We used as many shortcuts as possible to get the job done quickly yet provide a safe and livable home. Amazingly, the total cost of building the house was around $500...that seems impossible compared to building today.

Imel, Rachel and his daughters (L-R), Janet, Anita, Sandra
at their home in Bloomington, Indiana ca1947

Indiana University Enrollment

The front gates of the Indiana University campus

Scores of men and boys were returning to or entering college for the first time after being discharged from their military service. Over 10,000 students registered at Indiana University that year. It was the largest enrollment in the university's history and classes were overflowing. Most, if not all, of the boys who were attending school after the war were doing so under the G.I. Bill. This government program was available under the Veteran's Administration and provided for tuition payment and school supplies.

The V.A. (Veteran's Administration) also paid veterans a subsistence allowance equivalent to unemployment benefits. Having my schooling paid for and getting the subsistence income was a blessing, as I would not have been able to return to college without financial help. In addition, I received a small disability compensation as a result of being wounded during the war.

I registered for classes in math, physics and other required courses in the School of Education. Some credits were allowed for the courses I had taken at Purdue University. Imel had completed two years at Indiana University a few years earlier and he enrolled in advanced education classes that would soon qualify him for a first class teacher's license. He had been teaching on a conditional license. We were able to take a few classes together. He needed some additional math credits so we took several math courses together.

College life at IU was quite different from Purdue. Purdue seemed to have an air of country living about it; the atmosphere was one of simplicity and the students were unpretentious. IU was more formal. The campus was more crowded and I got the impression that those students were more sophisticated.

Imel and I usually left home early, walked to our classes, and stayed on campus most of the day. In the hours between classes, we went to the university library to study and do our homework. Rachel began working at the Bloomington RCA plant to help with expenses. During the day Berline was busy caring for Imel and Rachel's children, cleaning house, and preparing meals.

My new bride was always happy to see me when I came home from school. Our evenings together were wonderful hours of talking (often dreaming of our future) and laughter that confirmed my thoughts of what a lucky man I was to have found her. We spent our time dreaming of our future. Those were contented days for us even though money was scarce and I was busy with schoolwork.

Imel and I had verbally agreed to help each other build a house. After I helped him build his, in which both families would live together, then he would help Berline and me build ours the next year...if we could save enough money for it. That winter, Berline and I spent time drawing plans for our first home. We settled on a small three-room house, approximately 500 square feet. Finding a place to build was not difficult since undeveloped land was plentiful. A lot was purchased three blocks from Imel's place for $250. Our goal was to begin building during our summer break.

Vacation to North Carolina

By December, Berline had been in Indiana almost six months. It would be the first time in her life she had ever spent Christmas away from her family, and I think she was starting to feel homesick. Naturally so, because she did have a very close relationship with her mother, whom she still called *mama* in her sweet Southern accent. When it came time for Christmas break from school, Berline asked, "Could we make a trip to see my family during your two-week break?" I replied, "I would like very much to visit your folks. We have a good Chevy pickup that would easily make the trip. But I'll have to see if we have enough money."

We managed to save $30, from my Veteran's allowance, for the trip. I estimated we could make it on that amount because gas was only 20 cents per gallon. We would have no money for anything else along the way, so we needed take food to eat and we could not buy anything while in North Carolina. We also did not have the money to pay for repairs if we had a breakdown along the way. We were simply putting our trust in God to get us there and back without incident.

Our trip took twenty-four hours, with me driving all night. Even so, it was an enjoyable trip driving through the mountains, seeing the scenery and many Christmas lights along the way. By the time we pulled into Fayetteville, we had used half of our travel money. I began to worry I had miscalculated the cost of our trip and we might not have enough money to make it back home.

Berline's family was very happy to see us. Even her dad greeted me in a friendly way and gave us a hardy welcome. The formality that had once been expected by virtue of being strangers was relaxed and I was able to call Berline's parents by their first names, Melissa and Otis, instead of Mr. and Mrs. Barefoot. I think they both sensed how much I truly loved their daughter. During our short time with them, we took the opportunity to visit a few of her many relatives. Some of them made sly remarks and I suspected they were thinking, "Who is this Yankee guy that Berline has married and that has carried her away up North?" As our pleasant time together came to an end, we went to visit Berline's granddad and he gave her a sack of collards to take back to Indiana. It was the first time I had heard of collards.

The warmth and generosity of Berline's family touched me. I think my greatest surprise was the difference in how Otis treated us. He truly had a turn of heart. He knew we did not have much money, so when we were getting ready to leave, he said, "James, let's drive down to a filling station. I want to get you some gas." He filled up the gas tank of our truck not knowing how worried I was about having enough money for the return trip. My former enemy had become a friend indeed!

What a wonderful gesture from my formerly resentful father-in-law! It was a real blessing and it enabled us to buy a sandwich along the way to supplement the food Berline's mama sent with us.

Our return trip went smoothly until we reached Tennessee, where we ran into a snowstorm. However, we had to keep going because we had no money to spend on a room for the night. At one point, it got so bad the windshield wipers clogged up and I could not see the road. I had to roll down my window and stick my head out to see where I was going.

We finally got through the worst part of the storm and arrived at Mom and Pop's store by noon the next day. We stopped only briefly to say hello since we were anxious to get on home. The weather was still bad, as it was cold and sleeting. It looked like it could get worse.

North of Petersburg we started across the White River bridge when suddenly, I had no control of the pickup! I was driving on a sheet of ice! Somehow, I managed to keep the truck going down near the middle of the bridge by weaving back and forth. My progress looked like a dog's wagging tail.

We almost made it! Twenty feet before we got to the end of the bridge, the left front of the truck struck the bridge side rail. That put the truck sliding sideways down and across the bridge. Frantically, I cranked the steering wheel around, but on the ice, the truck would not respond. Then the other front corner of the truck hit the opposite side of the bridge. Both headlights had been knocked out and it was getting late in the evening.

Thankfully the truck was not too badly damaged so we continued on our way, shaken but unharmed. It was a race to get to Bloomington before nightfall. It became almost too dark to drive without lights by the time we got there. For a while afterwards, we could only drive in the daytime. Eventually, our insurance company paid enough to get the truck repaired.

The next day after we arrived home, Berline prepared the collards that were a gift from her granddad. She knew just how to cook them with the right seasoning. It was the first time in my life that I had ever liked eating any kind of greens. I have liked collards and other greens ever since that day Berline introduced me to this Southern dish. Imel and Rachel also enjoyed the collard feast! There is just no substitute for good Southern-style cooking.

Imel began looking to buy a new automobile in the spring of 1947, because his family had depended on my vehicle for transportation. There was a long waiting list to buy a new car, because automobile factories had stopped building passenger cars for five years during the war. He discovered he could get a new Hudson sooner than any other car. Within two months his name came up and he purchased a new 1947 Hudson for the extravagant price of $1,800. When he came home with his beautiful sleek automobile, he announced, "I never believed that I would ever pay that much for an automobile in my lifetime!" Before the war a new car could be bought for about half that price!

Imel's 1947 Hudson Hornet

Building our First Home

By the summer of 1947, we had saved enough money to make it possible to start building our new home. That was made easier since I was concentrating so much on my schoolwork, there was no room for distractions or time to spend money on frivolous entertainment. When school was out in July, it was time to begin construction.

Building a house was a simpler process in those days. A person could build their own house with a simple set of plans, or even without plans, if they were building on their own land out in the country. Even in the area where we were, not far from the campus, building permits were not required.

We used Imel's molds again for making the concrete blocks. Over 800 blocks were needed for the basement. They were made with sand, pea gravel, and cement mixed with just enough water to give the mixture a stiff consistency. The concrete was tamped into the molds, afterwards the molds were carefully removed leaving the block sitting on a small board, which was set aside to cure. The wet blocks had to sit in place for two days to dry and harden. We could only make 80 blocks at a time because of the limited number of boards and small storage space we had for the wet blocks.

While the blocks were curing, we were digging the basement, pouring the concrete floor, and cutting wood for the framework. Berline was eager to help. When the blocks were cured, she would remove them from the boards and stack them up while Imel and I mixed concrete for the next batch of blocks. She also helped tamp the concrete in the forms. It was hard working during those hot summer days but she never complained.

We started by digging a basement with Pop's old slip scraper. He had used it in earlier years to mine for coal. It was designed to be pulled by horses but the only horses we had were under the hood of my Chevy pickup. So, we hitched it up to the scraper, thus using mechanical horses to do the work. Imel and I took turns, one driving the truck and the other loading and dumping the scraper. One of us would drive the truck into the basement area where the loader (the person operating the scraper), would tilt the scraper, which caused the blade to lower into the ground, cutting into the dirt. The dirt was scooped up into the bed of the scraper and drug around to the back yard. At the end of a run, the scraper handles were lifted to empty the dirt and the truck pulled the scraper back around to the basement for another load. Round and round we went until we had a pit large enough and deep enough for the basement.

The whole house was planned to be 16 ft by 22 ft, but during construction we decided to add a 10 ft by 12 ft extension on the backside for a kitchen. That was an added blessing to our living space and it was all completely enclosed by the end of July. The interior finishing, plumbing, and electrical still had to be done, but we decided to take another trip to North Carolina since we would have plenty of time to finish the house before school started. We felt it was safe to leave the completion of the house until we returned, but little did we realize how wrong we were.

On that second visit, I began to learn about the real life and culture of Berline's people. Her family had moved to the country where her dad had bought a small tractor and was working a small farm. It was in the midst of their tobacco harvest. I decided to pitch-in and help even though I was completely opposed to the use of tobacco in any form. The strong smell of the tobacco dust made it difficult for me, so I was unable to do much work.

One day I drove to a mill in Clinton, 20 miles from their home, to see if I could buy flooring for our house at a bargain price. I found some three-inch-wide pine flooring for half the price that it was in Bloomington. I had the measurements of our floor space, so I was able to buy the amount we needed at a considerable savings. With our '42 Chevy pickup, we could easily haul the load.

An unpleasant surprise was awaiting us upon our return to our new home at 1101 South Dunn Street. All the new windows were gone from the house! Someone had cut the window cords on each window and taken every window. We had not put locks on the windows, but merely closed them. The theft was reported to the police but no trace of the windows was ever discovered.

It was necessary to return to Petersburg, where we had bought the windows, to purchase replacements because the lumber store there would sell them to me on credit. Imel helped me install the flooring and the new windows. We also invested in a new Montgomery Ward refrigerator and electric stove. All work was completed before the start of the fall semester. With our newly completed house and modern appliances, we felt like rich people...living a life of luxury in a new home of our very own.

James and Berline by their 1942 Chevy pickup
in front of their house

Our house at 1101 S. Dunn St. in Bloomington, Indiana. Photo was taken
in the summer of 2014. There have been a few changes made to the house,
but it still looks pretty much the way it did when we built it.

The war had provided the driving force for many new inventions and product developments such as the microwave oven, nylon, and a greater understanding of the atom. In 1947, the transistor was invented paving the way for a revolution in electronic innovation and miniaturization. In the political scene, Harry Truman was elected president in 1948. He had been serving as president since 1945 after Roosevelt died in office.

The New Store Building

We found Mom and Pop in a despondent mood when we visited during a short break from classes in the spring of 1948. Mr. Jones had been given them a 30-day notice to vacate their store business.

After Joe Hurst bought Grandma Belle's property at her estate auction in 1934, he tore down the house and built himself a modern house in the same location. He owned a grocery store a few miles away and had the whole building moved onto the property close to his new home. In 1945, a Mr. Jones bought the property including the store building.

He did not want to operate the store so he rented it to Pop and Mom. They had been managing the store for about two years and had a good business, for a small country store. Mr. Jones saw the thriving business and decided to evict them so he could take over the running of the store.

They explained their dilemma to us and Imel came to a quick solution. He told them by law Mr. Jones had to give at least 60 days to move. Imel told them not to fret, "I will deed you a one-half acre of land across the road which will be a better location than this, and we will build you a new store building. You have five ambitious sons and two dedicated son-in-laws. We can start right away and, with all of us pitching in as we have time, we can have it built in 60 days."

Mom objected, "You can't do that, and besides you all have your own things to do. We need to make plans to move back down to our home and forget about the store business."

Imel said, "You just watch us and see what we can do!"

He notified Mr. Jones of the law whereby he would have to extend the time for them to vacate the business. Then he set the wheels in motion for the construction of a new concrete block store building with living quarters on one side and gas pumps in front for automobile service.

Imel, Wesley, Morris, Orace Wayne, and I began construction on the new store. During the week, while Imel and I were in Bloomington attending classes, our brothers were hard at work to accomplish as much as possible. Imel and I spent long hours every weekend and during our spring break assisting with the work to meet the deadline for the completion of the store.

Imel (in the foreground pushing the wheelbarrow)
James (in the background - on the right)
working on the store foundation

Within six weeks we had the building completed. Then new shelves were installed and modern refrigerated display system was put in for the meat and milk. Marathon Oil Company soon had tanks and pumps installed ready for service.

Willis Grocery store my brothers and I built for Mom and Pop in 1948

Mom and Pop in front of their store

Moving day was a fun time, and the old store was left vacant for Mr. Jones. The new Willis Grocery Store was open for business. The majority of Pop and Mom's customers followed them to the new store and their business continued to grow.

Mr. Jones soon ordered supplies to stock his store and opened for business as a competitor. It was interesting and kind of sad to see him sitting out in front of his store waiting for an occasional customer, while people came and went from the Willis Store all day long. Within a few weeks he realized the mistake he had made and closed his store business.

Our family came together for a reunion that summer. Pop and Mom were living in their new store mostly, but had not completely vacated their home by the canal. It brought back memories of earlier days...for us to meet at our old homeplace where we all grew up.

Family photo taken in front of the Clark's Station homeplace 1949
Floyd and Inez (seated)
(L-R) Wesley, Orace Wayne, Lelah, Imel, Marybelle, Morris, James

Family reunion photo in front of the Willis Grocery 1949
(L-R) Back row: Gene, Gerald, Wayne, Wesley-holding Roger, Pop, Imel,
Morris-holding Sherry, James-holding Bonnie
Middle row: Rachel, Lelah-holding Brenda, Marybelle, Berline-holding
Hervey, Mom and Mary-holding twins Juanita and Jennetta, Norma-
holding Carol, Mary (Joey)-holding Danny, Orace Wayne-holding Aron
Front row: Janet, Sandra, Marsh and Anita, Floyd, Jack, Millicent

The community was still called Clark's Station at that time. But in the summer of 1958, that changed. Wesley's son, Roger, started walking along the highway from the Willis Store toward Petersburg and he watched in astonishment as the highway department put up a sign with the word...*Willisville.* Roger ran back to the store to tell Mom and Pop what was happening. Then, they saw the highway department truck go by toward the south, then Roger ran out to follow the truck and watched the sign being put up on the south end. From that point forward motorists then knew they were passing through *Willisville.* The Willis Store finally had a town where it belonged. That caused quite the stir of excitement! We were so happy to have a community named in recognition of our ancestors who originally settled in that area in the mid 1830s and the many descendants who have resided in the area.

There is nothing official about Willisville and it's really not clear who should receive the credit for getting the signs placed on the edge of the community. It has been said that a friend of Mom and Pop, Forest Braden, was instrumental in getting the state to put up the signs. That may be the closest we will ever be as to *who did it*. It is possible this will always remain a mystery, because when asking local residents this question you will get a variety of answers.

Clark's Station unofficially became Willisville in 1958

First Two Wiggley Waggley Dees

The most important event for us soon happened–the first addition to our family. It was a cold, blustery night, in the midst of a big snowstorm, and the roads were covered with snow. I called the doctor and told him to come right away. After a long wait, there was still no sign of the doctor and I began to wonder if he would arrive through the storm in time for the delivery. To our relief he finally made it, although with difficulty. That night on January 22, 1948, Bonnie Mae was born. To us, she was the most beautiful baby in the whole world. Of course we were very partial! She was a wonderful blessing from God. Bonnie came right at the time I was having first semester final exams, so I could not skip any classes. Page Morris, Rachel's dad, came over from Imel's house, where he and his wife were staying, to keep the house warm while I had to be gone. I had installed an improvised coal-fired furnace in our basement and Mr. Morris kept the fire going. In fact, he almost kept it going too well. The house was often too hot for comfort. He must have felt that he should err on the side of caution for the health of mother and baby.

A few days later our new baby became colicky, and the best way to ease her discomfort was to lay her on my shoulder while I rocked her in our rocking chair. During the night I fell asleep with her lying on my shoulder. It frightened Berline when she woke up and discovered me dozing with Bonnie sleeping on my shoulder. Fortunately, Bonnie did not fall from her comfortable place. The colic had eased and Bonnie slept by her mother through the remainder of the night.

While living in Bloomington, Berline and I established regular attendance at the Church of God. The pastor's name was Reverend Albert Bridwell. He was a wonderful man of God who made us feel like a part of the church. We were looking forward to taking our new family member to church with us. As soon as Berline felt able to get about, she dressed our new live doll up in a pretty outfit and tied a little pink ribbon to a lock of her hair. With that, we introduced the congregation to our baby and thanked the Lord for giving us this beautiful life.

All our children were beautiful and very precious to us and never knew when they started attending church. Eventually, we became friends with some of the young married couples at the church. Two of those couples closest to us were Herb (Hervey) and Mona Rose Lawrence, and Dale and Wanda Freeman. They were good Christian people. We spent much of our social life with them while living in Bloomington. We even named our first son, Hervey after Herb because the name was unique and he was a fine Christian man.

Berline's mother came to stay with us when it was time for the birth of our next child. Her help was greatly appreciated and it allowed me to concentrate on schoolwork. Hervey James, our second child, was born on February 22, 1949. Hervey was also a beautiful baby and we were proud of our little boy. He was especially alert of everything around him and I loved to hold him and explain my calculus or physics problems to him. He also was born in our little home in Bloomington. With the sudden doubling of her workload, Berline was grateful to have her mama's help in taking care of our two babies, Bonnie and Hervey.

By transferring some of my credits from Purdue University, I was able to complete the requirements to graduate with my bachelor's degree in the spring of 1949. That was a very exciting time for me. After all the studies I had been doing for the last three years, I was finally graduating from Indiana University. However, I declined the privilege of attending the graduation ceremony because of the expense and the mass of graduates. I received my Bachelor's Certificate in Education with a major in Mathematics and Physics. That qualification allowed me to apply for a high school teacher's license in those subjects.

James Willis
Indiana University
Bloomington, Indiana
Graduation - spring 1949

Chapter 15

MY EDUCATIONAL CAREER

Shew me thy ways, O Lord;
teach me thy paths. (Psalms 25:4)

Monroe County Schools

By the fall of 1949 I was ready to begin my teaching career. I had finished my Bachelor's Degree in Education and earned my Indiana Teacher's license.

The years following the end of the war were a time of transition for Americans. Factories were returning to producing consumer products after years of manufacturing war materials. In addition, folks seem eager to join in on a spending spree after the war, during which many items had been rationed or simply unavailable. Once again there were plenty of goods to buy and Americans were buying.

There was also a rapid rise in the birth rate during that era. Consequently, the sudden increase in school age children resulted in a need for grade school teachers. The need for elementary teachers became so great during that time the state began offering a special program to attract college students to become teachers. Any graduate who took nine credits during the summer would be given a two-year conditional elementary teacher's license. I had enrolled in that program and earned my Elementary Indiana Teacher's license.

The local schools in Bloomington and surrounding Monroe County were in dire need of elementary teachers. I began to look for a position in one of the local schools. By working close to Indiana University, I could continue my studies for my Master's Degree. The trustee of an elementary school at Harrodsburg, just 10 miles south of Bloomington, hired me to teach a combination of fifth and sixth grade classes.

Before school started, Berline and I decided to celebrate

my graduation by taking another trip to visit her folks in North Carolina. We had purchased a better traveling vehicle from Imel–his 1947 Hudson. He was looking to trade his vehicle for a 1949 Hudson, but found they would not allow him much for his '47. He sold it to us for the discount price of what they were giving for the trade. I had been working part time which gave us a little extra money, thus we could better afford the trip than previous ones. It was only fair to Berline that she have the opportunity to see her folks occasionally.

James Barefoot, Berline's brother, had been staying with us for about six months while he worked at some part-time jobs in Bloomington. He wanted to return home, where he expected to find better employment, so he traveled with us. Since we also had two little ones riding along, we took our time for a more relaxing trip. The Hudson was a luxury car and made it comfortable for traveling.

At that time, the Barefoot family was living near Salemburg on another small farm and they were in the middle of harvesting crops. I helped a little with the cotton picking just for the experience...it was quite an ordeal. I canceled out on the tobacco work after trying it just a little, because the strong smell was so repulsive. I did help pick some cucumbers, though. It was enough to realize that the Southern farm life was hard work, and not as interesting as it had been in Indiana. We had a chance to attend a Southern family gathering for a Sunday feast and meet some of her relatives. There was no shortage of great Southern cooked food for lunch–and plenty of Southern talk! Our return trip to Indiana was uneventful and enjoyable; we never tired of the beautiful, scenic drive, winding our way through the mountains.

When we returned to Bloomington, Mildred Barefoot (Berline's cousin) came with us to stay for a while. Mildred had been living with her father since her mother died. We thought perhaps Mildred would find in Berline a positive example and our home would be a wholesome atmosphere for her. I believe she missed her mother greatly. Mildred was starting the ninth grade that fall so we enrolled her in a local country high school, got her books, and other supplies she needed. We soon found that getting her to school was a challenge. Mildred was a late sleeper and it was difficult to get her up to make ready for school. One morning I set off a firecracker under her bed. After that, she would respond to our wake-up call a little better.

Berline (left) and Mildred in front of our house on Dunn Street

It was a busy semester for me. During the day I taught school at Harrodsburg and at night I took classes for my Master's Degree at IU. The job at Harrodsburg turned out to be a test of my inexperience. Mr. Smith, the principal of the small school, taught the seventh and eighth grades. He was very helpful in giving me some advice in conducting my large class of 39 fifth and sixth grade students. I considered it an effective initiation to be given such a large class for my very first year of teaching school.

Harrodsburg Elementary School - it has since been torn down.

During Christmas break, we took a trip to Atlanta, Georgia, to visit Berline's sister and brother-in-law, Melissa Jr. and Bill Maloy. Our trip to Georgia was pleasant and we were fascinated by the sights of beautiful mountain vistas and stately southern pines.

Bill and Melissa were gracious hosts and they took great pains to make sure we felt welcome in their home. It was the first time I had met them. They had a big garden that had given them a good harvest and when it came time for us to leave, they gave us some wonderful southern produce to bring back to Indiana. We also purchased oranges, sweet potatoes, and collards from a market place.

As the end of the school year was nearing, the Superintendent of Monroe County Schools offered me a position at a little country school (in the same school district) named Knight Ridge. The classrooms would have fewer students and he thought that would be good fit for me.

I felt my year at Harrodsburg School was reasonably

successful even with the large number of students. I learned more about teaching school that first year than I had during all three years of college! I was really anticipating the smaller classroom for the next year.

By the end of the school year, Mildred was homesick and anxious to return to North Carolina. She wanted to go back and live with her dad. Perhaps attending the country school also had something to do with her decision.

As soon as school was out, we took our usual trip to North Carolina to visit the Barefoot family and Mildred was able to return home.

It was enjoyable to make a few stops while traveling. Many of the winding mountain roads ran alongside a stream of cool clear water. At one stop we let Bonnie climb upon a large rock for her picture.

Trip to North Carolina 1950 - we traveled in our 1947 Hudson

During our stay in North Carolina, Berline felt concern for her mother, who was pregnant and nearing her time of delivery. Berline thought she could be helpful to her mother and we agreed that she and our children would stay with her. I had to get back before school started but I was not going home alone. Berline's brother, Oscar, went back to Indiana with me. He would be attending Bloomington High School.

After our arrival to Bloomington, Oscar and I began adding a room onto the house that would be a bathroom. We were not close to a city sewage line, so we needed a septic tank. The neighbor across the alley from our lot had built a house with a septic tank, so I asked him if he would give me instructions on building one. He taught me how to build a two-compartment septic system with concrete blocks, using glazed tile for intake and outlet to the field tile into the yard. He claimed that his design would outlast factory made tanks. Since then I have built at least six septic tanks for myself, relatives, and friends. I never had any report of them malfunctioning. When Berline came home, we had a completed bathroom–an important feature to our humble little home.

Knight Ridge School 1950

Teaching at the Knight Ridge School was a wonderful experience. It was a small two-room school out in the country. I had the secondary classroom, consisting of the fourth, fifth, and sixth grades. There were 24 students in my room. The primary classroom, which included the first, second, and third grades, was taught by Anna Lee Gross. She was also from Bloomington and we shared rides throughout the school year. On the snowy and icy days of winter she always asked me to drive.

Knight Ridge was in a depressed area where children often brought meager lunches, if they brought any at all. A few times in the winter I cooked a pot of beans on top of the classroom stove during the morning. (Many rural schools still had coal or wood stoves in the classrooms for heating.) Then at noon I would serve beans to all who were interested. I never had any beans left over!

In my fourth grade class was a girl who could play the piano and sing quite beautifully. Her performance was such that it seemed as if she may have had some professional training. Sometimes she would play a song the other students knew so the class could sing along with her. The kids really loved to make music.

In December Ms. Gross and I had the kids present a beautiful Christmas program to a room full of awestruck parents. My fourth grade piano girl played and the kids sang with uninhibited joy. At the end she played and sang "A Winter Wonder Land" as a solo, to the delight of everyone present. Recently, I learned from a couple of my former students at Knight Ridge, Don Bray and Connie Gross, it is probable the girl was Rosemary Rogers. The whole program was exceptionally beautiful and everyone was enthralled with the evening's entertainment.

Our Third Child

Late in the evening on February 20 of 1951, Berline started going into labor with our third baby. We called our regular doctor who was willing to make home deliveries (he had delivered Bonnie and Hervey at our home), but he was out of town. Therefore, I had to call a different doctor. I was able to get in touch with Dr. Ramsey, for whom I had been doing some part-time work. He agreed to take Berline as a patient but would not make home deliveries. I took Berline to the hospital where Patricia Lou, our second beautiful girl, was born on February 21, 1951. It was a weekday and I was still at the hospital when school started. I called Ms. Gross and asked her to open the doors between our classrooms and watch after my students until I got there.

After the delivery, I was able to hold baby Patty and make sure Berline was okay before I needed to leave for work. I really did not want to go to work that day; my mind was on Berline and our new baby.

After school, I rushed back to the hospital to find the hospital staff had parked Berline's bed in the corridor because there was a shortage of rooms. I did not like that at all and asked to check her out of the hospital. I thought she would rest better at home anyway. In addition, they would have charged us for another day's room for her to sleep in the hallway.

Berline and baby Patty got to ride home in the comfort of an ambulance. At home, Bonnie and Hervey were excited to meet their new sister. It was a little rough at first, having three little ones, but we soon adjusted and settled into a routine.

In those days a teacher's pay stopped at the end of the school term, therefore many of us needed a summer job. When school was out in the spring, after a short job search, I was hired at the General Motors Allison factory in Indianapolis where they made jet engines. I worked in the parts receiving department and was making more money than at teaching. I had been working there about a month when the manager, who thought highly of my work and attendance record, offered me full-time employment. I turned down the offer because I thought my divine calling was to be a teacher. So, when fall came and school was ready to begin, I left my good paying job at Allison's to return to the classroom.

Ellettsville School 1951

Ellettsville High School

At the end of the school term at Knight Ridge, I was offered a different job for the fall. The superintendent, Mr. Stewart, informed me that the school in Ellettsville, Indiana, needed a physics and science teacher for their junior and senior high school. The position fit right in with my qualifications and since the school was close to Bloomington, it would allow me to continue taking night classes at IU toward completing my Master's Degree in Education.

Upon meeting the principal, he told me they were just starting to offer the course in physics. He wanted me to meet with the science supply representatives to order the basic supplies for that new class. The budget for the program was somewhat limited, but it was fun. I had the freedom to select whatever materials I wanted, design the curriculum, and then teach the school's very first physics course! Only eight students signed up for the class that year. I also taught science and biology, but the physics class was my favorite.

Oscar enrolled at Ellettsville and we rode to school together each day. It was his sophomore year in school and he was in my biology class. That was my third year of taking night classes and teaching during the day, so it was again a very busy year for me. It was a very demanding time for us during 1950, 1951, and '52, as I had been working toward my Master's Degree in School Administration.

Berline was very patient with me during those three years. Through it all, she was devoted to being a good mother and an understanding wife. It would have been difficult without her strong support. Having three lovely children was a real joy, but it also added to our parenting responsibilities and financial needs. She willingly worked part-time during the evening when I could be home with the children. It helped a great deal with our bills.

At the end of that summer I had completed my goal, and was qualified for elementary and secondary principal's licenses in Indiana schools. I could finally move ahead with opportunities in the educational career that I wanted to pursue. Still, I wasn't exactly eager just yet to move up into an administrative position.

The previous few years had been trying on us because of our limited finances and my concentration on schoolwork. We were looking forward to the freedom to have more family time together and possibly afford a few extra conveniences for our small family. We knew it was likely we would have to move if such a job became available and we would miss the familiar places and friendly people of our home in Bloomington.

Even with our tight budget there were many things we had enjoyed about Bloomington and the surrounding countryside. The university offered free programs in their large music hall. There had been a free organ concert given when they installed their first pipe organ. A live production of Peter Pan had been one of their best shows.

The minister at the Church of God, was greatly

appreciated for his wonderful services and we received inspiration for our spiritual life. Attending the church functions had been our most important social life while in Bloomington. It is there we made many good friends.

In beautiful weather we could not resist a drive out through the wooded hills of Monroe County. Occasionally, Imel and his family would join us for an outing or an excursion to the beautiful Brown County State Park, some 40 miles away.

Our six years of living in Bloomington had given us many wonderful lasting memories, including building our first home and starting our family. I was content to stay with the satisfying job in Ellettsville. But the Lord has mysterious ways of leading in unexpected directions during our life journey.

Griffin School 1952

I learned of a position open for a principal in a little town called Griffin, located in southern Indiana. I met with Mr. Crawford, the Posey County superintendent, and Mr. Redmond, the township trustee, who were in charge of the school. Schools were mostly controlled by a politically appointed township trustee in those days. The rural schools of Indiana, and many other states, operated under the township trustee system for years. They were pleased with my interview and my three years experience as a teacher. I was hired for my first job as a principal at their combined elementary and high school.

We found a large farmhouse to rent in the country near Griffin. It took three trips using our little trailer to move our furniture and other items. Oscar was a big help to us in making the move. That year he enrolled as a junior in the Griffin School.

Several oil pumping stations were in the area, some of them vented the natural gas from the well into the air. I got permission from one of the well owners to tap into a natural gas line, which was right near the house. I then connected a pipe to the line and ran it to our house, giving us free gas for heating and cooking. We bought a new gas cook stove at the local hardware store to make use of the free fuel.

Even though it was not a big school, the job at Griffin was an initiation into the business and politics of school administration. Nevertheless, the job had its rewards and challenges. The school's enrollment consisted of approximately 250 students in all grades, one through twelve. I was required to teach two classes, Algebra I and Algebra II, along with being in charge of the school.

Things went smoothly for a while, then I was suddenly faced with a crisis. It might have been the first emergency decision I had to make as a principal. While it may seem trivial now, for those students involved–life hung in the balance. The incident concerned the senior class play which, just three days before the opening, became the center of controversy. One of the girls who had a major role fell ill. The question suddenly became, "Will the show go on?" I didn't see any way they could get another student prepared in three days. They would need to make arrangements for the play to be delayed. However, some teachers recommended a very bright sophomore girl who could possibly rescue the show. She was given the part and in two days she had all of her lines memorized! Opening night for the play went on as scheduled and was a big success. The young actress performed her part like a Hollywood movie star!

We made many good friends in the community of Griffin. We found a simple country church to attend, full of wonderful Christian people. The townsfolk were friendly and outgoing people, living as they were, in the midst of the farm belt. It was rich fertile farm country and the community included several small farmers with enduring devout families who loved working the land. In those days, a man could live well and provide for his family by farming a few acres of land either by himself or by hiring a hand.

One farmer, a close neighbor of ours, was not so friendly toward us. To my dismay, it even seemed as though we were destined to be enemies at one point. That particular neighbor's name was Vertis Matz. Vertis planted a field of corn on the other side of the lane, which went beside our house back to the fields. The cornfield was soon full of growing seedlings.

One day Bonnie and Hervey, with two-year-old Patty tagging along, went across the road into the field when the small corn plants were three or four inches tall. They went down two rows pulling up about 30 feet of the sprouts that had recently come up. The children were excited about making a little garden of their own and neatly arranged the tiny plants in a box. They carefully brought their box with transplanted corn seedlings back to the house where they could tend it. At age five and four they were very innocent and did not realize any harm of their actions.

I had not noticed what the kids had done until Vertis came knocking on our door one evening. He was furious! He began ranting at me about what the children had done. I told Vertis, "The children did not realize any harm was being done, but I'll pay you for the damage." He retorted, "I don't want any pay. I just want you to keep those kids out of my field!" Vertis turned and walked angrily off the porch. Although he did not swear at me, he certainly let his temper rage. The most astonishing thing to me was that Mr. Matz was well known as a good man in the community and an active deacon of the Church of Christ in town.

Jesus teaches us to *love your enemies and do good to them that hurt you.* Well, I was deeply hurt over that ordeal! So, I wondered if there might be some way I could do a good favor for Vertis. Soon after that, on a hot Sunday afternoon, the opportunity came for me to use Christ's lesson and heal the hurt in both of us.

One Sunday afternoon, Vertis was in a different field working the ground with his tractor. I had Berline make a big jar of ice tea so I could take to him. Then the kids and I took the tea and walked back to where Vertis was working. He acted so thankful and drank as if he was quite thirsty.

His hired hand would not work on Sunday, so his other

tractor was parked by the side of the field, hitched to a disc. I put the kids in a nearby wagon that was sitting under a big shade tree. Then I got on the idle tractor and helped him finish cultivating the field. When we finished, he gave us a ride in the wagon back to our house.

Vertis thanked me for the tea and for helping him disc his field. From then on we were very good neighbors and friends. Vertis never offered an apology for his previous actions, but eventually he had a chance to prove his true friendship in another way.

Bonnie, Hervey, and Patty 1953
In the picture here, they appear very innocent of any mischievousness. That is really true! They were just ambitious and adventurous. This picture was taken shortly before the corn seedling transplant incident with Vertis.

The Good Samaritan

Berline's parents and her brothers (James and two-year-old Herman) came to stay with us while we lived at Griffin. We had plenty of room in the big, two-story farmhouse we were renting and their presence was a welcome addition. While they were with us, Herman became very sick with pneumonia.

The local doctor in Poseyville gave Herman an examination but did not think there was anything serious to worry about. He prescribed some medication to give him and sent us home. Later in the night Herman went into convulsions and we took him to the emergency room at a hospital in Evansville, which was 30 miles away. That night the Lord called Herman home; he died in the emergency room soon after we arrived. The lengthy drive to the hospital deprived him of the precious time he needed for the doctors to save his life.

Otis and Melissa wanted to have Herman's body taken to North Carolina for burial but they could not afford the cost of transportation. They were blessed by an unexpected miracle. The Poseyville funeral director and his wife were going on vacation and would be traveling through North Carolina. They offered to transport Herman's body in his casket free of charge.

When Vertis Matz, my befriended enemy, heard the news of Herman's death, he transformed into a Good Samaritan! He came to me expressing his sorrow for our loss. To my surprise, he offered to let me drive his new Hudson automobile to North Carolina for the burial. He knew I had an older car and he said he worried my car might not make the trip without problems. I think he just wanted to make restitution for his former behavior and to show his appreciation for my friendship.

Otis and Melissa decided they wanted to return to North Carolina to stay, so they packed all their belongings in their car and were ready to leave the next day. They planned on living with friends until they could find a place of their own.

We had been discussing the possibility of spending an entire summer in North Carolina and decided that summer would be a good time for such an extended visit. We could be near Berline's parents and possibly be a comfort to them in their time of loss. So when school was out in the spring, we went there and stayed most of the summer.

While there, I attended the University of North Carolina in Chapel Hill. I earned the college credits I needed to qualify for an additional Administrative Certificate in Education. I also worked for the university in my spare time.

Tennyson School 1954

In order to further his political career, Mr. Redmond contrived to give my job at Griffin to a supporter of his political party. Of course I did not think it was right, but I trusted God would lead me where He would provide. We had enjoyed the country living at Griffin for two years and had made some good friends. But it was time to look for another position.

I had become close friends with the superintendent during my time at Griffin. I discussed my situation with him and realized he could not help me. I thought it ironic that the superintendent of schools had no authority over the township trustee or at least did not exercise his influence in the selection and dismissal of school staff. Mr. Crawford wrote a very nice recommendation and suggested some places that might of interest to me.

There was a school at Tennyson, which was in a different county, that needed a principal for a combination elementary and high school for one year. When I applied for the job, I was told the chairman of a political party would be coming to assume the position the following year. Even though the job was for only a year, the experience would be beneficial and I could seek other employment at a greater leisure.

Berline and I found a nice house to rent in a little settlement west of Tennyson called Degonia Springs. That was the year for Bonnie to start her first year of school. Soon after we settled in our new place, we had to get her ready for the big day. She was excited to be starting school. She would be riding to school with me instead of taking the bus.

Bonnie's teacher, Mrs. Haas, told me one day, "Bonnie is left-handed and she tends to write backwards. When she's at the chalkboard, I have to place her at the left end to keep her from writing backwards." After that, we took some extra time at home to help Bonnie with her writing. We never discouraged her from using her left hand, and eventually she began to write forwards with greater clarity. She eventually developed a very beautiful handwriting style.

Our fourth child, Alvin Eugene, was born at home in Degonia Springs on January 25, 1955. He was a healthy boy from the start, but within a few months it was clear he did not like the confinement of his crib. He would stand holding the side rail, scream, and shake the bed until someone came to his rescue. We would have to get him to sleep before placing him in his bed. As soon as he awakened, the whole house would know it. Alvin was our only child who reacted with such distress about his crib. The problem went away when we got a set of twin beds for him and Hervey.

There were some really rough characters in the Tennyson High School, and it stretched the limits of my experience to know how to handle them. Their parents were tactfully solicited to help with their problems and it made a big difference in the cooperation and behavior of those students. I had to teach three periods of math each day in addition to my principalship duties. Although I enjoyed the teaching jobs, it was a considerable distraction from my real duties of administration.

Mr. Henderson, the superintendent, came to visit the school every now and then. On one of his visits he said, "I don't know what you principals do with all your time." I wondered if he was joking, but he seemed serious and did not act like he was trying to be humorous. Maybe he did not understand the many responsibilities required of the principal's attention. I began to feel relieved that it was only a one-year contract.

Regardless of a few difficult situations, the teaching staff was very supportive and appreciated my efforts to make a better school. There were some rewarding accomplishments, including taking the senior class on a trip to Chicago. They acted very respectful throughout our whole trip and seemed to enjoy their first time on such an excursion. They had become dignified seniors ready for the graduation. My brother Orace Wayne (often called O.W.) was invited to be the speaker for their graduation ceremony.

O.W. became a Christian during his teenage years and later, an ordained minister. He was an excellent choice for a speaker, as the Lord blessed him with an eloquent way of presenting the truths of the Bible and speaking to the heart of people. I wanted the seniors to have some solid spiritual words to guide their footsteps along their continuing life journey.

We enjoyed our stay in the community and had an opportunity to visit several interesting places in southern Indiana. One trip included seeing my maternal grandparents' homeplace and their gravesite near the town of Richland City, Indiana. My great grandfather, William Parker, had operated a large general store in Hatfield, which was still standing but unoccupied.

Otwell School 1955

When I started searching for a job for the next school year, it wasn't long before I was blessed to find an opening for a principal at Otwell, Indiana. It was close to Petersburg and the community where I grew up. Otwell was politically controlled by one man, Paul Hollis, the township trustee. He informed me it might be a two-year job, and I was willing to take the job on those terms. I would be required to teach a seventh grade math class and to oversee a two-room elementary school in Algiers, which was a small community five miles away.

We moved to a vacant farmhouse near Algiers. That was the year Hervey started first grade. He and Bonnie rode the school bus to the small two-room Algiers School.

A displaced visitor came to our house while living at Algiers! A beautiful black mama cat showed up at our door, which thrilled our children. Soon thereafter, the cat had three babies and that excited the children even more. When the kittens grew to about half-size, Alvin thought it would be fun to see if one of them could swim. So he lifted the cover to the well and tossed one in.

The little kitty was swimming and crying desperately. One of the children came yelling, "A kitten in the well!" I fastened a short board onto the end of a rope and let it down to the water. The kitten crawled onto the board and I hoisted it up to dry land. Alvin and the others learned not to pitch a cat in the well. In fact, they were all firmly instructed to not remove the cover from the well—for any reason.

Most of the time the activities of the school went well, even though I had to teach the math class each day. I was lacking a secretary, as they were not hired for small township schools. So I asked a smart senior girl if she would volunteer to sit in the office when she was not in class, to act as secretary. I found that practice to work well from the success of it at my previous schools.

I implemented two successful projects at Otwell School. The first was to have a 20-minute assembly every Monday morning in the high school. Each week I would invite a different local minister to give a devotional talk to the high school students. That was in the days when we could still have prayer in our schools. The parents in the community appreciated our having Monday morning devotions. The second project took longer to get off the ground. When I first started my job at Otwell, there was no lunch program consequently the students either brought their lunch or they went home if they lived close by. That was out of step with most Indiana schools at the time.

I talked to Mr. Hollis about remodeling a section of the school basement for a kitchen and dining room. He was willing to back the project and provided the funds to hire a contractor to begin work. I contacted several kitchen supply companies to find bargains on the equipment we needed, which was paid for partly through township funds Mr. Hollis made available. I arranged a payment plan with the suppliers for the balance, which would come from the money we collected for lunches. With a subsidy of funds and free commodities from the state's school lunch program, we could serve wholesome meals for 25 cents per student.

Mr. Hollis said he knew of two local women he wanted to hire to be the kitchen cooks. We would soon learn that the women, although good cooks, were not experienced in cooking for large groups and they were not up to the task. But Mr. Hollis was responsible for hiring them and I'm sure he had reasons for his choices. Within two weeks the construction was done and everything was in place for a trial run to feed the students a good lunch.

First Day Visitors

Mr. Hollis and Mr. Buechle, the county superintendent, both came to observe, maybe thinking of it as a ribbon cutting ceremony! The episode revealed the inexperience of the cooks, who had never before worked in a school cafeteria or restaurant. The lunch period was a disaster! It took two hours for all the students to get served, and the two observers were very critical of the service they saw. I wondered if Mr. Hollis felt partially responsible for the muddle of our first lunch. I reminded our visitors that it was a trial run and a new learning experience for the cooks. I suggested they come back the next week to observe the operation again after we got it running smoother.

I made a special effort to help the cooks improve the serving arrangements and find ways to move the students through faster. A couple of responsible students were offered a free lunch to help on the serving line. By the third day we had an efficient operation that anyone could be proud of. The lunch program became a real success and was a big boost to the functioning of the school. Of course, I knew it would be successful if given the chance to operate the way I intended. By helping the cooks plan nutritious meals, being frugal with purchases, and using state donated commodities we were able to pay for the equipment in a short period of time.

Otwell was a very successful and interesting part of my school career. We had an excellent teaching staff who worked together as a team to promote an outstanding school program. We had introduced some progressive teaching methods and had a dynamic curriculum. We also leased new typewriters for the typing class. Students were respectful and the percentage of graduates was high. There were only a few students who dropped out before graduating.

A Teaching Hiatus

Toward the end of the second year of my job at Otwell, a refined lady came to my office to talk about the World Book Encyclopedia, published by Field Enterprise Educational Corporation. I was somewhat familiar with the World Book Encyclopedia and had always wished I could have a set. I just never could afford it.

The woman was Nellie Young, a district manager with the company. She told me about a sales training class that was being planned for the week after school was out. It was going to be held at the library in Washington and she invited me to attend so I could learn of the opportunities as a salesman for Field Enterprise. She also told me I could earn a free set of the World Book Encyclopedia by going to the training seminar.

Imel was principal of Baldwin Heights Elementary School in Princeton, and I knew he would be out of school in time for the class. We had always enjoyed doing things together, so I invited him to accompany me. Nellie Young was a compelling teacher and we attended all five days of the class.

The class was exceptionally motivating. Imel and I both were eager to earn a free set of the World Book Encyclopedia. I had never been a salesman and knew I had to follow the instructions I learned in the training class. I was soon making more at sales work than I had made teaching. Both Imel and I earned a set of the World Book. I was offered a full-time job with Field Enterprise Educational Corporation (publisher of the World Book Encyclopedia), as an area manager and school consultant covering a few local counties. The company guaranteed me a higher wage than I had made as principal of Otwell School. My brother, Morris, joined us in the World Book business sometime later. He became a district manager and went on to become the corporation's top World Book salesman *in the world*. No other representative or manager has ever sold as many World Books as Morris Willis.

A Special Arrival

After school was out for the summer, I took a job as a substitute delivery driver for the Meadow Gold Milk Company in Jasper, Indiana. We continued to live at Algiers, as we had an enjoyable country home. A big barn was on the premises of our home but the children were young and we did not permit them to go there alone. They were especially excited when I would take them to see where the animals had lived and let them play in the loft. We needed to relocate for my job with Field Enterprises, but decided to postpone the move since Berline was expecting our fifth baby and a move would be difficult.

A minister at our church, Rev. Curtis, talked of his daughter, DeAnn, often and we became fond of the name. We decided to use that name for our baby, if we had a girl. When it was time for delivery, Berline was taken to the hospital in Washington, Indiana. She wanted a girl and she got the desire of her heart on July 10, 1957. We named our beautiful new baby Barbara DeAnn. During the time Berline was in the hospital, the other children were loaned out to various relatives while I was at work.

The hospital did not permit visitors during the babies' feeding time because visitors were not to have contact with the newborns. I had the privilege of holding each of our other babies soon after they came into this world. Even when Patty was born at Bloomington Hospital, the nurse brought her out to see me soon after she was delivered. I did not want to be deprived of that joy. I learned when the feeding time was and I violated the hospital rules by sneaking in the back way to get to Berline's room when my baby was there. Then, for the first time, I held tiny Barbara DeAnn in my hands. She looked just like the others and was equally as beautiful. Berline was afraid a nurse might come and find me, but what could they do? To avoid any problem, I soon left out the way I had entered and no one else knew I had been there.

Mother and baby came home in a few days. The other children had been anxiously waiting. I gathered up the children and brought them home to introduce them to the delight of seeing their new little sister, Barbara DeAnn (we called her DeAnn).

Chapter 16

WALKING A NEW PATH

But the path of the just is as the shining light, that shineth more and more unto the perfect day. (Proverbs 4:18)

Brief Stay at Oakland City

By the end of summer, we found a reasonable place to live in Oakland City so I could be in a location central to the district I had been assigned as a sales manager with Field Enterprise Educational Corporation. We moved there before school started so we could enroll Bonnie, Hervey, and Patty in the Oakland City Elementary School. It was quite a comfortable and convenient place for us to live. Oakland City was a small college town about 15 miles south of my original homeplace in Clark's Station.

We had a friendly next-door neighbor, his name was Willie Young, and he was exceptionally cordial to our family which made us feel welcome to the neighborhood. He had a truck with a big tank on it, which he used for hauling water. Little did we know that we would be calling on him to bring us water in the future.

A Little Tot's Journey

The elementary school was about a half mile from our house and the children usually walked to school. On school mornings, Alvin would stand at the street corner and watch them till they were out of sight. When it was time for them to come home, he would run to the corner and wait for them. He missed his playmates.

One day, soon after the children left for school, Berline got a call. The school secretary called and told her, "We have a little boy here that has come to school to be with his brother and sisters. He says his name is Alvin."

Berline hurried to the school to get Alvin. He was only three and one-half years old at the time. After having gone with us to the school, he had remembered the way there. It was almost a direct 10 blocks south of our house. Alvin had to cross some streets and a busy highway by himself to get there. He received some stern instructions and a talk about the danger of his trip after which he never tried that again.

Headquarters at Whip-Poor-Will Hill

Imel came to our home one evening and discussed a proposition with Berline and me. He and Rachel owned a house and 40 acres near Union, a small community in southwest Pike County. It was situated way back in the remote and wooded area on a gravel road. The house was lovely and well cared for, with some fruit trees and big maple shade trees all around. It sat on a 10-acre strip of land on the north side of the gravel road. The remaining 30 acres to the south of the road was where Imel kept some horses...20 acres of which was in Pike County and 10 acres was in Gibson County. Imel was living elsewhere and had no further use for the property. He offered to sell the property to us on contract until we could arrange our own financing. Berline and I loved the place and agreed to buy it. I believe that was the best purchase we ever made.

Imel brought his pickup to help us move to our new home on Thanksgiving weekend in 1958. The house had four rooms and a bathroom downstairs, with the attic space having been converted into three bedrooms. It was well built with a front porch and plenty of space for our family. Rachel's grandparents had built the house in the early 1900s. Her parents inherited the place and lived there several years before Imel and Rachel acquired it. Our family was blessed with the opportunity to have it as our home.

Photo taken ca1927 when the house was owned by the Harveys

James and Berline getting in the old buggy
taken in the winter of 1959-1960

We inherited four riding horses as part of our purchase. Their names were Molly, Ginger, Starlight, and Buttons. The children were too small to ride by themselves, but the horses captivated their attention and interest in animals. Buttons was a very gentle old horse and we could let the older kids ride him alone. He would walk slow and obeyed the pull of the reins.

Half of the 40 acres was covered with trees, so we called it a tree farm. The canopy of trees over the road, leading to our place, made for a beautiful drive. In the summertime, it was like driving through a tree-lined tunnel. Often it was called the Old Lonesome Road.

Originally, when the Harveys built the house, it was heated with a cast iron stove on the main floor that burned wood and coal. Later, a coal-fired furnace was installed in the basement. When Imel and Rachel lived there, they used that furnace, which sat on the dirt floor with a bin of coal next to it.

We used the coal furnace at first but it was dirty, hard to operate, and not something we wanted to contend with. So, we tore out the old coal furnace, carried out a lot of dirt, leveled up the ground, and poured a concrete floor in the basement. I found a used gas furnace to install in the basement to heat the house. We had the gas company install a large propane gas tank close to one side of the house that fueled the furnace and kitchen stove.

We enrolled Bonnie, Hervey and Patty in the old school at Union, the small town that was about two miles from the farm. Warner Ammerman, my first grade teacher at Willis School, was teaching at Union. He was Bonnie and Hervey's teacher. In 1961 Alvin became a proud student at Union School. He had a great teacher, Mrs. Doris Harvey, who had been Patty's teacher the previous year. He came home telling us, "Mrs. Harvey is a good teacher. She gave us a treat today and she let me sit right up next to her desk!" We wondered if Mrs. Harvey had a good reason to move him up near her desk! She was a wonderful teacher and all the children loved her.

DeAnn started first grade at Union School in 1963 and she also had Mrs. Harvey as her teacher. Like all of our children, she was excited to be going to school. Mrs. Harvey was generous and rewarded students, who received an A in all their subjects for the entire school year, with a silver dollar.

Doris Harvey's husband was a distant relative of the Harveys who had built the house where we lived.

It was coming winter when we moved to the farm. Little could be done around the place except feed and care for the horses. We enjoyed our new location far out in the country, even on the coldest winter days. Snowstorms were a serious inconvenience to our travels, but it made our place like a winter wonderland. The kids and I took advantage of those times to play in the snow. With snow tires and chains, the snow did not usually delay us much in our travels.

On one occasion that we had such a storm, Berline was stranded within a mile of the nursing home where she worked and she had to get the car towed into Petersburg. She spent two nights at the nursing home before the snowplows made it possible for her to get home. The children and I were stranded at the farm, even without electricity part of the time. We played games and lived in the kitchen, which was the only place where we had heat in the house. We bundled up and had fun playing in the snowdrifts, but was nice to get to the kitchen to warm up and have hot chocolate with some snacks.

James with Patty, Alvin, and DeAnn - Hervey pulling the sled

Berline with all our children

During our first winter on the farm, we made plans for improvements we wanted to make when the weather got better. Some fences needed fixing and our horses needed a better shelter. Early in the spring we put to use a large garden spot that was behind the house.

We also wanted to make some changes to the house. Originally it had only four rooms on the main floor. The attic had been remodeled and we used the space for bedrooms. One of the first modifications we made was to remove a wall on the main floor that separated the living room and dining room. That gave a more spacious appearance to our living space.

Another project that needed to be done was to clean out the cistern. We did not have a well, so our water supply came from the rain that collected in a cistern beside the house. When our water ran low, we had more hauled in. Willie Young, the neighbor of ours when we lived in Oakland City, made the delivery to us. Periodically the cistern had to be cleaned out and sanitized.

The school at Union was a long two-mile walk for the

children, so we transported them in the car most of the time. There was no school bus route for those who lived out in the country. The next school year, the Clay Township Trustee decided to hire someone to drive a route through the countryside so the children could more easily get to and from school. Berline went to the Union schoolhouse to bid on the job. She was the lowest bidder and got the contract.

For two years Berline used our car to serve as the Union "school bus". She drove one direction, for our children and others along the way, to the school. Then she went out another road west of Union, for students in that direction. She had to make those two trips morning and afternoon.

Our family ca1960
(L-R) Front row: DeAnn, Berline, James, Alvin
Back row: Patty, Bonnie, Hervey

Berline in front of our old Whip-Poor-Will Hill home

Bonnie in high school band uniform

(L-R) Hervey, Alvin, DeAnn, Patty - all dressed for church

Alvin and DeAnn - beside a redbud tree in our front yard

Barefoot visitors

After school was out in the spring, Berline took the bus to her parents' home in North Carolina. Her dad was seriously ill and she wanted to be there to help with things as she could. After he recovered, Otis and Melissa decided to drive Berline home and stay with us for a while.

However, Melissa would not come without her chickens, which there were about two dozen. Clever as always, Otis fixed a wire netting over the bed of his pickup so they could bring them. In that manner, they brought Berline and chickens to Whip-Poor-Will Hill. Berline said it was quite embarrassing to her when they pulled into a gas station early in the morning and the rooster started crowing.

When they got to the farm, we fixed the chickens a small pen next to a shed. That gave them a little range and a roost. They could not run free because they would soon become food for a fox. They were an added attraction to our farm and we welcomed the supply of fresh eggs.

We were in need of a barn and Berline's dad was enthusiastic about helping me build one. A good location was across the road, near the Harvey's original log home, where a barn had stood in earlier days.

We discussed what kind of plans I had for the barn and what features I wanted for it. Cost was a consideration and we talked about ways to economize in the construction. There was no requirement for a building permit or for wildlife impact studies; we didn't even have blueprints. We did have some drawings of what we wanted the barn to look like and with that we were ready to build.

We designed the barn with a symmetrical roof line, tall in the middle for a large hayloft and two low wings, one on each side for livestock. The west side was enclosed with stalls for the horses and a crib for storing corn. On the other side, the roof extended at the same shallow pitch but was open. Inside, the middle of the ground floor was open for storing equipment and had access to mangers on both sides. Stairs had been built on the east side to make it easier to access the loft. Although we had only horses at the time, I thought someday it would be nice to have some cows. The cows would use the open side shelter for feeding.

Otis used his truck to get the materials we needed. He did most of the work, with me helping as often as I could take time from my World Book business. Of course, the kids wanted to help as much as they could, too.

The barn was completed before cold weather and the horses had a dry shelter. Soon we had corn in the crib and hay in the loft from our own fields.

The barn still stands yet today, although there is another owner of the property. It is a strong reminder of Otis' token of love; the gift of his time and labor.

Following is an article from the local newspaper about our Christmas barn party in 1963:

Unique Christmas Party Held In Barn

The annual Christmas party of the Floyd and Inez Willis family took a unique twist this year. The party, which includes the children, grandchildren and great grandchildren of Mr. and Mrs. Willis, was held this year in a newly constructed barn at the home of James Willis near Union.

The new barn, with a big hayloft, was completed just in time for the occasion. The electrical wiring was the last part of the barn completed and it was turned on at 5 p. m. Saturday, just before the party began at 8 p. m.

The barnloft was decorated with bales of hay around the wall for seats, a stove to make it cozy and a large Christmas tree decorated with lights, trimmings and piles of gifts for the members of the large family.

Invocation by the Rev. Orace Wayne Willis began the party. Refreshments were then served in a "help-yourself" style, which included sandwiches, pie, coffee and potato chips. The special treat was a large, old fashioned hickory nut cake baked by Wesley Willis.

During the evening, some of the children repeated Christmas verses, under the direction of Lelah Pancake. Rev. Willis gave a short talk about Christmas and what it means to people in America. A Christmas film portraying some artists' ideas of the birth and life of Jesus was shown. Marybelle Gray and Wesley Willis distributed the presents to all present.

Those who attended the party were as follows: Floyd and Inez Willis with their children and spouses and their children's children; Imel and Rachel Willis, Bob and Janet Ray Breidenbaugh, Sandra Bell and David, Anita and

(Continued to Page 4)

Barn Party

'Continued from Front Page'

Floyd Imel; Gerald and Marybelle Gray and Denny; Wesley and Mary Willis; Roger, Juanita, Jeanita and Timmy; James and Berline Willis, Bonnie, Harvey, Patty, Alvin and DeAnn; Wayne and Lelah Pancake, Jackie and Carroll, Floyd, Brenda, Terry and Ronnie; Morris and Mary Fay Willis, Sherry, Danny, David, Randy and Carla; Orace Wayne and Norma Willis, Millie, Marsha, Aaron, Carroll, Steve and Debra; and Arba Willis. Also relatives of Berline Willis attending were: Otis and Malissia Barefoot of North Carolina; Bill and Malissia Maloy, Cathy, Billy and Bobby of Atlanta, Georgia; and Oscar and Carolyn Barefoot, Mike and Lissa of Texas.

300

The Barn Christmas Party

That winter of 1963 we put the new barn into use for a special event. Berline and I decided to host the annual Willis Christmas party. Mom and Pop had a tradition of inviting their seven children with their families to a Christmas party each year. One or two of us would always help with the arrangements. I sent word to Mom and Pop and to rest of the family telling them I wanted to have the party at Whip-Poor-Will Hill that year. They loved the idea of having the gathering in our new barn.

There was much excitement as we began fixing up the barn. First on Berline's mind was our guests' comfort. It was winter and likely to be a cold party without heat. Electricity had been run to the barn but something had to be done to make the loft warm. I bought a used wood stove, set it up in the loft, and arranged the stove pipe to exit a hole I had cut in one of the loft doors.

Bales of hay were arranged around the loft for seats. A plywood table was set up in the middle for food and presents. Christmas lights were strung around the inside giving things a bright and cheerful look.

Then the Lord blessed us with enough snow on the day before the party to make the countryside pretty as a picture. The long snow-covered road through the woods to the farm was quite enchanting.

Otis and Melissa were there to enjoy the party and he received many compliments on his fine work on the barn. Melissa Jr., Berline's sister, and her family came from Atlanta, Georgia. Berline's brother, Oscar, and his wife were also there.

All of my brothers and sisters came to the party with their families. Over 50 people gathered in the hayloft of our barn for fun and a feast on the food everyone brought. The animals were having their feast of alfalfa hay in the stalls below us. They did not seem to mind us celebrating in the loft above them. Maybe it gave them the Christmas Spirit! The smell of hay and the rustic environment enhanced the festivities as we sang Christmas songs and exchanged gifts.

In those days, our custom was for everyone to bring a present and names would be drawn at the party for a gift exchange. Among my brothers and sisters, we had some extra fun by giving unusual gifts to each other; it might be a slingshot, or some other novelty. My sister, Marybelle, was a sales representative for Stanley Home Products. She always gave something from her Stanley products to all families. It was often a contest to see who could come up with the most outrageous gift.

Orace Wayne gave a Christmas devotional and a prayer for God's blessing as we parted. To those who were at that party, it remains the most memorable of the Willis annual Christmas gatherings. From time to time a recollection about our *barn party* come up among family members and it still invokes fond memories.

Flame

I came across an American Saddlebred horse farm near Orleans, Indiana. Those beautiful horses were too expensive for me, but the owner told me he had a two-year-old unbroken stallion he would sell for $100. That was still a lot of money, maybe about the same as $1000 today.

I bought the stallion and returned a few days later with my trailer, with racks on it, to take him to Whip-Poor-Will Hill. When we got home and opened the rack for him to unload, he jumped out of the trailer and took off. He was so wild we could not get close to him.

Hervey and I built a corral in which to corner him and on our first attempt to get a rope around his neck, he climbed over the fence rails. Fortunately he did not hurt himself. We built the corral higher and that time we had him trapped. He trembled and struggled, the whites of his eyes showed his fear as we put the rope around his neck. We tied the rope to a heavy wheel so he could not run fast, then turned him loose. He was still too wild to catch. After he drug the wheel around a few days, he started getting a little brave to let us get closer.

One day I found him in a fence corner, hemmed in by the tractor, where he could not get away. I talked to him gently and attempted to pet him. But he was not ready to be touched and, in his effort to escape, he threw himself over the fence landing on his side. The wheel, however, did not go over with him. As he struggled to move, the rope became entangled with the fence. The more he struggled, the tighter the rope became around his neck. With the rope strangling him, he soon lay lifelessly on the ground.

I jumped over the fence and frantically worked at the knot in the rope, trying to free it before he choked to death. I barely got it loose in time. I rubbed his head and neck looking for any injuries while talking soothingly to him. Flame, as we had named him, lay on his side a minute then jumped to his feet and staggered away some distance. He stood still for a few minutes, then ran into the field.

After that episode, any time we could get him in the barn or into a close place and lay a rope on his neck, he would stand perfectly still. It seemed ironic that after having been strangled with a rope, he would finally let us put a rope on him. By petting him and making friends, we were eventually able to get a bridle on him. He flinched and resisted the bits at first, but he soon took them.

One day I had a bridle on him and told Hervey to get on while I held the reins. Flame flinched a little but accepted the rider without much resistance. After leading him around a little, I handed the reins to Hervey and Flame was ready to go. Flame was a beautiful but spirited horse. He loved to run. Few people could handle him but Hervey. I rode him a few times but did not let him have the reins as he liked. He never offered to kick, bite, buck, or hurt anyone. I think Flame grew fond of us and realized we were his friends.

Two of our horses – Flame and Ginger
To the right, it is possible to see where Flame broke the fence

Ginger had a filly we named Stardust. Within three years, Stardust grew to be a fine young riding horse and she was bred to Flame. When it was time for her to give birth, we were away from home. Aaron, Orace Wayne's son, happened to be hunting on the farm and found the newborn stuck in a groundhog hole. Stardust stayed close by, her concern for her baby was evident as she watched Aaron closely. Aaron got the baby out of the hole and carried it to the house. It was weak and could not stand. When we arrived home, we had to hold the head of the colt to its mama to nurse. After it gained some strength, I took it to a vet in Princeton to give it an examination and patch up its injuries.

We had a dog, named Trixie, that was a good watchdog. One day Trixie kept running around at the barn and barking as if something was wrong. When we investigated, we found the corn crib door open and the horses inside. Evidently, Flame dominated the situation, as he was the only one that got sick from eating too much corn and he foundered.

The veterinarian came out and helped me get some kind of oil down Flame's throat. He said we had to keep him on his feet and walking for at least 12 hours. If not, he might lay down and then he would die. The vet said Flame's feet would probably swell, but the walking would help keep the swelling down. We took turns walking him through the night and all the next day. Flame recovered from his great adventure in the corn crib, but his feet did swell and he was never quite the same. If it had not been for our faithful little dog Trixie, we might have lost Flame as well as some of the other horses.

Keeping horses on the farm was rewarding yet full of hard work and surprises. Hervey was getting to the age that he needed the responsibility and experience of caring for our horses. It was necessary too, as I could not be there every day to see to their needs due to my World Book business.

Animal Fun

There was the time we attempted to make pets out of some baby skunks. The kids and I were on our way to church one evening, when we saw a mama skunk crossing the highway with a string of young ones behind her. We thought they were cut and a spur of the moment decision was made to catch some of them. I figured a veterinarian could fix them so they could not spray and they would be unique pets. It was easy to corner them because they are not fast runners...they don't need to be, as one spray is enough to deter their attackers! Hervey managed to grab three or four of the babies and put them in a burlap bag, which I had in the trunk of the car. Even though they were tiny, there is no such thing as a little skunk odor. Hervey held the bag of skunks out the car window as we drove off, but there was no escaping the stench. The skunks were taken to a vet who removed their scent glands, and then they smelled better. They did make cute little pets.

Alvin was especially fond of cats. We had a yellow cat and one day he decided to paint it green. He just got a stripe painted down its back before it got away. The cats were pretty tolerant of his attentions and would sometimes sit in his wagon as he pulled them around.

Alvin with his cats

Our farm also offered some interesting experiences with cattle. One summer, Cleo Collins wanted to sell his cows because he did not have enough pasture. Our fields had an abundance of grass so I bought his 12 cows. In the fall, when the cows could longer graze, my supply of hay was not sufficient and I would need to buy some feed. Therefore, I sold them to a farmer who was into the cattle business as well as a large grain farmer.

Some years later, while temporarily living elsewhere, I decided it would be good to have some livestock on the farm again. I first bought two black Angus cows and they were both due to have calves soon. One time I went to spend the weekend at the farm and there were two baby calves in the pasture. I returned the next week just to make sure they were still doing fine and then there were three little Angus babies in the pasture! When I saw two of the calves following after one of the cows, then I realized she had given birth to twins.

Later I bought a few Charolais cows and one of those cows also had twin babies. It is very rare that cows give birth to twins. I felt very blessed to have two sets of twin calves in my herd. Among the small herd was one Charolais bull that was very gentle and like to be petted. We could go to him and he never showed any signs of aggression.

We had rented the upstairs portion of the house to Tom Hensler and his family. Tom liked to be around the cattle and look after them when we were away. He mistakenly taught the young bull to be playful by getting him to butt his head at Tom.

Tom meant no harm and did not realize the seriousness resulting from that because thereafter the bull always wanted to play when we approach him. The bull could playfully overpower you and create a difficult situation. One day Berline was stooped over pulling some weeds. The bull came up behind her and almost lifted her off the ground. Then he just stood looking at her innocently. He was not mean, rather he had just learned a mischievous game.

Because of our interest and work in different directions, regretfully, it was necessary to part with the cows. They had been a very big part of the interesting experiences of living and working at Whip-Poor-Will Hill.

James and our German Shepherd, Joe
Joe was the only dog that took a real liking to me. Every time
I stepped out of the house, Joe was right there with me.

Chapter 17

SOME AUDACIOUS DECISIONS

My son, despise not the chastening of the Lord;
neither be weary of His correction: (Proverbs 3:11)

Seattle World's Fair

While our children were young, we took many family trips together. We tried to make a visit to see the Barefoots in North Carolina at least once a year. We also made excursions to see the Maloys in Georgia. In the summer of 1962, we learned the World's fair was being held in Seattle, Washington. We decided that would make an educational and fun summer vacation. I had just bought a Rambler station wagon and it was in excellent condition for the trip. We began making plans, studying maps, and determining the best routes to take.

In those days, the Interstate Highway System was incomplete and existed only in fragments. Many miles were just two-lane highways with intermittent stretches of four-lane interstate expressways. There were also many detours due to road construction, so finding a scenic route and one where we could make good time was a challenge. We also looked for places where it seemed possible to camp overnight so we could save on expenses.

To round out the passenger list we invited my nephew, Roger Willis, to take the trip with us. He was near the age of Bonnie and Hervey and was a welcome companion to have along. His good humor and cheerful disposition would be enjoyed by all during the long drive.

It was a little crowded for the eight of us in the wagon even with packing most of our luggage on the roof rack. That station wagon had a rear-facing third row seat and could hold two or three people. It was before the days of seat belt laws and kids pretty much rode anywhere inside (or outside) the car, standing, sitting, or hanging out the windows! We practiced common sense safety rules regardless. No one was allowed to hang out the window.

We began our journey shortly after school was out. By the first night of our trip, we had reached Missouri. There we found a park where we rolled out our sleeping bags–at least those who wanted to sleep out under the stars. The ones who didn't (mostly Berline and the girls) slept in the car. An army cot was among the fantastic bargains I had bought at Camp Atterbury surplus store and I had taken it along just for that purpose. I unfolded it anticipating a restful night in the fresh air. It was a fine bed for Alvin and me. Any others who slept outside used a sleeping bag on a grassy area.

James and Alvin, Hervey on the right

The next day we reached Yellowstone National Park where we got a cabin. DeAnn had become sick and we were greatly concerned. We did not want to continue traveling if it was going to make her, or everyone else, feel miserable. We spent two nights in Yellowstone until DeAnn was feeling better and we were able to continue on our way.

Even though there were warnings about not feeding the bears, people still wanted to be friendly so the bears were looking for a handout.

We were in mountainous country as we left Yellowstone Park. The Rambler was taxed with a heavy load going up those steep grades and the motor began to overheat. The car was like new so it was difficult to understand why it was overheating. There were no repair shops around to look at it, so I kept driving hoping the problem would not worsen. After we got out of the mountains the problem seemed to let up, thus I decided to push on. That evening, as we arrived in Missoula, Montana, I was beginning to worry about the car again. The overheating problem continued, and we still had the Rocky Mountains to go through. Something had to be done to prevent the motor from becoming permanently damaged.

I found a service station where the mechanic discovered the wrong type of water pump had been installed. He was willing to exchange it yet that night. We found a place to stay for the night while he made the repairs. He installed a heavy-duty water pump, which was the correct one for our car. It solved the mystery and we never had a problem with the car overheating again for as long as we owned it.

We were soon on our way again with the Rambler

churning merrily along. From there we traveled on Highway 90 to Huson, where we turned off on Nine Mile Camp Road. I had been hoping to have enough time to drive up to the camp. The kids were anxious to see the place where I had spent my summer with the forest service 20 years earlier.

The winding road up to the campsite seemed like thirty miles instead of *nine*. I had no idea if the camp was still even there. I figured the beautiful mountain scenery was worth the drive even if we did not find the camp. Along the way, we saw the ranger station where the mules had been broken and trained to work. Although there were no mules around anymore, the ranger station was still in use.

Eventually we reached the campsite where we found an archway with a large sign overhead that read *Nine Mile Camp*. That structure was built by the CCC workers who used the camp in the 1930s, before it became a camp for the Smoke Jumpers and other forest fire fighters. Everyone got out to explore the area.

All the buildings were gone, but we found some concrete steps where they had been. I showed everyone where my barracks stood, the place where we made a swimming hole, and the kitchen location. The post that the bear had climbed was still in place and the surrounding forest resembled a beautiful park. It brought back memories of the bustle of activity that went on at the camp when I worked there. It was an intriguing restful stop and we were soon on our way back down the mountain.

We traveled the remainder of the day and all night to make up for the various delays. It also saved us a little money; as we had not anticipated having the car repair cost. The next day we traveled through the rugged snow-capped mountains in Washington and reached Seattle in the late evening. We found the housing agency at the World's Fair Information Office and they gave us assistance in locating a small apartment to rent for the few days we would be visiting there.

The fair had so many fascinating and enticing things to see and do. We decided to let the older kids pair up and explore on their own, with instructions that we would all meet at a specific spot at a certain time. Each child was given an equal amount of money to spend on whatever they wanted. Patty lost her money and she was very upset about it. We gave her a little more to replace what she lost. Even though we did not have much money, we did buy a few souvenirs and some raincoats. It rained almost the whole time we were there.

Things were expensive, so we looked through the pavilions, browsed the exhibits, and took in the activities that were free. We found a great variety of appetizing and unusual foods, the best of which was waffles topped with strawberries and whipped cream!

The exhibition was full of amazing attractions and wonderful new inventions. It was a memorable event for each of us. We all have priceless memories of the wonders that we saw, such as: the giant *Bubble Elevator,* Futurama, the Monorail, and the Musical Fountain that was operated by an organist.

The most popular attraction was the tall graceful Space Needle with its rotating restaurant and observation deck at the top, which resembled a flying saucer. Long lines of people waited to ride the glass elevators that glided up the center support, giving passengers a breathtaking view of Seattle, Puget Sound, and Mount Rainier.

The Musical Fountain was a marvel of engineering and art combined. An organ was connected to the fountain so when the organist played, the fountain would literally dance to the music. It was synchronized with the sound, changing the shape of the sprays in beautiful and intricate patterns. At night it was even more spectacular as colored lights, built into the base of the fountain, flooded the display...illuminating the water droplets so they appeared as millions of glittering diamonds.

We spent two enthralling days at the World's Fair. It was filled with wonders beyond what we had ever experienced. Berline and I appreciated the exhibits of the various nations, but the children were more interested in the rides and moving attractions.

Patty

Before we left Washington, we took a ferry ride to visit Rachel's brother, John Morris, who lived on Vashon Island across Puget Sound. He was quite an inventor who liked to tinker and experiment with electronic gadgets including model trains (which he collected). He had one entire room in his house filled with a model train layout that was intricate in detail and fascinating to watch.

In his garage he had even built a robot, although simple in design compared with today's standards, was a marvel in 1962. That was during the early days of electronics, when robots were fabrications of science fiction novels. John asked us if we would like to see his robot and our suspense heightened when he took us into his workshop, closed the doors and warned us he would be turning off the lights. He carefully explained that we should not try to get in the robot's way or try to touch it.

The room went dark, and suddenly–as a hidden switch was thrown–the robot came alive! It moved in fits, jerking and shaking. It made a terrific noise, flashing its lights while sparks went flying. It rolled around on wheels making a terrible racket, apparently just to scare people. To that extent, it was successful as it caused the children to panic and want to run. It was an amazing sight to see and even a little frightening to the younger children. To see an actual operating robot was practically unheard of.

John also took us to visit the Battleship Missouri, which was anchored in the harbor at the Bremerton Naval Shipyards. It was upon the quarterdeck of this mighty battleship where the unconditional surrender terms were signed by Japan at the end of WWII.

We spent four exciting days in Seattle before starting back home. The return trip was very tiring but we found many historical and entertaining sights along the route. When we arrived at the border of Colorado and Kansas, we stopped at the archeological site of the Dinosaur Monument. At the visitor's center, we went up into a glass observation building to see where they were excavating and digging for bones of dinosaurs. Some skeletons of prehistoric animals were on display along with information booths.

We found a campground nearby where we could stay the night. That evening, Berline tried to cook supper with our crude facilities. The wind was brisk and blowing the sand, which made cooking a challenge. She fixed hamburgers and hot dogs, which due to the weather were well mixed with sand. They tasted good in spite of a little grit.

After supper, the camp director invited us to an area where he showed a film and talked about the animals and plant life in the surrounding desert. Berline and the girls slept in the car that night. Roger and Hervey used their sleeping bags and I got my favorite cot down off the car. During the night, the cot developed a big rip, dumping Alvin and me onto the ground. I put him in the car, rolled myself up in the blanket and slept on the ground. Next morning we got up a little stiff from the cramped and hard sleeping places but refreshed enough to be on our way home. We lightened our load a little by disposing of the cot.

On the last night of our journey, I got very sleepy but it was not necessary to stop for a nap. I let Bonnie sit close beside me to drive. By using her foot on the gas while she drove, it allowed me to close my eyes and rest for a few hours. She could drive good at age 14, but had no license. I cautioned her to wake me if there seemed to be any uncertain situation.

When morning came, we stopped at a restaurant and had breakfast. Bonnie's driving gave me enough relief that I could take us the rest of the way home. Our overloaded station wagon finally turned down the road to Whip-Poor-Will Hill and we reached *home sweet home*. It had been a wonderful and memorable trip.

It was time to come down "out of cloud nine" and settle back into our routine of living. Berline's driving contract for Union School bus route had ended. She wanted to find another job and found out about a Nurse's Aid position that appealed to her. She went to work at the nursing home in Petersburg, often having to work nights. It was a relief to our growing financial needs but it was difficult working hours for her.

The Rambling Fiasco

It was in 1963 that Imel, Morris, Orace Wayne, and I listened to a Rambler Automobile representative who gave a presentation for a Rambler Dealership in Princeton. We were convinced the business looked attractive and discussed how we could join together in the venture. We agreed to a four-way partnership to start a dealership and garage. The Rambler representative sat down with us to explain the rules and requirements of the Rambler dealer's contract.

We called the business *Willis Bros. Rambler* and we divided our responsibilities somewhat arbitrarily. Imel and I would be General Managers, Orace Wayne the Sales Manager, and Morris the Repair Shop Manager. We had the utmost trust in each other and knew each one of us could attend to any part of the business.

317

Each of us made a capital investment of $1,500 to begin the business. From the start, we were selling several cars and had a nice profit from the mechanical work in the garage. We hired a sales person, two mechanics, and a secretary. Orace Wayne's son-in-law, Bill Thompson, was excellent at auto paint and body repair so we hired him to work in the body shop.

As the days went by, the business required more expenses than we had anticipated and our sales did not grow enough to keep up with our obligations. We never generated enough income to have any profits to share. After a year of business, sales were slow and getting slower. We were losing money. We finally discovered our hired salesman was actually selling cars below cost, but by the time we realized what was happening...it was too late to recover. It was evident we would have to close our doors. The inventory of new cars were returned to the company. We sold off the few remaining used cars and had an auction to sell the tools and equipment.

It would have been easy to point fingers and try to lay the blame for our failure on each other but we did not do that. There were no hard feelings between any of us as brothers, or toward any of our employees. We just did not manage the business properly and learned the hard way that the automobile business was not our calling! As it often happens, the Lord has a way of redirecting our lives. Sometimes it takes a hard lesson to get the message we are working contrary to His will. We marked the venture off to experience and got back to devoting our time to the professions we felt the Lord had for us. Each of us ended up with a new or used car at wholesale price as the only reward from our audacious pursuit.

Building a New Home

In the spring of 1965 we lost our Whip-Poor-Will home to a fire. We decided to build a new home on the hillside of a 30-acre plot we had purchased a few years previously. The land adjoined the north side of the original Whip-Poor-Will Hill property. It had been owned by two sisters who lived in Indianapolis. They had sold the parcel of land to us for $600! The location would allow us to build on a small hill, overlooking a pond I had built three years earlier, and we could include a basement opening on a lower level.

Berline and I spent several hours, using our experience in building and remodeling, drawing plans for our new home. It would be our dream house. The plans for the main floor included four bedrooms, two bathrooms, a kitchen with a formal dining room, a utility room, and a large living room. It would have a full size basement, where I could have my office as well as a single car garage. It was a very ambitious plan, but we figured by being conservative with doing most of the work ourselves and the help of others, our project was attainable.

When we were ready to begin construction, I hired Babe White, a neighbor who had a bulldozer, to dig out the hillside for the basement. Then the kids and I dug a trench around the sides for the footing. After we prepared the foundation, I hired a concrete man from Oakland City to lay the concrete blocks for the walls of the basement. Later he came back and helped pour the basement floor.

Gerald Gray had been building houses in and around Oakland City for a few years and I hired him for assisting with the carpentry work. He came with his helper and built the framework, including the roof, and installed of all the doors and windows. The house was soon totally enclosed. Gerald then built the custom designed kitchen cabinets.

I did all the plumbing and electrical work, which included the installation of radiant heating coils in all the ceilings on the main floor. Berline and I spent several hours fastening the small heating wires to the ceiling with staples placed every two-inches. Then we hired a man to plaster the ceilings and the walls of three bedrooms. In the basement, we installed baseboard heaters.

Berline did most of the painting and finish work. We set up sawhorses on which she stained and varnished every piece of trim work and baseboard before I installed it. Berline invested many hours of work towards the completion of the house. She was as anxious as I was to make it an enjoyable and comfortable home. Everywhere I worked, if she was available, she was there to help in whatever way she could.

We would eventually panel the walls of the other rooms and cover the outside of the house with limestone from Bedford, Indiana. Piles of the cut limestone blocks were brought in and stacked in the front yard. The limestone veneer job took about seven years to complete, meanwhile those piles of stone sat in the front yard waiting for time and opportunity. Imel helped me lay some stone on the basement end of the house. The remainder of the exterior walls were simply covered with outdoor cellotex, a fibrous material similar to sheets of rigid insulation but made from cellulose and covered with a black weatherproof material. It did not make for a very attractive home but it would eventually be covered with the beautiful limestone. I wanted to lay the stone to save expenses and for the experience.

We were ready to move into our new home by November. There was still a lot of work yet to be done though. The floors were unfinished and bare wall studs were exposed in many areas. One bathroom was finished but the other could wait. Even though the house was far from being finished, the whole family was excited about moving into our dream home.

The insurance from the fire loss and a small bank loan had been sufficient to complete the house to the point where it could be occupied. The incomplete projects would have to wait until funds were available and we had time for them.

We compare the first year in our new unfinished home to that of a continuous camping experience. Some floors had no covering over the crude sub floor, the windows were lacking drapes, and the large future living room had the appearance of a barn. The front porch deck had not been built and the back door landings were unfinished; we had improvised steps at the entryways. We were comfortable, however we were looking forward to the day when our dream home would be completed.

The back side of the house with the black cellotex

Our German Shepard, Cindy
at the back door on our improvised entryway

The older children had been attending Mt. Olympus High School during their high school years. That fall, Bonnie, Hervey, and Patty rode the bus to Petersburg High School along with the other high school students from the Union area. Alvin and DeAnn continued going to school at Union.

That was the senior year for Bonnie and Hervey. When they had attended school at Union, Hervey had been moved from the sixth to the eighth grade. His teacher, Preston Potter, had requested Hervey be moved up so he could be in the same grade with Bonnie. Mr. Potter claimed Hervey was already doing eighth grade work anyway.

Berline was working for the Hurst Manufacturing Company in Princeton and she was making better wages than she had been as a nurse's aide. However, she missed the opportunity of caring for the elderly people and felt that some day she would like to get back into a nursing career.

Even with maintaining the farm, the Rambler business, the distractions of building a new home, and the many other things requiring attention...my World Book business was growing strong. I had advanced to a regional territory manager and it was serving me incredibly well. My region was one of the top producers in the zone. It was quite a shock when it was suddenly taken away.

Despite the success I had in building up my region, George Smith, my manager notified me in 1965 that it was going be assigned to Fred Ingram, a regional manager from across the Ohio River in Owensboro, Kentucky. I could not understand George's motives because my region had been more productive than Fred's. In my new assignment, I would be working as a district manager under Fred Ingram and taking a 15 to 20 percent income reduction. I was discouraged and tempted to quit the company immediately.

Maybe the Lord was giving me a message for a different direction in my life. However, I did not listen to His call at that time. I accepted the situation as it was and tried working for Fred. It lasted about 10 months. My heart was no longer in my work and I fought to still the feelings of injustice. I felt that my work in building up a successful region had been unrecognized and my efforts unappreciated.

The region began to lose business under the leadership of Fred. I often wondered if George Smith, who was loosing money as a result, ever regretted making the change. I soon decided to leave. I learned later that Fred became a failure and he left the business too.

I began to look for a job in the teaching profession. It was in the middle of the school year and I anticipated a search might take weeks. However, I just prayed that God would lead me where He wanted me. I was trusting the Lord for the next steps of my journey.

I am reminded of the scripture:

Trust in the Lord with all your heart, and lean not on your own understanding; In all your ways acknowledge Him, and He shall direct your paths. (Proverbs 3:5-6)

Chapter 18

RECALL TO PROFESSIONAL WORK

For all things are for your sakes, that the abundant grace
might through the thanksgiving of many redound
to the glory of God. (II Corinthians 4:15)

Shelby County Superintendent

Indiana University placement office indicated the possibility of teaching vacancies in Shelby County. I drove to Shelbyville to check it out. It was an unusual time of the year to look for a teaching job, being as it was in the middle of the school year. Yet, that did not deter me because what mattered to me most was that I was working in accordance to God's will. His timing is perfect in all things.

I located the County Superintendent's office using the directions someone had given me. I introduced myself to J.O. Smith, the Superintendent of Eastern Shelby School District, and explained the purpose of my visit. Mr. Smith asked a few questions about my experience and education, then he said, "I am in need of a fourth grade teacher in a school five miles south of town. I have been using substitute teachers for a few weeks. Would you be interested in that?"

I could hardly believe my ears. What a miracle! God had provided an answer to my prayers on my first contact. I replied, "That is a very good grade to teach. I would be pleased to take that fourth grade class."

He explained that the former teacher had resigned and he had not been able to find a replacement. He had brought in three different substitute teachers for that class but he had not found anyone fully qualified for the position. He was very pleased to have a licensed teacher for the class and he wanted me there the next day!

The next morning Mr. Smith met me at the school to

introduce me to the principal, the secretary, the other teachers, and my new class. Everyone was very friendly and expressed delight in having a young man as the new teacher.

It was a major turning point in my life. I loved that fourth grade class from the first day. Through the following years that I was at Shelby Elementary School, each day with my fourth grade students was an inspiration to me.

It took a few days for us to find a place to live and we finally found a house in Shelbyville. We were not happy about its condition, however housing was in short supply so we accepted it and made plans to move in. We spent a couple of days cleaning and painting rooms. I had to be at school the day we were to move in, so it was up to Berline and the kids to get started. Only something happened along the way that changed our plans and we never moved into that house.

Hargett's Place

Hervey, along with his new wife Sharyn, and Berline were pulling the trailers to Shelbyville to unload them. Along the way, they passed a nice house in the country that looked empty. They turned around to go ask about it. Sure enough, it was for rent and ready to be occupied. Berline inspected the house and was impressed with its cleanliness and homey atmosphere. Its charm and character, qualities the other place lacked, won her approval. Mrs. Hargett, the owner, was very happy to rent to us after hearing Berline's story and learning I was a teacher.

The house was a white wood frame, two-story home with a full basement. There was a small guesthouse next to the main house and it was where Mrs. Hargett lived. The Hargetts had once farmed the surrounding land. The house was nestled between fields of corn and had two barns. One barn was rented to a farmer who sometimes kept cows and equipment in it. The other barn was close to the house and used as a garage and for storage. We lived in that nice home for three years.

Since we moved in the middle of the school year, it was a little challenge to get Patty, Alvin, and DeAnn enrolled into school. A brand new school called North Decatur, for grades seven through twelve, had opened near Greensburg and Patty would be going there. Alvin was in the sixth grade and DeAnn was in the fourth grade. Every day, for the rest of the school year, I got to have them with me as they both finished out the spring semester at Shelby Elementary. DeAnn became one of my students and was the only one of my children to ever be a student in any of my classes. The following year she continued her schooling at the elementary school in St. Paul and Alvin enrolled at North Decatur.

Patty and Alvin liked North Decatur but the bus ride was very long in the morning because we lived at the beginning of the route. Occasionally there were days when Patty could have the car and she would drive them to school.

One dreary cold morning I had to stop at the county highway garage concerning an accident Patty had involving one of their trucks. A few days earlier, one of them backed out onto the highway in front of Patty as she and Alvin were on their way to school. I felt kind of sorry for those hard working men who had to get out in all kind of weather from extreme cold to blistering heat, to work on the roads.

One man asked me where I worked. I replied, "I teach school up west of Waldron." He said, "Oh, I feel sorry for you!" I answered, "You need not feel sorry, because I am anxious to get there every morning." And that was the truth. I was always eager to get there and make interesting plans for all those young inquiring minds.

Shelby Elementary School

Shelby Elementary School was small, having grades one through six with about 15 students per class. I had 13 wonderful students in my class. I had been there only three weeks when the sixth grade teacher (who was also the

327

principal) was absent. A substitute came for two days to take his class. On the third day of his absence, Mr. Smith came to the school and called me into the office. No sooner had I sat down when he said, "Jim, you're it!" I wanted to know what he meant.

Mr. Smith said, "You're the principal starting today! The sixth grade teacher got into some trouble in town and he is terminated from his job!" I had discussed my credentials and previous principal jobs at our first meeting. Therefore, he knew I had a principal's license.

When Mr. Smith assigned me to be principal of the Shelby Elementary School, he asked me if I wanted to take over the sixth grade class since it needed a teacher. It was customary for the principal, if he were going to teach, to take the teaching position for the highest grade. I chose to stay with my fourth grade class, because I enjoyed the students and they had already had four different teachers that year. I thought it best I remain as their teacher so they would not have further disruption to their learning. It was a pleasure to be the principal and the fourth grade teacher, which I was able to enjoy for six years.

I taught my students the classroom was a place of learning. I played games with them and I took them on field trips. On one such outing, I took the whole school to Brown County State Park. I also worked with the music teacher to produce some outstanding programs each year.

Mr. Smith was a very practical educator in many respects. He strongly believed in helping every teacher be successful rather than cast a critical eye on their shortcomings. His methods inspired the best performance from those who worked for him. He sometimes offered me constructive suggestions, but never any criticism.

One day at noon, Mr. Smith came to the school and said, "Jim, give your class some assignments and have the secretary sit in your room. I want you to go with me to Terre Haute." That was about a hundred mile trip, so I knew we would be gone the rest of the afternoon.

His purpose for the trip to Terre Haute was mainly to bargain for some school supplies at a major school supply store. His reason for inviting me was that he just wanted someone to talk to about the school situations while he drove. He especially wanted to discuss some plans for building a new school to consolidate the two small elementary schools in the south part of our school district. Mr. Smith liked my ideas about schools and appreciated my conservative values.

At one of our principal meetings, the other three elementary principals were discussing the serious financial problems of their lunch programs. Mr. Smith told us he would ask the school board to approve a supplement of $300 to each of our school lunch funds.

After the meeting, at my first opportunity, I told Mr. Smith my lunch fund was in the black with a good surplus and we did not need the supplement. He was glad to hear that, but said, "Just accept the $300 and feed your kids something special." So, I bought a steer from a local farmer and had it processed so we could have quality meat for the lunch program.

We had an excellent cook, Mrs. Woods, who worked with me to plan good nutritious meals. I was able to acquire government commodities that were available to schools and she made good use of those items including the beef I had purchased. Even while being very conservative, she still served our school kids great lunches!

In 1971, a few weeks before the fall term of school was to begin, the principal of the Morristown High School resigned. Mr. Smith was having difficulty of finding a replacement because of the shortage of teachers and administrators at the time. I reminded Mr. Smith that my high school principal's certificate was on file in his office.

In discussing the situation with him I asked, "Would you like for me to take that position for a year and give you more time to find another principal? I love my job at Shelby Elementary School but would be willing to take the high school for a year if it will help the system. If so, I would appreciate your holding my job by hiring a replacement teacher there for one year." Mr. Smith appreciated the offer and he promptly presented the arrangement to the school board. Unanimously I was accepted for the position based on my successful few years at the Shelby school.

I arrived on the new job just two weeks before school was to begin. The biggest challenge was that no classroom schedule had been made for the year! With the help of one of the efficient secretaries, we were able to prepare a schedule that only had to be altered in a few places after school began.

I also started a book rental system for the school similar to the one I had started at Shelby Elementary. Most parents were very pleased with the new service and school got off to a good start. Of course I stood out like a new gate in a barnyard for the animals to see! The students, teachers, parents, and the eyes of the community were anxious to see what kind of person had taken over their school in such a short notice.

Greeting Senator Birch Bayh, Morristown School

There was one special highlight that occurred while I was at Morristown. Senator Birch Bayh came to speak at a student body assembly. It was an honor to have met the former governor of Indiana.

The high school position was more challenging, but I loved the opportunity to make some changes and direct the variety of activities in the school. Overall, things went well and I was accepted by the great majority of the staff and students. However, the divided responsibility of being in charge of both the elementary grades and the high school called for occasionally neglecting one while attending to the needs of the other.

I explained to Mr. Smith that I would live up to my offer of taking the Morristown school for one year, but then I wanted to return to my position at the Shelby Elementary School the next school year. He accepted my request and was able to find a well-qualified man as high school principal for the next year.

A Summer Vacation

Bonnie & Berline at Hargetts

While in college, Bonnie met a young man named Steve Powell. After they married, Steve joined the Air Force and he was stationed at a training center in New Jersey. Bonnie stayed with us at Hargett's place until Steve learned married personnel could get approval to live off base. He wanted her to help find a place for them to rent.

Since summer vacation was coming up soon, we decided to drive Bonnie to New Jersey. From there, we planned to take a weekend trip with Steve to the World's Fair (Expo '67) in Montreal, Canada. When we got to New Jersey, my big army surplus tent was put to use. We stayed at a campground near the base where Steve was located. It was a nice campsite for the few days we needed it.

During our time there, we drove through the New Jersey countryside, sightseeing and visiting historical sites. On one of our drives, we came upon a large strawberry patch. I asked the man if we could pick some and how much it would cost. He said, "Pick all you want and you can have them free. The patch has already been picked by the pickers." There were plenty of strawberries and we picked about five gallons of them. We feasted on the strawberries for several days.

We made preparations to leave as soon as Steve got off duty on Friday, then we began our journey to Montreal. It was raining most of the time at the fair and we did not enjoy the trip as much as we expected. On our return, we drove through New York City, visited the Statue of Liberty, and went to the site where the New York World's Fair had been some years earlier.

We returned to New Jersey just as Steve's leave was up. We gathered up our supplies, which included the strawberries, and started back to Indiana. We left the tent for Steve and Bonnie to use until they could find a place to rent. On our return trip we stopped in Philadelphia, Pennsylvania, to see the Liberty Bell and other historical places including the well preserved buildings where the U.S. Government was formed.

Loss of our Parents

Berline and I both lost one of our parents while we were living at Hargett's place. Pop died in the spring of 1968. Orace Wayne and I were at his beside the night before he died. He seemed rational but was unaware of us at his hospital bed. We heard him talking, but he was not speaking to us. He was praying to the Lord and naming each of his five sons and two daughters. He was asking the Lord to protect and watch over them but he did not mention his own condition. It was as if he knew his time had come to meet the Lord and he was making his last requests known to God.

Pop had read the Bible quite often and could quote some familiar scriptures, but we had never heard him pray or express any commitment as to his salvation. We knew he believed in God and to hear him pray was a special consolation to Orace Wayne and me.

Pop was well known in the community where he had spent his entire life, and his reputation was above reproach with those who knew him. He knew enough about the Bible to believe in a God who was the creator and giver of life. He was a strong believer in Christian morals. His condition was not good and we were thrilled to hear him express faith in God and pray in faith, believing for the protection his loved ones. It was evidence of his faith in God and was a source of comfort to us and the best testimony we could have had from Pop.

Pop was allowed to go back home the next morning where he died later in the day. Mom and Pop lived in the house Joe Hurst had built, which was on the same spot where Pop's original home had been–the home where Pop was born and raised. Pop died and left this world within 20 feet of the place where he was born into it!

Wesley had kept the Willis Grocery going during the last few months of Pop's illness. Soon after Pop's death Wesley wanted to return to other activities, so Mom ran the store by herself. She became very sick within a year and underwent gall-bladder surgery. She seemed to recover and went back to the store business. The family objected at first because it seemed it would be too much for her. But then we could see she was doing fine and the store business was her enjoyment. In a few months Mom had to return to the hospital.

Dr. Gene Gray, her grandson, diagnosed her with cancer. She never returned home but remained hospitalized until her death June 6, 1970. Her passing was a tremendous loss of a love beyond description to all who knew her.

In memory of
Floyd Hunter Willis (1897 - 1968)
Goldie Inez Parker Willis (1897 - 1970)

Mom and Pop 50th Wedding Anniversary

Berline's mother, Melissa, was killed in a car wreck in October of 1968. She had gone into town for an appointment. She had pulled out of a parking lot to cross the street with plenty of margin for safety (according to witnesses). But there was a drunk driver among the oncoming cars, who was going about 80 miles per hour. He hit Melissa's Buick broadside. Seat belts were not required in those days and, as Melissa was not wearing one, she was thrown from her car. A woman in an oncoming car said that she saw the lady flying through the air like a big rag doll being pitched from the car.

Although paramedics tried to revive her in the ambulance, she was dead upon arrival at the hospital. The man who hit her lived but was hospitalized for a long while from serous injuries he received in the crash. The inside of his car was full of empty alcohol bottles and reeked heavily of alcohol.

We received a phone call about the accident a few hours after it happened. Early the next morning we left home and drove straight through to arrive in Fayetteville the following afternoon. Melissa had many relatives and friends who mourned her death. There were so many people at the funeral, it caused the church to be overflowing. We spent a couple days with Berline's father, assisting him with business matters, before returning to Indiana.

Berline Nursing School

Berline found a job near Shelbyville helping a man in the sign business doing various odd jobs. It was an interesting job, however, she had to quit as she had developed medical problems that required surgery. As she was leaving her workplace, the boss expressed his appreciation for her good help. He told her to return when she was able and they would have a job for her. After her recovery though, she decided to further her education and seek a career in the nursing profession. She felt that vocation could be her life's work.

For many years Berline had aspirations to work where

there was a meaningful purpose–something that would help others. Ever since she had worked as a nurse aide in Petersburg, she felt that becoming a nurse was her calling in life. With the hopes of fulfilling that dream, she decided to go to nursing school. She found a nursing program in Indianapolis where she enrolled.

We could hardly believe 25 years had passed since we were married. Our children came together to help us celebrate that important date, which also marked the beginning of a professional career in life for Berline.

Our 25th Wedding Anniversary

It was enormously brave of Berline to go back to school at that time in her life. It was not an easy decision. But she did have our unquestioning support and her example had an immeasurable influence on each of us.

Berline was allowed to take some entrance exams that qualified her to enroll into the nursing school. She studied hard and stayed up late at nights reading, memorizing, and writing.

Achieving her goal took much courage, determination, and work. She had to drive 60 miles round trip each day while attending school. Completing her education was a milestone in her life. She graduated with a Licensed Practitioners Nursing (LPN) degree in the spring of 1972.

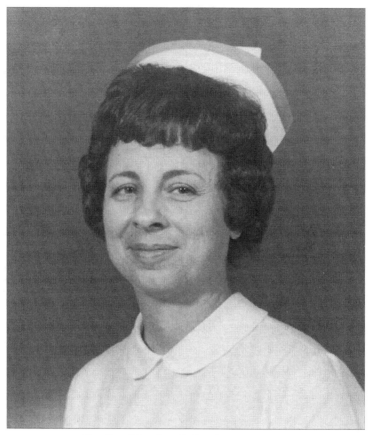

Berline Nursing School Graduation

It was highly rewarding to Berline when she obtained her nursing diploma. I really admired her commitment and determination to make more of her life. It was an honor to introduce her and explain to people that my wife was in the medical profession as a nurse.

Boat Trip to Texas

During the previous years when we lived at Whip-Poor-Will Hill, I had hired a man with a dozer to build a large dam at the south side of our property. The lake that was created covered about five acres and I bought fish from the state fishery to stock it. I even acquired a boat to go on the lake. A neighbor gave me an old Chris Craft wooden motorboat that was in need of repairs. The boat was called *O-So-Slo,* as it had to be rowed because the motor would not run. It had been an expensive boat in its day, with sleek lines and a V6 inboard motor. However, years of neglect had taken their toll and the wood was bare in many places where the varnish was peeling and blistered. I was not sure the boat would even float.

We put the boat on the lake and it proved to have a sound hull. With some tinkering, Hervey attempted to get the motor running, but it had several problems so he gave up trying to fix it. While we were away from Whip-Poor-Will Hill, *O-So-Slo* sat in a state of disrepair.

Late in the fall of 1970 Hervey moved to Greenville, Texas, with his family. Hervey had used my trailer for moving, but there was not enough room for everything. Their remaining personal belongings were stored in our house. After he got settled with his new job, he asked about getting the boat so he could get it running.

At the time, our 1966 Plymouth had 110,000 miles. It was using oil badly and needed mechanical work. I was debating on trading it off, but Hervey thought the engine just needed an overhaul and he made me a deal. If I would pull the boat to Texas for him, he would overhaul the motor in the Plymouth.

I had been planning to take a trip to California with Alvin and DeAnn, during the Christmas break from school, to visit Imel. Hervey agreed to let us use his new Dodge Charger to go ahead to California while he worked on our car.

As we prepared for the trip to Texas, we filled the boat

with as many of their things as possible and put some items the car too. Towing the boat, with it being fully loaded down, would be a strain on the engine. The Plymouth was not in the best condition for making the trip even without pulling a load. However, it had been a faithful automobile and I had confidence we could make the trip.

That year the annual Willis Christmas party was being held in the Church of God fellowship hall in Petersburg, Indiana. Our plans were to attend the party, then after it was over we would continue on our way that night to Texas. I knew I would have to keep an eye on the oil level as we traveled. I checked the oil just before we left for the party and the level was fine.

The party was a joyful time as usual. All my siblings were there, plus the food and festivities were enjoyable. When the party was over, we began our unforgettable odyssey to Texas. I checked the oil level again before leaving Petersburg and thought it strange that it was already two quarts low. We had traveled only 120 miles since the last time I checked it. I added two quarts and we continued on our way.

After we had traveled 50 miles, the oil light on the dashboard came on. We stopped to added the quart I had taken along. That got us across the Wabash River into Illinois, where I could buy more. Common sense should have told me we could not drive 1,000 miles to Texas with the car drinking so much oil. However, we had promised to take Hervey the boat, and we were anticipating an enjoyable visit in California. I decided to buy oil by the gallon and stop to add some every 30 miles. We did not want to be cheated out of our trip or be delayed any more than possible.

Most stations in those days had used oil that could be purchased for a few cents a gallon. On the trip I took advantage of that, but sometimes they would just give it to me. I figured the used oil would work just as well. Since the engine was burning it so fast, it wouldn't matter. We kept on going through the night, stopping frequently to add more oil. We were burning oil and leaving a cloud of smoke behind us. I expected to see red lights flashing behind me most any time, but maybe the police had sympathy for us.

Whenever we stopped for fuel–or more often when we stopped to add oil–I always asked for some used oil. When we pulled into one such place, an attendant came running with a fire extinguisher. He thought the car was on fire! I explained it was not on fire, the motor was just burning oil.

We arrived at Hervey's house greatly relieved and tired from the long trip. We had used *14 gallons* of oil! I wish I had counted the number of stops we had made. However, we were able to keep the engine going for trip–laying a smoke screen all the way.

We spent the night at Hervey's and the next morning we helped unload his things from the boat before starting ahead to California in his new Dodge. We breathed a sigh of relief, as we drove off in a good comfortable car with a feeling of confidence that we would not have any problems. Or so we thought!!

On to California in Luxury

Unfortunately, our difficulties were not over. One never knows what to expect when traveling, even with a new car. In Arizona, we stopped at the Cactus National Park for a break. There, we took a scenic drive through the park enjoying the sight of many different kinds, colors, and sizes of cacti. The car just stopped running while we were driving through the park. We coasted to a place where we could pull off the road and it just would not start.

I walked to where I could use the phone. Since the car was new and still under warranty, I called AAA road service to tow the car to a Dodge dealer in the nearby town. It was Saturday, and when the tow truck driver arrived, he reminded me it would be Monday before anybody would work on the car. We did not want to wait two days to complete our trip to California.

The cars of that era still had relatively simple electrical systems and I was somewhat familiar with how they worked. I suspected there was a problem with either the alternator or a malfunctioning voltage regulator. I asked the tow truck driver if he had a piece of insulated wire. He searched around in his junk box and found just what I needed. I connected the wire directly from the battery to the voltage regulator, which would allow current to the coil and distributor. Then the car would run as long as there was a charge in the battery, but it could not be started using the key in the ignition. I used a tire tool to jump power between terminals on the starter solenoid.

That started the car and we were to be on our way. Each time we stopped and turned off the engine, we had to open the hood and use the tire tool to start it, therefore we seldom turned off the engine. With the alternator not charging the battery, the car could only go so far before we would have to stop and get a charge on the battery. Every electrical draw on the battery decreased the distance we could travel on a charge, so we tried not to use the turn signals or do anything to pull power from the battery.

All went well until it started getting dark. We were getting close to where Imel lived and we didn't want to have to stop when we were so close! We could not turn on the headlights until I found another piece of wire and wired the headlights directly to the battery. That lasted several miles, but without an alternator, the battery went down much faster. We stopped at a service station to get a quick charge put on the battery. We were close enough that one battery charge would get us to Imel's house.

Within a half mile of Imel's, suddenly my rear view mirror lit up with flashing red lights! I had forgotten to connect the taillights to the battery. The patrolman ordered me to get off the freeway at the next exit and would not allow us to continue further. There was no one at the station where we exited that could fix our problem and I had no more wire to connect the taillights.

I called Imel's house to see if someone could come and get us. Floyd, Imel's son, was the only one at home and he was not yet driving age. I studied the map and found a way to Imel's so we could stay off the highway. We were able to get to his house yet that evening by carefully finding our way down back streets.

The next day a Dodge dealer repaired the car and we didn't have any more auto problems the rest of our trip. Our return trip to Texas was uneventful. Hervey had repaired my Plymouth and it was running good. I hitched up my trailer, which he had used for moving, and pulled it back home. The pleasant trip back to Indiana was also uneventful. The entire return trip home was quite a contrast to the challenging adventures of our getting to California. That Plymouth lasted another 50,000 miles before I had to trade it off.

Career Enemy

Politics have always played a bigger hand in school operations than people realize. J.O. Smith knew there had been some political adversaries elected to the school board. They were not really opposed to him, but they had in mind a political friend for his position. J.O. could see "the handwriting on the wall". He would soon be out of a job if he stayed, so he resigned and took a superintendent's job in Kokomo, Indiana. Shelby Eastern School Corporation lost a good Christian man. J.O. used common sense and professional approach to all school issues. He was one of the best superintendents in the state of Indiana.

In 1973, the school board hired Gerald Carmony to be the new Superintendent. The fiasco of Carmony's leadership was that he was not qualified to be in such a key position where diplomacy and tact were needed. He had a negative approach to every school problem and was constantly interfering in affairs that he didn't understand.

Our bi-weekly principal meetings became a waste of

time, as they were no longer interesting and all six of us principals dreaded to attend them. Those meetings with Mr. Carmony were not constructive discussions but lectures on what was wrong and what had to be done. He would visit our schools occasionally, with a critical attitude looking for any fault he could find and he never gave a compliment. He was not friendly to me, and the derogatory remarks he made showed the anger in his heart.

Mr. Carmony did not like J.O. Smith and said he knew I was J.O.'s pet teacher. That statement, while shocking to me, was at the same time gratifying. I had immense respect for J.O. I told Mr. Carmony that regardless of how much J.O. Smith and I enjoyed working together, he treated every principal and teacher in his district with courtesy and dignity. I wanted him to know J.O. did not play favorites and treated us all equally.

One day Mr. Carmony summoned me to his office under the pretense of questioning me about how things were done at my school. He had a folder with my credentials lying open on his desk and mentioned that my license qualified me as a superintendent. He asked me about it and wondered if I would like the job of superintendent.

It suddenly dawned on me the cause of Mr. Carmony's antagonism toward me. He was afraid I might try to get his job. He had reason to feel insecure because his rise to his position had not been earned through his past accomplishments or performance as a school administrator and because of my good reputation in the community.

I let him know that I had no experience for the position and neither did I want the responsibility. Nevertheless, it seemed like he still thought I was a threat to his job. He continued to meddle and find fault in the way I ran my school. For all the good that discussion did...I might as well have told him that I was applying for his job!

Each year the state declared a National School Lunch Week. Schools were encouraged to offer special incentives to encourage more students to participate. With our lunch program finances being in such good shape, I decided on a rather grand plan. I sent a notice to parents letting them know we were offering free lunches for one full week to all students. I wrote that we would like to have 100 percent participation. Children who normally brought their lunch could eat free all week.

We had plenty of money in our lunch fund to give the free lunches and still have a substantial balance. I also had the secretary write up a short article for the local newspaper about how we were participating in National School Lunch Week. That might have been a mistake. But the Lord works in mysterious ways and I believe He had a hand in all the events of my career. Nevertheless, I was caught off guard by the response I received from that well-intentioned effort.

Mr. Carmony exploded when he read the article. It was ammunition he needed with which to attack me. He came to the school the next day and called me to the office, then proceeded to give me a very rude lecture, almost to the point of using curse words. Mr. Carmony let me know I had no authority to give free lunches–only the school board had that authority. He also claimed it made the other schools look bad. In my entire school career, I had never received such a hateful and demeaning diatribe from a superior.

I felt like asking, "What did the other schools do in honor of National School Lunch Week?" However, I held my peace and let him make a fool of himself while trying to degrade me. The secretary was in the outer office and heard it all. She said that she had never heard such a rampage from a school official. She felt as if she had contributed to the lecture by helping me plan the week. I assured her that Mr. Carmony was after me and not her. I offered my appreciation for her assistance because it was my idea in the first place.

The issue was pointless because Carmony had already made clear he was biased against me. After that harsh ordeal over the lunch week promotion, I finally had enough of his heavy handed complaining and decided I no longer wanted to work under such oppression. The next week I gave him my resignation to be effective at the end of the school year.

That was just what he wanted! After that incident, Mr. Carmony treated me decently for the remainder of the school year. Perhaps he felt the threat to his job had been removed. He had accomplished his mission of getting me to leave the school district. I had no idea at that time where I would go, but I was confident the Lord would lead me where He wanted me.

I learned of a position opening that fall, for a combined elementary and middle school principal, in Markleville, Indiana, near Pendleton. I contacted Mr. Cousert, the superintendent, for an interview. I took a day off from school to go to his office in Pendleton for the meeting. He hired me for the job, which meant an increase in salary. It was a real blessing to find a good job with a good supervisor. I was looking forward to the end of the school term when I would be free for the summer months.

Stone Veneer to Whip-Poor-Will Home

Alvin graduated from high school in the spring of 1973 and enlisted in the U.S. Navy. He said to me one day, "Daddy, I'm leaving for the Navy in August and I would like to help you complete the stone work on our house at Union this summer." His offer was readily accepted and we spent the entire summer laying stone on our home at Whip-Poor-Will Hill. A small portion of the house had already been veneered with the stone with the help of Imel, Wesley, and Steve Powell. Time had not permitted me to continue with the stonework until then.

Alvin learned quickly how to cut and dress the limestone blocks. We used a skilsaw to score the stone where we wanted it to break. Using a chisel and hammer, the broken end would be squared and cleaned up, making it look nice and straight. Most pieces were not cut completely through with the saw because that wore down the masonry blades too quickly. However, some special pieces did need a through cut and it took extra time and care to make them perfect.

Each piece of the thousands of stone blocks we laid had to be dressed. Some stone blocks did not need to be cut, but every one of them had to be dressed, whether they were cut or not. Probably 80 percent of the stone blocks had to be cut to fit. Using the saw produced a generous amount of dust. It would get in your hair, your ears, all over your clothes, and even in your eyes if not protected. Everything within a 10-foot radius of the saw became a dust magnet. We quickly learned we had to pour a little water on the stone as we were cutting in order to keep the dust down. Still, the fine dust particles built up and got inside the saw, eventually the saw would quit working. We had to stop and clean out the saw occasionally during the project.

We used three different sizes of stone, which was determined by the height. As I laid the stone, I alternated the different sizes. It not only created a unique pattern, but also helped hide any imperfections in our work. It was like a gigantic puzzle. Alvin sometimes figured out a pattern and cut the stone ahead of me. Often I would call for a certain size of stone with the dimensions and he would cut it to fit. Sometimes those cuts would be off a little and we would joke that there was something wrong with the saw. Actually, all mistakes were used somewhere so they were not really mistakes. They were just made to fit elsewhere.

Alvin usually mixed the mortar, but I would mix it if he was busy cutting stone. There was only so much mortar that could be mixed ahead of time. If the mortar sat too long, it became unusable. We had to judge how much mortar we would need based on what kind of work we were doing. The pace of laying the stone varied, depending on the architectural features of the house. Corners, openings, and other details required more time so we had to consider those things when we prepared a batch of mortar.

The masonry work that summer also included building a chimney from the basement up through two stories. Inside, we built a fireplace in the basement and a corner fireplace in the upstairs living room. We also built a barbeque pit in a corner of the chimney next to the kitchen. The chimney on both floors was then finished with the veneer of limestone. We extended the stonework from the fireplace to include a fountain in the upstairs living room and a small aquarium in the basement. By the end of that summer we had laid over 8,000 square feet of Bedford limestone.

Working on the fireplace and fountain upstairs

Finished fireplace and fountain upstairs

Built-in grill beside the kitchen

Finished fireplace in the basement

I am standing at the south end, which overlooks the pond

Our Whip-Poor-Will Hill home

[A.E. Willis illustration]

Alvin designed and painted the sign, as well as the mailbox

Markleville, Indiana

We found a nice house to rent in Pendleton, which was close to my new job, and moved there before school started. DeAnn enrolled in the Pendleton Heights High School where she would graduate two years later. Berline continued her nursing job at Shelbyville and drove the 80 miles round-trip to work.

When I became the new principal of the Markleville School, I could see the job would be a challenge right from the start. The school was a combination of elementary and junior high school students. That meant I would have responsibility for grades kindergarten through the eighth grade. Still, I thoroughly enjoyed the challenge for the two years I was there.

In my teaching experience, there have always been a few memorable events that occur every school year. One day a woman from the small town of Markleville came to school to report an incident about a boy who I will call Johnny. Johnny, an eighth grader, had apparently stolen a light from a city traffic barrier. The woman was really wanting to protect the boy from trouble and was hoping I could help him do the right thing. His father had been killed in the line of duty as a policeman. She asked if I would have some influence in getting the light back.

Johnny had been kind of a problem boy and the teachers warned me I would have trouble with him. But I had no trouble with him and found him a very likeable boy. Because of his reputation, the woman thought the street department suspected he had the light.

When I called Johnny to the office, he walked in with a troubled countenance. I accepted him in a friendly manner to relieve his fears. Then I said, "Johnny, the town is missing one of their barricade lights." At that his eyes lit up and I could see the sense of guilt in them. I followed with a request; "I would like to help you get it back to them before they come to your house looking for it." He quickly responded, "How did you know about that?"

I replied, "A little bird told me. Would you let me have the light if I take you home after school? Then I can return the light and no questions will be asked." He readily agreed to that arrangement and the light was returned. The person in charge thanked me and seemed to know from where it came.

I never had any trouble with Johnny before or after that. Rather, it seemed we developed a friendship. I think Johnny deeply missed his father; perhaps I became a surrogate. One day after the incident with the light, Johnny brought me a small packet with some drugs in it. He had bought them from another boy and turned them over to me as an effort to stop the drug business. I reported the incident to the boy's parents and left it to them to deal with his problem.

I helped solve another problem, involving a girl who had been repeatedly missing money from her locker. I contacted the state police and they gave me some bait powder. I baited a one dollar bill and put it in the girl's locker. I then notified the teachers to have a hand inspection early in the day. One boy showed up with red hands. His mother was called and she was devastated to learn her son had stolen the money. She paid the girl back the estimated amount that had been taken. The boy was in bad trouble with his mother and I offered no other punishment from the school. I also left that problem for the parents to handle.

In 1975, a new school building and consolidation of schools was under way. The other elementary principals in the school system had seniority over me for the leadership positions at the new school. However, I could have taken a teaching position, but I thought it would not be feasible. I began to think about looking for a job elsewhere.

Berline, James, and DeAnn (in prom dress) at Pendleton
In front of 1965 Plymouth

James and Berline by their 1972 Chevy pickup

Chapter 19

THE EMPTY NEST

Wait on the Lord: be of good courage,
and He shall strengthen thine heart:
wait, I say, on the Lord. (Psalms 27:14)

The Captains Sandwich Galley

After being away for six years, we returned to Whip-Poor-Will Hill once again. I looked for a teaching position but finding work in the school system was not as easy as it had been in former years. During that time, we were brainstorming ideas for what we should do next. Our nest was empty and we were at liberty to try new adventures. After many long discussions, we decided to start our own business. It was not something exactly new to us, as we had tried a few ventures in our lifetime. Some were more profitable than others, we now had the inspiration of a successful model.

In 1975, Steve and Bonnie started a restaurant in Indianapolis called *Sandwich Machine*, specializing in submarine sandwiches. In the intervening years, their operation prospered. We had watched their business thrive and believed we also could do well if we copied their techniques. We decided to open a submarine sandwich shop in Evansville. Now when I look back, it is hard for me to understand why we undertook such an ambitious project. Yet, we had faith it would be a profitable venture.

We found a site that met our requirements: a building with plenty of space in a good location. The building had great potential but needed a considerable amount of cleaning and repairing before we could set up shop. The owner, Mr. Schweitzer, offered it to us rent-free for six months, then at half price for the next year as compensation for the improvements we made.

Even though he was an elderly man, Mr. Schweitzer helped us get the building fixed up–he clearly wanted us to succeed. It was Mrs. Schweitzer who suggested we name our little restaurant *The Captain's Sandwich Galley*. We thought it was perfect.

I called on Steve for advice several times as we struggled through the myriad of details and red tape. He gave us helpful suggestions; his experience with his sub shop venture provided us with invaluable ideas and smart insights. He loaned us equipment he had in storage and we shopped around at restaurant supply stores for other items we needed.

We had help from other family members too. DeAnn had recently married a fine young man, William Flint (Bill), whom she met at college. Bill had grown up on a farm in Colorado and he was no stranger to hard work. Together, they jumped in to help us prepare the restaurant for its grand opening. It is mind boggling all the work we had to do just to open our doors, never mind the day-to-day management involved once we were up and running. However, once we were into it, there was no turning back.

After about six weeks of making plans, renovations, and preparations, The Captain's Sandwich Galley (we often just called it *the Captain's Galley* or *the Galley*) was ready to open. The business was slow at first, but it increased as people learned about the restaurant, the quality of our sandwiches and other great food items.

After we had been open a while, Bill and DeAnn rented an apartment in Evansville. When it was Berline's turn to close, she would spend the night at their apartment. That helped everyone feel more rested, as it avoided the daily drive back and forth between Evansville and Whip-Poor-Will Hill, which was 40-miles (one-way).

We soon began to feel more relaxed with the routine of day-to-day operations. Along with our success, we had two break-ins. We thought one of them was an employee because the thief went right to where the money was hidden, without disturbing anything else. Despite our suspicion, we could never prove it. From then on, we never left any money on the premises after closing. If we could not put the daily receipts in the bank deposit box, one of us would take all the money home.

One night, it was my turn to close and I had over $600 to take home. I drove to the farm by myself, as Berline was spending the night with Bill and DeAnn. After I went to bed, I heard a noise in the closet of the bedroom next to mine. It startled me because I had never heard strange noises in the house before. I lay still, listening to see if it would happen again. I heard it a second time and it sounded as if some boxes were being moved around or stacked about in the closet of the adjacent room. It was too much of a scuffling sound to be a mouse or a rat. Anyway, we had never had a rodent problem in the house.

I do not believe in ghosts and am not easily scared by noises in the dark, but that night I was definitely feeling uneasy. When I heard the same noise a third time, I quietly slipped out of bed and dressed. Then I grabbed the bag of money and left the house as quickly as possible. I was not interested in trying to find out what was making the noise or if someone was in there, when I had so much cash on hand. I drove to Evansville and went to Bill and DeAnn's apartment for the night.

The next day we returned to the house only to have the mystery deepen. Upon inspection of the closet, where I had heard the sound coming from, nothing was missing and everything in it seemed untouched. Likewise, we found no evidence of anything missing or disturbed anywhere in the house. It has always been a puzzle to me what made those sounds that night. I do know the noises were real–I was not dreaming and I did not imagine what I heard.

Berline got a different kind of scare as she was closing the Galley by herself one night. She had already cleaned up the equipment and put away the food items when a scraggly dressed, rough-looking man came in asking for a sandwich. She was leery of the man but her tenderhearted nature overcame her apprehensions. Typical of her willingness to help someone in need, she began making him a sandwich in spite of the extra work it would cause her.

As she prepared his food, they were talking and the man came around behind the counter into the area where she was working. It gave her a real scare, but she acted calm and kept the customer engaged in conversation. She gave him his sandwich and he paid, leaving without incident.

A little over a year after we opened the Captain's Galley, the school bell rang once again. In February of 1979, Steve Willis, Orace Wayne's son, told me of a vacancy for a principal position in Crawford County where he worked. He asked if I would be interested in the position. Returning to school was an easy decision for me to make because teaching is what I have always felt was my calling in life. But since Berline and I together had made the commitment to the restaurant, I wanted us to be in agreement about the decision. Berline was very understanding and was willing to continue operating the Galley with Bill and DeAnn's assistance, if I were to be offered that principal position. With the business established and a few part-time workers hired, it was not critical for me to be there on a daily basis.

Steve Willis helped arrange for me to meet with the school board's selection committee where I was told the details of the position and was asked about my previous experience. The next day, I was invited to meet with the school board and there I was introduced to the superintendent, Ralph Hanger, and the other board members. Our discussions were productive and I felt a good rapport with everyone in attendance.

I was hired to be the principal over five small elementary schools and asked to report for work immediately. At the request of the school board, I took my credentials to Superintendent Hanger's office where I signed a contract. Then he took me around to the five schools in the district, introducing me to the head teacher and secretary in each one.

The first week, I commuted the 50 miles between Whip-

Poor-Will Hill and English, Indiana, where my office was located. Then I found a place to rent in English, but I continued driving home on weekends or going directly to the Captain's Galley on Friday evenings to help with the restaurant's weekend business (we were closed on Sundays).

I felt blessed that God had provided a way for me to get back into the work I loved. I still feel that way, only with a deeper sense of thankfulness because it turned out to be the best job I ever had. It was also the last principal position of my career. Yet, I had mixed emotions about it. I was excited about my new job and yet felt it was unfair to leave the daily operation of the Galley to Berline, Bill, and DeAnn. However, they were well qualified and knew the business, and I was confident I could leave the responsibilities of managing the business to them.

Although we did hire other employees, Bill and DeAnn were our main assistants. It gave Berline and I great peace of mind to have complete trust in their ability to run the business.

Within a few years, it became apparent our hearts were seeking fulfillment in interests other than the restaurant business. The Captain's Sandwich Galley had provided us a goal and direction, but each of us felt drawn to pursue other dreams. When it was time to put the Galley up for sale, it wasn't long before we found a buyer.

Our earnings from the business had been small, but we had kept up with expenses and paid off most of the equipment we had purchased. However, we did realize a little profit from the sale. We didn't lose money on the venture and we did gain a wealth of experience about the restaurant business.

Crawford County

As principal in the Crawford County school system, I enjoyed the challenges of my administrative duties. The five schools were located in small towns throughout the county and each bore a distinctive character. However, they all had the special charm that I always found appealing about rural schools. Each school had a good head teacher who reported their needs and concerns to me. I would visit the schools each week to take care of details that needed my attention and would leave instructions with the head teachers. My job really amounted to being a liaison administrator between the superintendent and the five schools.

Since my office was located in the school at English, that is where most of my time was spent. One of the most delightful aspects of the job was getting paid to travel to the various schools. I was even reimbursed for my travel expenses. It was a pleasure to drive through the scenic countryside, seeing the colors of the beautiful hills and woodlands change with the seasons. I never tired of those peaceful drives and seeing God's handiwork in nature.

The room I had been renting was in the home of an elderly couple. They were members of the Wesleyan Church and knew Orace Wayne (a Wesleyan minister) and I were brothers. I soon learned Lois Blevins, one of the school secretaries, owned a house near the school that had a room for rent. The English School coach, Monte Eckart, and I both rented a room there, sharing a kitchen and other facilities.

At the end of the school year, I moved all of my belongings back to Whip-Poor-Will Hill so I would not have to pay rent while school was out. That summer a great flood came through English with a rush of water 10 feet deep. English sits in a valley and all the homes in the area suffered severe loss and property damage. There were even buildings that floated off their foundations. Mrs. Blevins's house was solid but had a lot of damage. Everything that she and Monte had in the house was ruined, because the water came up in the house about six feet. As the waters receded, a coat of foul smelling mud was left behind on everything. Mrs. Blevins had no interest in fixing up the house because the extent of the damage was too oppressive and the repairs were beyond her abilities. She just wanted to sell it as it was...and her price was a bargain.

Berline and I bought the house intent on making the place livable again. After a lot of hard work cleaning and fixing, it was a decent comfortable place for us. After we sold The Captain's Sandwich Galley, Berline found work at a nursing home in Leavenworth, a town about 15 miles from English. During the school year, we usually went back home to Whip-Poor-Will Hill on the weekends unless Berline was on duty at the nursing home. There was always work that needed to be done around the farm.

In my experience, I have found that locust trees make excellent fence posts. We had many locust trees on our Whip-Poor-Will Hill property and occasionally I would cut down a few to use for repairing or building fence. The best method for making locust fence posts is to fell the tree during the winter when the sap is down. This makes the posts more durable.

One Saturday, I wanted to use my new chain saw to cut some locust trees that were the right size for fence posts. There was a fresh layer of snow and it was a pleasant day for outside work. A few trees were felled, measured, and cut into proper lengths. Then the accident happened. As I cut one big tree, it fell onto some smaller ones, preventing it from landing properly. That forced the trunk to swing up...straight at me! It all happened so fast and before I could jump out of the way, the cut end of the tree slammed into my left leg, knocking me to the ground.

I knew immediately my leg was broken. At first, I thought I could hop on my right leg to the house. Gingerly, I tried to pull myself up off the ground. Oh! Oh! Ouch! That would never do! So I began crawling on hands and knees through the snow, dragging the broken leg along as gently as possible, back toward the house. I had a long, painful journey through the woods, across a field, down a bank, and over the gravel road before reaching the yard. There, I began to yell for help. Berline heard me calling and came out to see what was the matter.

By the time we got to the Oakland City Hospital where

my nephew, Dr. Gene Gray worked, my leg had swollen. Dr. Gray could not do much because of the swelling, so he put my leg on ice and kept me in the hospital. He wanted to wait a couple of days until the swelling went down, to do surgery on my leg. Gene explained he was going to put in a metal plate to hold the bone in place. Then he would put my leg in a cast to keep it immobile while it healed.

The cast slowed me down but it did not stop me from getting chores done–it has always been hard for me to remain idle for any length of time. Four weeks after the surgery, I still had the cast on and I was mowing around the farm on my Snapper riding mower. I got too close to a pile of lumber and accidentally drove into a board that was sticking out at just the right height to hit my injured leg...exactly where it had been broken! When the pain didn't to go away, I had to return to the hospital so the doctor could look at it. The results of an x-ray showed the metal splice was broken. It had to be removed and Dr. Gray commented to the attending nurse, "He broke that darn leg again!"

I was on crutches again for another six weeks, but even so, my leg injuries only kept me away from school a few days. By the time school was out in the spring, my leg was completely well and I could engage in normal activities.

During my fourth year at Crawford County, I was confronted again with decisions based on school politics. A new school board was elected and they began to make sweeping changes in the guise of saving money. The biggest change was to allow the head teacher in each of the five schools to become a *teaching principal*. That allowed the school board to appoint each head teacher to act as a principal, even if they did not have a principal's license. Consequently, my job as the elementary principal was eliminated at the end of school in 1983.

As I looked for other work, I discovered vacancies for school teachers or administrators were harder to find than they once had been just a few years earlier. Salaries had improved considerably and more college graduates were attracted to the teaching profession. While I continued to look for a job in the school system, I found temporary work at the Crane Naval Center. I worked there for the next year commuting to Crane while we lived at Whip-Poor-Will Hill. I shared rides with other Crane workers from Petersburg in order to cut down on travel expenses.

Abundant Life School

In time, Bonnie introduced me to the pastor of their church, Reverend Vibbert, who wanted to start a Christian school in their church classroom facilities. He hired me to start an elementary school at the Abundant Life Assembly of God Church in Indianapolis. I would be the principal, but also teach as needed.

Berline looked for work around Indianapolis and found plenty of prime opportunities to choose from. She was soon offered a job at a new nursing facility, Regency Place, close to the Powell's home. She was hired as a nurse and soon promoted to Charge Nurse. Along with greater pay, it gave her administrative responsibilities.

At the Abundant Life parochial school, we had six classrooms available for grades kindergarten through six. The facilities were nice, but there was inadequate promotion of the school's opening that contributed to a low enrollment. We had full kindergarten and first grade classes, but the second and third grades together totaled 12 students. There were only 10 students for grades four, five, and six, so I taught them all in one room. In addition to keeping records and attending to other details as principal, I looked for ways to advertise our school and increase enrollment.

With so few students, we barely met expenses and there was no extra money the first year to promote the school. Reverend Vibbert expected the school to make him a profit and decided the number of students in the school could not support the cost having a principal. I clearly saw a potential for increased enrollment for the next year but he was more interested in the money than the education of the children. Reverend Vibbert thought he could make the school more profitable by letting go some of staff.

His decisions played right into my needs. I really wanted to get back into a public school for better pay and to add more years to my retirement account with the Indiana State Teacher's Association. Working in a parochial school did not contribute to my retirement pension fund. The more years I worked in the public schools, the greater my nest egg would be when I retired.

Orleans School

I began searching diligently for a position within the Indiana school system. My teacher's license in math and physics contributed to my success in finding a position in Orleans, Indiana, 60 miles south of Indianapolis. The position was for a physics teacher who also had a license to teach math.

The distance was too far of a commute, so I needed a place to live in Orleans. At that time, Orace Wayne was the Indiana South District superintendent for The Wesleyan Church and his home in Orleans served as his office. The district headquarters was located outside of town on a large tract of wooded land where they had a campground for their church functions. There was a mobile home on the grounds that I was able to rent from the church.

The first year at Orleans, I kept busy with class preparations and making repairs on the trailer. Sometimes I would visit with a minister who lived in a mobile home next to mine. He was the pastor of the local Wesleyan Church and very helpful to me with work that needed to be done on the place.

During my second year, Berline took leave from Regency Place Nursing Home to come to Orleans to be with me. She found work at the Orleans nursing home, which kept her involved in her career. That fall, when she met our uninvited guests, she was ready to move back to Indianapolis.

The trailer was right beside a popcorn field. After the popcorn was harvested, there was an abundance of food for the mice and they came from all over the countryside for the feast. In frosty weather, the mice began looking for shelter from the elements and they found cracks and holes in which to enter our living space. I began setting traps and continued catching mice for three weeks. After catching 67 mice, we never had any more of the pesky guests.

The job at Orleans teaching algebra and physics was a relaxing change; it was a relief to be free of the administrative duties of being a principal. The algebra classes and general math were fun and easy to teach but the physic classes were more demanding. I had to review some of the scientific principles, which had come so natural to me in college and early in my teaching career at Ellettsville High School.

Departures From the Nest

In the fall of 1967, Bonnie and Hervey were first to make their departure from the family by starting to Anderson College, in Anderson, Indiana.

Bonnie met a young man, Stephen Powell, who was also a student at Anderson College who soon became her husband. Steve spent two years in the U.S. Air Force, and Bonnie was able to travel with him to different places where he was stationed. After he was discharged, they lived at Muncie, Indiana, where Steve attended Ball State University to complete the necessary college credits for an Indiana teacher's license. When we were still living at Whip-Poor-Will Hill, Bonnie had attended and graduated from Vincennes Beauticians College at Vincennes, Indiana, by driving the 50 mile round trip each day to earn her Indiana beauticians license. She worked as a beautician in Muncie to help them meet expenses while Steve was in College. Steve accepted a teaching job for one year, but determined he wanted do something else. He took a job as insurance adjuster for Hartford Insurance Company until he the opportunity to start a submarine sandwich restaurant. He and Bonnie owned and operated the business, which they named *Sandwich Machine*, successfully for almost 30 years. Bonnie and Steve have two children, April and Erik, as well as one grandchild.

Hervey also met a student at Anderson College, Sharyn Maffit, who would become his wife. They were married in 1968 and they both withdrew from college. They began looking for employment and making plans to establish a home for themselves. Hervey was more interested in mechanics and technology than attending college. He wanted to look for opportunities of employment along those lines of work. He and Sharyn had two children, Melissa and James (he is known as Jamey), while they lived at Gas City, Indiana. Hervey worked for a company in the area until they moved to Texas.

Soon after Hervey was in Texas he completed training to be a Texas State Policeman and then served as a state patrolman for about a year. He eventually worked with a company in Texas building computers. Then he became supervisor for a large computer company in Dallas for a few years. His main ambition was to operate machinery, so he left the computer business to work for construction companies using heavy equipment. Hervey eventually moved back to Indiana where he has successfully worked at operating heavy equipment on various construction jobs building roads, bridges, and other projects. After moving back to Indiana, he married Kimberly Toomey. They had two children, Julie and Dawson. Sharyn remained living in Texas with their two children and she has worked for NASA Space Center for many years. Sharyn is still like a daughter to us. Jamey and Melissa, have also found successful employment in the area.

Patty was the third one to "fly the coop". She attended Vincennes University School of Nursing and became a Registered Nurse. Soon thereafter, she married Edward Turner whom she had met while in high school at North Decatur. Ed served as a pilot in the U.S. Air Force and upon leaving military service he enrolled in Purdue University at the Indianapolis campus. While he was working on his degree, Patty worked as a nurse in an Indianapolis hospital. In recent years, Patty has taught some nursing classes and has been in a close running with her mother as being the best cook in the world! Ed was hired by Allison General Motor's plant in Indianapolis upon graduation from Purdue University. Edward and Patty have five children: Benjamin, Susan, Rebecca, John, and Stephen. They also have several wonderful grandchildren.

Alvin was next to leave the nest. After his high school graduation, he joined the navy and was inducted that fall. When he was discharged from the navy, Alvin decided to live in the area of Seattle, Washington. He liked that part of the country and wanted to study at the University of Washington. He met a young woman, Jana Kennedy, who was living in Bremerton, Washington. They were married and established residence in Bremerton. He and Jana moved to our Whip-Poor-Will Hill home in Indiana and lived there two years. While there, he enrolled at Vincennes University to continue his studies toward a technology degree. He graduated from the Vincennes University School of Electronics Technology two-year program. He and Jana had their first child, Penny, while living in Indiana.

They moved back to Bremerton and Alvin attended the University of Washington in Seattle, by traveling back and forth across Puget Sound by ferry, for one year. He then entered Pacific Lutheran University and graduated cum laude with a Bachelor's Degree in Computer Science. Among other things, Alvin worked for a large engineering company with the responsibilities to make computer installations and computer repairs. He worked there until he decided to start his own computer business. He and Jana had a second child, Gabriel, after moving back to Bremerton.

Then, we had only one of our flock left at home. Maybe DeAnn enjoyed life at home without having to compete with

369

the other siblings for attention. We can hardly express the joy of having her left at home–to travel with us and go places together. When I was at Markleville School, she was my helper there on several occasions. She stayed very busy and was involved in many school activities. She was active with the church youth group and through our church she had the opportunity to go on a mission trip to Guyana, South America. DeAnn graduated from Pendleton Heights High School and attended Anderson College. While there, she was able to go on a missionary trip to Guatemala. After she married Bill and they helped us with The Captain's Sandwich Galley, they moved to Colorado for a short while. They eventually returned to Indiana and lived in Indianapolis, where he worked in the computer department at Walker Research and then at Evergreen Healthcare Headquarters. After 10 years, they left Indianapolis to work as missionaries in Japan. Upon returning to the United States they enrolled at Indiana University in Indianapolis to earn their Bachelor degrees.

They were instrumental in helping us remodel our home in Indianapolis. They have been a real asset to help us in many of our projects and our way of life. Around the year 2000, Bill said to me, "Mr. Willis (as he calls me), you need to get a computer and learn how to use it. I will help you find one and teach you how." I objected to the idea, thinking it would be too complicated. I thought I could never learn to use a computer, but Bill insisted I would like it and could learn.

I finally decided to give it a try, so Bill helped me to select a computer and the other things needed. It took a special amount of patience to teach this old-timer to learn even simple things about the computer. He would not just sit down and show me what to do...he had me to sit at the keyboard and have me do the work. I'm glad I went ahead with learning how to use the computer, because it has been an invaluable asset while writing my books.

Evidently, the places of learning have been drawing cards for our children to find their spouse. God has blessed each of them in special ways through their journeys in life. We feel fortunate to have 14 grandchildren and a host of great grandchildren. Berline and I are especially thankful that our children and their spouses respect and love us. They are all concerned about our well being and are ready to assist our needs in whatever way possible.

Following are the graduation photos of my children:

Bonnie Mae 1966

Hervey James 1966

Patricia Lou 1969

Alvin Eugene 1973

Barbara DeAnn 1975

Chapter 20

COASTING THROUGH RETIREMENT

Now also when I am old and grayheaded, O God, forsake me not; until I have shewed thy strength unto this generation, and thy power to every one that is to come. (Psalms 71:18)

Retirement

In the spring of 1988, after two years of teaching at Orleans, I decided to retire from teaching. At the same time, Berline left her job at the Orleans nursing home and we were free of our employment responsibilities. When the last of our children left home, Berline and I thought we had completed our parenting days. We assumed we would be free to indulge in interests of our choosing. We took for granted that we could just enjoy the grandchildren and leave all their needs to their parents. However, we soon learned their concerns and interests were ours too, whether they were looking for advice, counsel, help, or just some companionship.

Berline and I never really thought of retirement in the same light as many folks. For us, it was impossible to simply quit work and live a life of rest and relaxation. While some people retire to hobbies, travel, or a retirement center, none of that was for us. Our idea of retirement was having time to finally tackle our list of long delayed projects. We wanted to make improvements on our home at Whip-Poor-Will Hill, and help our children where we were needed. Our involvement with them and their families was a privilege we lovingly cherished.

Our grandchildren enjoyed going to the farm as there were plenty of things to experience at our home in the country. My Ford tractor was one of the most interesting novelties. I would let them ride with me as I used it for various tasks around the place.

April and Erik (Bonnie's children) learning to drive my tractor

Patty's children *helping* on a project

a favorite hobby - my ducks

Retirement Excursions

Our goal to find useful service to our family was given a direction soon after our retirement. Alvin and Jana had bought a mini-farm near Bremerton, Washington. We wanted to help them with some improvements they had been wanting to make. The term mini-farm was new to me but I figured, with my farming experience, I could find some chores that needed to be done.

On our way to Washington, we went through Dallas, Texas, to visit Hervey. I was able to make a couple of needed modifications to his shop. First, I added airdrops for his compressed air system by installing the needed piping and connectors. Then I ran electrical wire and installed a new power outlet where it was required. When those projects were completed, we continued on to Washington.

The questions I had about a mini-farm were answered when we reached Alvin and Jana's home. They had a five-acre lot, part of which was fenced for pasture, with a modest barn next a two bedroom house. I saw the potential for several projects that fit right in with our retirement goals.

The first job we tackled was relatively simple yet urgent; the back porch roof had deteriorated beyond repair. We bought new Plexiglas and other materials at a local building supply store to replace the roof. Alvin's children, Penny (age six) and Gabriel (age four), thought it was fun to watch the old roof coming down and wanted to help. Within a couple of days, we had the new roof completed. It made an improvement on the appearance of the backside of the house. It seemed to be the season for roofing work. Our next project was to replace the gambrel roof on their 24 ft by 30 ft barn. A neighbor across the street joined us and we completed it in a few days.

Alvin had a nice two-acre pasture where he kept a horse, but since the barn was not connected to the pasture, the horse had no accessible shelter from the hot sun or the elements. If someone did not take him to the barn when the weather was bad, he had to stand out in it. I found discarded materials at the many construction sites in the neighborhood and built a shed in the pasture with a hay-rack and feeder trough. I figured the horse appreciated the shelter because he did use it.

Soon afterwards, Berline and I undertook the building of

a guesthouse. Since their home had only two bedrooms, the extra space would be handy for visitors–such as us. In their back yard was a small structure that could be used as a sleeping room. We actually attached the new building to the smaller structure. We salvaged most of our materials from the housing projects in the area plus we bargained for used cabinets and a stove. Then we purchased new Sheetrock, roofing, and siding. When we were finished, the guesthouse measured 16 ft by 22 ft and was nearly a replica of our first home in Bloomington.

As always, Berline was a big help with those construction projects. She also found time to can a lot of blackberry jelly from the abundant supply of berries that grew everywhere. We enjoyed finding the abundant patches of berries. Not many people in the area took advantage of the bounty of berries that were free for the picking along roads, in parks, and even backyards. She also made plum jelly from a plum tree in Alvin's front yard.

In time, Berline learned about a very nice nursing home in a town called Poulsbo, just 10 miles north of Bremerton. She was anxious to earn some extra spending money and activated her Indiana nursing license, which was valid in Washington. She went to work at the Poulsbo nursing home soon after we completed our building projects. Berline was readily accepted by the residents at the nursing home, and soon became loved for her caring and gentle ways. She was such a favorite that when we left Washington, the manager told her that she could have a job there any time she ever wanted to return.

We have always found great satisfaction and enjoyment in worthwhile projects that benefit others. Even though our work around the mini-farm was fun, we did find other pleasant activities to appreciate while we were there.

One weekend we traveled through the rugged, beautiful mountains southeast of Bremerton to see the destruction caused by the powerful eruption of Mt. St. Helens. Words cannot explain the devastation caused when the mountain exploded. The enormous blast permanently changed the shape of the mountain and surrounding landscape. In some areas, the stark treeless hills resembled a moonscape–devoid of life. In others, the slow reforestation process was gradually rebuilding a new growth of trees replacing the ones the volcano had leveled like dominoes.

On another occasion, we traveled to Mt. Rainier, also an active volcano. We drove to a ranger station, which was high up on the mountain and at the end of a road. From there, we hiked up the mountain to the point where there was snow on the ground. We were near the foot of the mountain's glacier, which rises several thousand feet to the top, crowning Mt. Rainier's granite peak in white.

Our trip to Bremerton was rewarding and constructive. We met many interesting people, traveled to fascinating places, and accomplished a considerable amount during our stay. The most enjoyable part of our visit was spending time with our grandchildren, which included attending church with them. However, the time came when we felt the need to return home and see what else the Lord had in store for us.

When we returned to Whip-Poor-Will Hill, we spent some time making a few improvements. It was kind of a hobby with us to find things that needed to be built, rebuilt, remodeled, or otherwise improved. We began spending more time in Indianapolis with our families. Bonnie and Steve needed help with some landscaping and outdoor projects. I helped Steve build a large utility shed, shaped like a small barn, on their lot. We poured concrete for a large patio behind their house. Then, using chunks of stone I built an in-ground water fountain. Then Bonnie wanted a stone wall to line the walks and edge their property boundary. That required going to various places to find the right kind of stone. Most of the summer of 1990 was spent doing her stonework.

Berline by Bonnie's house

Berline and I helped with landscaping by planting shrubs, flowers, and trees. Then we helped paint their entire house. Following that, Steve and I built a gazebo and put a wood fence around it.

During our stay in Indianapolis, Berline obtained a job as a nurse at Regency Place. I made excursions to Whip-Poor-Will Hill, sometimes taking the grandchildren with me to work on things or just for a fun trip. Erik went with me more often than anyone else. In time we began to realize maintaining our home in southern Indiana was beyond our means. The farm required a lot of attention and we could not foresee returning there to live and care for it properly. With much deliberation and uncertainty, we decided to sell our beautiful home in the country where so many memories were rooted. It was a very emotional and extremely difficult decision.

Israel Trip

My brother, Orace Wayne, and his wife were going with a group of people from his church to Israel and he invited Berline and me to go along. Bonnie and Steve also made the excursion with us.

It would be hard to say, out of all the places I have traveled, which has left the greatest impression on me. Yet, I have often remembered our trip to Israel as being the most moving and spiritual journey of my life.

It was an inspiring pilgrimage to the Holy Land to see the places where our Savior lived, traveled, taught, and was crucified. We walked the streets of Jerusalem, stirred by the inescapable feeling of His presence. Antiquity surrounded us everywhere we went, but the history was alive. It was thrilling to walk in Jesus' footsteps, to be where He preached and performed miracles. We were taken to the lower level of a great cathedral that was built in honor of the birth of and over the birthplace of Jesus. A large brass circle plaque, with a gold star the middle, designated the place where Jesus came into the world. In silent awe, we stood at the shrine of His earthly birthplace in Bethlehem.

From our hotel we could look across a valley and see Jerusalem–*The Holy City*. Beyond one of the gates facing us, we could see the Dome of the Rock where Solomon's great temple had once dominated the skyline. From the back of our hotel we could overlook the Sea of Galilee where Jesus traveled by boat with his disciples. Our group even took a trip across the water similar to one Jesus had made and Orace Wayne led the group in a devotional service as the boat traveled. It was a trip of a lifetime to be in the presence of Jesus' shadow and go to the places where He had actually traveled, taught, and spent his days while here on earth. It was very inspirational.

Our trip was extended with an excursion to Egypt. We had a military escort through the Sinai Desert while traveling to Egypt. The first day after spending a night in a famous hotel, we traveled by bus to historic places in and around Cairo. We also took a boat ride on the Nile River observing sights on the shorelines. Our group then boarded a small train, which ran alongside the Nile River. It was an overnight ride to where we visited Pharaoh's castle, the Great Sphinx, three large pyramids, and the Valley of the Kings. It was amazing to see the ancient sites and structures. It is hard to imagine the ingenuity and amount of labor it took to construct them.

We traveled back to our hotel in Cairo. While there, we witnessed an elaborate Egyptian wedding and were even permitted to partake of the elegant refreshments following the wedding. The military escorted our bus back through the Sinai Desert to Tel Aviv where we boarded our flight back to the USA.

After our trip to the Middle East, we were ready to begin some of our own building projects, although on a more modest scale than the marvelous wonders we saw in Egypt.

Our 50th Mile-Marker

Golden Wedding Anniversary

Our wedding anniversary has always been a time to reminisce about how God brought Berline and me together and how He has blessed us. We have been asked, "What is your secret for long marriage life?" The question is easy to answer..."We made a commitment before God to love each other until death do us part." Each year we have tried to have a simple celebration to remind us of that important time when God united us as husband and wife.

We were given a wonderful and blessed surprise for our 50th wedding anniversary. Bonnie and Patty with their husbands arranged a special dinner. Their whole families were there to celebrate with us. In addition to the wonderful meal, they had a beautifully decorated cake and some special gifts for us. I gave a brief story to the group of how God had miraculously brought us together, our chance meeting in the beginning, our limited courtship, and some details of our marriage and the honeymoon trip to Indiana.

God has richly blessed us over the years with more anniversaries and ways of joyful living. Each year has added new blessings and accomplishments that draws us closer together. We thank the Lord that He has helped us through difficult times and deepened our love and commitment to each other.

Move to Indianapolis

In 1997, after the sale of Whip-Poor-Will Hill, we bought a house in Indianapolis down the road from Patty and Ed's home. It is located where there are fields and wooded areas, which makes us feel like we are in the country.

The move confirmed our dreaded expectations of such a task to move from an estate where the large house, full basement, and double garage had all consumed more than their share of space. Some of the family went along to help on moving day. I had rented a large U-Haul truck for the occasion. As soon as we got to the farm, we had to rent an additional large U-Haul truck. We filled both trucks and my pickup truck for the first trip to Indianapolis. Many things in the garage, basement, and barn would have to wait until I could make a few more trips with the pickup to get them.

It was an overwhelming task to unload our belongings into a house just two-thirds the size of the home we left and only a one-car garage. At our new home, the garage was packed full and there was little more than a walking path through the house.

Not long after we got settled in Indianapolis, Berline was involved in an automobile accident. She has always been a good driver, but that does not prevent bad drivers from causing accidents. That particular situation involved a bad driver passing Berline on the interstate and attempting to cut in front of her before being completely past her, resulting in clipping the front of her car. The impact propelled Berline's car off the road and up a high embankment. The car crashed through a fence then slid to a stop between a large tree and the back porch of a house. The accident caused a lot of damage to Berline's car and her shoulder was wrenched during the collision. She suffered a great deal of pain from the injury she received.

After the accident, Berline could not twist or move her shoulder without having intense pain. She had to retire from her nursing job, as she was no longer able to push the heavy medicine cart that was used to deliver medications to patients.

After her recovery, we determined we would be able to do some traveling. We wanted to visit Berline's family in North Carolina and asked Bonnie and Patty to go with us. We considered it kind of a pilgrimage trip to visit some of the places in Fayetteville where we had lived and walked during our courtship days.

James at the Fayetteville train depot,
where he first arrived on his way to Fort Bragg in 1945

James and Berline in front of the Church of God
where they first met in 1945

Remodeling Wisdom

The kitchen in our new home was so tiny there was little space in it for eating. There was barely room for a small table for two. Another inconvenience was having the laundry room in the basement. While those features were cumbersome and unhandy, we could have managed to adapt and make out with the situation as it was. However, we got to figuring how we could take out an outside wall and extend the kitchen to make a more comfortable eat-in kitchen. Then we realized we could extend it further and add a utility room at the same time.

Early that spring we drew up several sketches and our remodeling plans became ever more ambitious. We decided to add a large section onto the house that would include a completely new kitchen large enough for a breakfast nook. The old kitchen would become a dining room. Then we made plans to add a bathroom beside the utility room. "Well," I thought, "while we are building, it would not cost much more to have an upstairs guest room and bathroom." By the time we were done planning, the addition almost doubled the square footage of the main floor of our home. However, it was in the middle of summer and I thought it best to wait and begin construction until the next spring.

Bill offered me some good insight and wisdom. He explained to me, "Mr. Willis, I think you ought to begin the work immediately while you're in good physical condition and I am here to help you. You are ambitious and in good health at present but in a year or two your health and strength could begin to decline to the point where you couldn't successfully complete the job." As a result of Bill's encouragement, we started on the remodeling of our home that summer. Often I have been thankful for Bill's advice, as I found the truth in his words when the work took longer to complete than I had expected.

With Bill as my right hand man, we broke ground and began building. He stayed with me throughout the entire project–clear to the finish. Berline and DeAnn were also right there to assist with the work. In addition to helping keep materials available as we needed them, they often kept track of tools when they got lost. Hervey rented an excavating machine and dug the crawlspace and trench for the foundation footing. Bill and I laid the foundation, then we went up with the framework.

We were blessed with some donated labor from a family we had met at church. We had been attending the Burge Terrace Church where we met a family by the name of Newfeld. At church, we enjoyed their talents as musicians when the entire family, including five boys and three girls, gave marvelous performances. We became good friends with the family and loved to hear them play. The father and his five boys were all carpenters and had their own construction company in Canada. When he heard of our project, Mr. Newfeld and two of his boys came to help with the framework. They helped only one day, yet it really boosted our progress because they knew how to make every move count.

One morning we went out to work, only to find our power tools and other equipment were gone. Although it was a setback, we still managed to get the structure enclosed with chipboard siding and the roof completed, plus all doors and windows installed by the time *Mr. Frost* came. We still had no heat inside and we preferred not to proceed during cold weather. All further work was put on hold until the following spring.

A Diverted Vacation

That winter Berline and I decided to take a trip to Texas to visit family. We planned to drive through Atlanta, where we would stop to visit Berline's family. When we got to Atlanta, we found Bill and Melissa Jr. in poor health. They had sold their home and were living with their youngest son, Bobby, and his wife. Bobby had built a new home which had been designed to have living quarters in the lower level for his parents. However, the downstairs apartment was still unfinished, so Bill and Melissa Jr. were living upstairs. Berline and I decided, if they would allow it, we would like to help finish the apartment before proceeding on to Texas. We talked it over with Bobby and he was thrilled to have our assistance. There was a complete set of used base and wall cabinets stacked in the kitchen area. We renovated and prepared them for installation. I also hung six doors, then finished the trim around all the windows and doors–while Berline was working on cabinets.

A drop ceiling was installed, we laid floor tiles in some areas, installed the plumbing fixtures, and new electrical lines had to be run for the stove, dryer, and a few other outlets. Bobby was very busy with his job, but he helped as he could.

In five weeks, we had the work nearly complete, almost ready for Bill and Melissa Jr. to move in. However, before we could finish the project, we received an urgent call to return home for some pressing business. We left with a promise to return. Within two weeks we were back and shortly we had them moved into their new living quarters.

They were as happy as newlyweds moving into a new home. We felt very blessed to share in their happiness and that we had been a part of bringing joy to their lives. Our labor was an expression of our love. Our sense of accomplishment was affirmed by their heartfelt expression of appreciation.

Then we felt free to continue our journey and made a leisurely trip to Texas. There we found a place for more volunteer work. Our grandson, Jamey, was soon to marry a young woman named Kim. He was in the middle of remodeling his house and preparing it to be their home. We spent a couple days helping him then took a few days to visit other relatives in the area before returning to Indiana.

The Unfinished Remodeling Project

At home, our unfinished remodeling project was waiting for us. As soon as we could work comfortably in the unheated addition, we began all the interior work. I took an electrician's test in order to comply with the city's regulations. I passed the test and was approved to do the electrical wiring. Then we hired a Sheetrock contractor to complete all the walls and ceilings.

When the weather was good, we shifted gears and began the finish work on the outside of the house. Berline took the pickup truck to Bedford and Bloomington looking for stone veneer. She hauled the stone while Bill and I laid it. We were almost able to lay it as fast as she could bring it. We put stone on the house from the ground up to the middle of the first floor windows. From there, we continued with vinyl siding up to the eves. By the end of the summer, we had completed the outside finishing.

When autumn came, we were ready to move back inside

and tear out the existing wall in the old kitchen. A lot of work was still ahead; we had to install flooring, cabinets, plumbing fixtures, doors, trim, and painting. Then we remodeled the old kitchen into a dining room.

We had really bitten off a big job. What had seemed like a simple project turned into a bigger undertaking than we wanted! It had taken us almost three years to complete the project, but we saved a considerable amount of money by doing it ourselves. We worked many long day, and I discovered my stamina was declining. I got to the place where I dreaded starting to work each day. But it had to be finished and it just wasn't in my nature to quit a job before it was done. Bill had been completely right about starting when we did. If we had waited another year or two, I would not have had the energy and determination to complete the project. I doubt I would have even had the courage to even start it.

Finding Retirement Adventures

I took a job delivering automobiles as it was interesting and gave me some something to do. The work was very flexible but I saw that it would not suit me for long. It eventually became obvious that I needed a more meaningful line of work. I inquired at the Indianapolis Public Schools (IPS) and discovered there was a big demand for substitute teachers. Teaching is my favorite occupation, so it seemed like a natural path to follow.

While substitute teaching for IPS, I saw how the inner city public schools had degenerated from places of education to little more than social centers for kids. It was disheartening to see teachers afraid to control disruptive students for fear of being reprimanded or even losing their jobs. Many of the young children had been taught their rights were more important than their education; they were empowered beyond the maturity of their understanding and skilled in manipulating authority rather than respecting to it.

Students came to school to socialize, join cliques, and be with their friends–learning was avoided. That may sound like an exaggeration, but I had students that absolutely refused to work on their lessons! It was often preferable for those students to put their head on their desk and sleep, so they would at least not disturb the others in the class. Even some children in the elementary schools, as young as eight years old, were disrespectful and argumentative toward the teachers.

The schools confronted more and bigger problems than I had ever experienced during my teaching career. Yet, I accepted the challenge to cope with the problems and had many enjoyable opportunities teaching children who were willing to learn. There was considerable apprehension about each job assignment; some situations I was put in were extremely stressful. I soon learned which jobs would be more desirable and I rejected those I knew would be troublesome.

Regardless of the school problems and the difficult students, I did feel a sincere sense of accomplishment when I had good students. I worked with the Indianapolis Public Schools for five years as a substitute teacher and met many good teachers.

Berline and I decided to spend some time in Texas with our family. While there I inquired about substitute teaching at a district north of Fort Worth and was informed that my Indiana Teachers License would be accepted. I was impressed by the staff's cordial manner and friendly service; they seemed willing to help me any way they could and were excited to have me working there. I thought to myself, "I could really like working in this school district."

After experiencing the battleground situations in Indianapolis, I was prepared for whatever might come. The teachers and other school staff were friendly and helpful, which made me feel welcome and wanted. I was pleasantly amazed at the cooperative behavior of the students, no matter what grade level. In every class, no matter what grade, they were respectful and courteous toward me as their teacher. Even the upper grade students came to class ready to do as they were asked and were well behaved.

It was hard for me to believe that I would have the opportunity to experience such a wonderful educational environment. Students are not this way by chance, it is evidence they have been taught values at an early age by loving parents that foster obedience and respect. My substitute teaching in the Northwest School District near Fort Worth has offered a rewarding climax to my teaching career.

I give thanks to the Lord not only for my accomplishments and blessings but also for the trials and tribulations. Through all things we all can see the hand of God that guides our footsteps through our journey of life.

And the journey continues.....

CONCLUSION

Miracles of My Journey

We are all students from our beginning to our end, for learning is a life long journey. Berline and I have done our share of learning to be compatible companions and trying to be good parents. We were not perfect at it but we were blessed with the care of five children, born flawless as the Lord formed them. Our faith in God has always been an important part of our learning and teaching. Our children cannot remember the first time they went to church because we took them along with us soon after they were born. One whole pew of the church was always reserved for our family of seven. The children all learned to respect the church and how to conduct themselves properly during services. God has sustained our marriage through the years and through our differences, God has taught us a deeper love and patience. It has been said that if two people agree on everything, then one of them is unnecessary. We accept that we will sometimes disagree and adjust as necessary so that we enjoy life together.

We believe miracle after miracle brought us together. God led me to the church in North Carolina where I met Berline and won her affections. That was a miracle. The Lord has protected me during my journey through life and I have seen His hand along the way. That I survived my journey to Montana to work with the forest service, fighting the fires, and my return home was a miracle. That God brought me home alive from Okinawa and that I was transferred to North Carolina was a miracle. The Lord has nurtured and carried Berline and I through perils; His hand has brought us comfort and peace in so many ways.

I am very thankful for the encouragement and love from my wife and children, which have been such a blessing to my life. As I have written this book, I have reflected not only on the path that allowed me to find my beautiful cherished wife and to have treasured children, but also the miracle of my birth and the family I was born into. My mom and dad never took me or any of my siblings to church, but they loved their children and taught good morals, respect, obedience, hard work and the value of proper living. I am grateful for having parents that were committed to each other and to their children to help them make a way in this world. I am blessed to have parents and the family of my youth that helped guide my footsteps and set me on the right path through this journey of life. I've had a very blessed and fulfilling life.

There is an old song that says, "Count your blessings; name them one by one." That is impossible for us because our blessings are too numerous. We can only say, "Thank you Lord, for giving us faith in You. Thank you for all that You have given us throughout our lives."

James and Berline with their children 1984
(L-R) Alvin, Patty, DeAnn, Bonnie, Hervey

Christmas Party 1967
(L-R): Imel, Marybelle, Wesley, James, Lelah, Morris, Orace Wayne
Pop and Mom (seated)
This was the last family Christmas gathering
that we were able to spend together.

ACKNOWLEDGMENTS

First and foremost, I give thanks to the Lord and Savior, Jesus Christ for blessing me with the courage, patience, wisdom, and wherewithal to complete this book.

I owe a debt of gratitude to all of my family for their variety of contributions. Without their help, this book would be lacking in quality and content for the reader.

I am very grateful for Berline's patience with me for all the time it has taken in the preparation and writing of my book. She and I have reviewed the stories for accuracy and clarity. Her constructive suggestions has been very beneficial. Berline has been vital to the writing of my journey through life.

Bonnie and Steve worked together to make a practical outline for organizing the sections of my writings. Bonnie has worked with me to edit many pages, contribute to the stories, help with the wording, organize the layout, as well as create the art concept for the book cover. I cannot begin to express how thankful I have been for her knowledgeable and relentless help. Bonnie has poured her heart and soul into this work and has been a great contributor and encouragement to the finish.

Thanks to Hervey for overhauling my computer in the earlier days of my writings. My computer was not performing properly and he made it like new. Without the computer I would have been handicapped for a legible manuscript.

Patty, my middle daughter, has offered encouragement along the way and has done some proofreading whereby she was able to offer suggestions.

I am ever so grateful for the work Alvin has done. He has edited and reviewed every page and has spent time to make the wonderful illustrations found within the pages. His research and recollection of places and things has enabled him to impart those elements with impressive accuracy.

DeAnn, my baby daughter, has been responsible for editing the pictures and putting them in place throughout the chapters. Bill assisted with solving computer related issues and making the manuscript ready for printing.

I shall speak about my daughters, as another man once said, "If Heaven is missing three angels, I know where to find them!" My sons have been a great help to Berline and me all their lives. Each of my children would do anything within their ability to assist us with our needs. God is surely pleased with the love and honor that our children give to their parents.

I am very appreciative to Arthur Miley for giving direction to his mother's book "Our People of Pike County, Indiana" for additional information regarding the Willis' history in the Clark's Station area.

Lastly, the staff at the Historic Remount Depot, the Ninemile Ranger District visitor's center, and the Missoula Smoke Jumper visitor information center were very helpful and kind to allow me to photograph their archived pictures to use in the section regarding my summer of forest fighting experience.

This book would not have been possible without the help and encouragement of family members and friends. It has been said that no man lives entirely by himself. I am reminded of our need for each other and our dependence on others for whatever we may wish to accomplish in life.

SOURCES

McClellan, Ruth - "Our People of Pike County, Indiana" c1978

Powell, Anita (Willis) - photographs and map of the Clark's Station community and permission for usage of the family history from "Plow A Straight Row" by Imel H. Willis. The stories in chapter 2, obtained from Goldie Inez Parker Willis and Aunt Mae in 1964.

Richardson, Juanita (Willis) - Canal photo near Willisville, Indiana, taken ca1980.

Schmitt, Stanley - research and historical information about the Wabash-Erie Canal in the southern portion of Indiana.

Strain, Paul - Harrodsburg School photo

Wikipedia (the Free Web-based Encyclopedia)

Willis, A.E. - Illustrated Drawings

AUTHOR'S NOTE

It was during a revival meeting, while I was in high school, that I committed my life to Jesus Christ and vowed to live a Christian life thereafter. My life took on a whole new meaning and resulted in a lifetime commitment.

Just like all of my ancestors have met their appointment with destiny, each and every one of us will have our own appointment. The Bible says it is appointed once for man to die. Our appointment with destiny is one that we will not miss. My goal is first and foremost to be ready for the appointment when the Almighty God makes that call for me. The end of our life is not something to fear or worry about...it is something to look forward to. Jesus said He has prepared a place for us to be with Him.

This journey of yours may be filled with sorrows and hardships, but we all have the same opportunity to find peace with God. My other goal is to make the best of all the remaining time the God of Creation allows me to remain here on this earth. When my journey comes to an end, I want to finish this race to hear the Lord's words "well done my good and faithful servant." I hope your footsteps through this life's journey will be destined by God's grace.

LEGACY

James Beverly Willis...those that know him, love him for his carefree, yet loving and gentle spirit. He has always had a penchant for mischievousness. He learned it well from his father and other kinfolk. It is apparent this is a Willis trait, based on the stories about his family and ancestors.

His capacity to meet challenges with resilience and rise above adversities, is evidence of the grace of God and strength from above. His success in life has not been measured by wealth or status, but by his steadfast love and faithfulness to his family and to the Lord. He is a dedicated father and husband who has worked hard to provide for his family. He loves them deeply and wishes nothing but God's blessings in their lives.

What better legacy could we receive, than these memoirs put to pen so we can know him better and remember the heritage we have through his life.

A Gift of Joy

With great anticipation, yet with anxious concern, the time was
near for the signs were evident their baby was about to be born!

As she waited, the sounds of spring were all around. She could
hear the birds singing and smell the freshness of the new day
morn...

Their baby boy came into this world healthy and strong
They were all thankful that all was well and that nothing went
wrong...

Her thoughts were full of joy as she held her tiny son.

It was an early spring morning, on Wednesday, April 23, 1924,
in their small 4-room bungalow home that sat beside the old
Wabash and Erie Canal, when I was born.

by Bonnie Powell

Psalm 139:14

I will praise Thee,
for I am fearfully and wonderfully made:
marvelous are Thy works;
and that my soul knoweth right well.

CONTACT AND ORDER

To purchase additional copies of this book:

indianamilitaryveteran.ecrater.com
Ebay.com
Craigslist.org
createspace.com/4839083

To contact the author:
James Willis
PO Box 39512
Indianapolis, IN 46239
317-495-2958

My other book for sale:

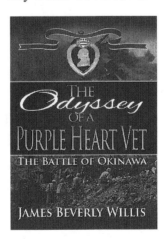

Made in the USA
Charleston, SC
01 May 2016